FREE
AS A JEW

A PERSONAL MEMOIR OF
NATIONAL SELF-LIBERATION

RUTH R. WISSE

WICKED SON

A WICKED SON BOOK

An Imprint of Post Hill Press

ISBN: 978-1-64293-970-5

ISBN (eBook): 978-1-64293-971-2

Free as a Jew:

A Personal Memoir of National Self-Liberation

© 2021 by Ruth R. Wisse

All Rights Reserved

Cover Design by Tiffani Shea

Post Hill Press

New York • Nashville

posthillpress.com

Published in the United States of America

1 2 3 4 5 6 7 8 9 10

CONTENTS

PROLOGUE

 *W*hose life is worth writing about?
Growing up in Canada, in the 1940s and '50s, I thought everything important in the world happened elsewhere—in Europe where I came from or in the Land of Israel where the Jewish people came from. During the war—which is how we always referred to the Second World War—I would return from school to find my mother inconsolable over a letter that had arrived from "over there" about one or more murdered family members. A letter was once delivered to "Leon Rojskes, Canada," although that was no longer Father's registered name; it had somehow reached us, courtesy of the dedicated postal service, from a no-longer-reachable sender. After the war people began arriving, still miraculously alive, to fill in news of those who weren't.

My childhood perception was not entirely false. All that made our lives remarkable was the *absence* here of what was happening over there: cruelty, hardship, starvation, inventive new forms of slaughter, and in Palestine, the unaccountably cruel behavior of the British who did not allow the Jews into their own land. Decades later, when Mel Brooks quipped, "Tragedy is when I cut my finger. Comedy is when you fall into an open sewer and die," I remembered my father's concern the day I accidentally sliced the back of my hand on a piece of broken glass and he bandaged it up rather than take me to the hospital. We both knew not to make too much of it. That may have been the very day my Bialystok cousins were shot, or my Kovno cousins transported to their death. We did not mock her logic when our mother told us to eat the crust because children were going hungry in Europe.

The restorative side of history likewise began to unfold not among us but where the Jewish homeland, under foreign domination for two thousand years, was being reclaimed. These were events we heard about at home and school, and at assemblies called to celebrate the achievements of the nascent state of Israel and to join us in solidarity with its defense. Foreign affairs were our domestic preoccupation. I did not wish to be in those more eventful places, but I knew that ours was not as consequential. The people who experienced or made that history would have something important to write about.

Meanwhile, where we lived, memoirs by nonfamous people tended to be about hardships overcome. Men and women who had wrestled with poverty, family trauma, physical disability, addiction, rape, racism, and discrimination could, through their stories, inspire grit and endurance in others. Between bouts at graduate school, I read Joanne Greenberg's *I Never Promised You a Rose Garden,* a personal story of teenage schizophrenia that is fictionalized, to be sure, yet revelatory about what I had not experienced and could only learn about in books.

MINE IS NO SUCH TALE. During the most momentous period in Jewish history, I had been whisked away from the centers of action to a land of peace and prosperity where a child could work to become anything she reasonably wanted. I came of age during the quarter century of grace between the establishment of Israel in 1948 and the 1975 passage of Arab-Soviet sponsored UN resolution 3379 defining Zionism as a form of racism and racial discrimination. During that interval, liberal democracy in North America was growing more confident, having triumphed over fascism and rallied against communism in the Soviet Union. In those precious years I tried to integrate my Jewish culture into my land of citizenship, certain that both would benefit from the give and take. I continue to think that they do.

But the passage of that infamous resolution marked the turning point from anti-Semitism that targets Jews in dispersion into anti-Zionism that targets Jews in their homeland. The regional Arab war against Israel morphed into the ideology of Jew blame that soon penetrated North America, undermining our liberal democracy, which is the actual target of anti-Jewish politics. All tyrannies, I realized, were not anti-Semitic, but all anti-Jewish ideologies are antiliberal. As a member of the Jewish people and dedicated student of modern Jewish literature, I was alert to the outsized role of Jews in political history, and what I saw unfolding was the erosion of the liberal confidence and strength I had come to rely on. Defense of Israel had become the Maginot Line against the enemies of our freedom, and as coalitions of grievance gained intersectional force in the media, the academy, and in the streets, I saw that line buckling before my eyes.

So I find myself at the heart of world events after all, a combatant in the war over the future of America. What might have been a life of uninterrupted good fortune with only private setbacks came up against unwelcome social and political forces. Many of my compatriots misjudge our situation, mistaking the imperfections of democracy for its vices, condoning barbarity out of misguided sympathy, holding Jews responsible for the aggression against them, confusing regressive with progressive governance, and neglecting to fortify all that is good. This makes it necessary to reestablish the obvious. Since antiliberal ideologies work through inversion (freedom as oppression, merit as inequality, the Arab war against Israel as Israel against the Arabs, and so forth) it keeps getting harder to straighten the record. Not everyone is as good at this as George Orwell, who set the standard for exposing the duplicities of our animal farm. I went about this in my plainer way, and this memoir invites readers to judge whether I have fallen short.

How I might have enjoyed recounting my rich life of love, friendship, marriage, motherhood, the myriad dimensions of family experience, collegial interaction, and the intertwined joys of learning and teaching! Much of that private life continues and will hopefully continue until my last breath.

In this memoir, however, I figure as a creature of my time and place, whose reflections and actions tell an often-overlooked part of the national and international story. Most of North American Jewry does not vote as I do. Most of my academic colleagues do not teach as I do. When it comes to moral-political values, I have more in common with the deeply Christian year-round residents near our summer camp in the Adirondacks than with some of my younger relatives. From an American perspective this is all to the good—less so from a Jewish perspective. The loss of Jewish and liberal moral self-confidence, which is the inevitable by-product of anti-Jewish and antiliberal politics, is the surest sign of civilizational decline. The last part of this book registers this apprehension.

My story is worth telling not because of what I overcame, but because of what we all have yet to overcome.

1

SURVIVAL

I was four years old when my parents engineered our escape from Europe, so I cannot pretend to have had a big hand in the matter. Had they not managed our flight in the summer of 1940, I would have remained a cute photograph in some Holocaust memorial museum. As we say in Yiddish, *moykhl toyves*—spare me those favors.

I'm not a great fan of Holocaust memorials and don't much care about the posthumous compassion of strangers. I just wanted to live. But having escaped the ash heap, I remain curious about the ratio of accident to enterprise in my own successful exodus.

Whose idea was it to leave? How close did we come to failure? And was I more an asset or a liability as we made our way across Europe? None of the escape was my own doing, but would we have made it had I not been fortuitously groomed for such an eventuality? These are some of the questions that continue to prey on me; probing them is one of the tasks I set for myself here.

❧

OUR DEPARTURE IN EARLY JUNE from my birthplace, Czernowitz—today's Chernivtsi—was so hurried that when the boy next door came by later that day to ask my brother out to play, he was stunned to find the door bolted and us gone. My father had asked one of his trusted former employees, a man with government contacts, to inform him immediately if Soviet troops ever approached the Romanian border, as he was certain they would.

When the phone call came, Father was already in Bucharest trying to arrange our exit visas. Mother packed us up and within a few hours we were on the train to the capital. She left behind two items that she had gotten ready and intended to take along in her hand luggage: a framed photograph of her father and a songbook by the Yiddish poet-songwriter Mordecai Gebirtig with an inscription thanking her, a good amateur performer, for how well she interpreted his songs. Leaving Czernowitz ended the brief fairytale chapter of my parents' life and cast us into the maelstrom of hundreds of thousands of Jewish refugees on the run.

Passport photo of Masza with children, taken in Bucharest, June 1940. Leo carried it in his wallet to the end of his life. Ben is shown similarly sheltering others in many subsequent family photos.

Europe was already at war when we began our flight. A year earlier the foreign ministers of Soviet Russia and Nazi Germany had signed the secret Molotov-Ribbentrop "Non-Aggression Pact," effectively dividing Poland and the rest of East Central Europe between them. Their invasions from

East and West ignited the Second World War, but though Hitler had proclaimed his intentions and had already begun his conquest of central Europe, the coordinated attacks from two ideological enemies took the rest of the continent by surprise.

My parents were still natives and formal citizens of the eastern "Lithuanian" part of Poland that was occupied by the Soviet army. They had not yet attained Romanian citizenship and could not have returned to Poland even had they wanted to. When Germany expelled its Polish Jews in 1938, Poland, fearing their return, decreed that all returning Jewish citizens needed to have their passports stamped anew. The border city of Zbąszyń became a transit camp for Polish Jews, trapped and unable to go either back or forward. Then, by the summer of 1940, the Polish government was itself in exile in London.

Romanian politics were controlled by the monarch, King Carol II, who was known to be under the influence of his Jewish mistress, Magda Lupescu. This led some Jews to hope that they would remain safe under his rule. In fact, it did not lessen the antagonism that was already palpable when we reached Bucharest and that erupted in pogroms just after our departure. Perhaps their formal statelessness helped my parents realize that they could expect no protection from local authorities. They were the only ones among their Czernowitz friends who fled Europe that year.

Whenever I am identified by my place and date of birth—Czernowitz, 1936—it is usually assumed that we fled the Nazis. I try to correct the mistake in the pursuit of truth and so as not to simplify the more complicated history. Though most of Mother's family and a large part of Father's were indeed murdered by the Germans, we actually fled a prior evil enshrined in the pact between the two parallel predators. My father deduced that Stalin, having invaded Poland, would also invade Romania. By 1940 every Jew knew the hazards of Hitler, but Father did not yield to the subtle moral blackmail concealed in the claim of communists that they were the only alternative to Hitler. He knew it was possible to have more than one enemy.

CR

LEIB ROJSKISS, LATER LEO ROSKIES, was a short, slight man with dark, tight curly hair and thick glasses who had come to Czernowitz in 1932 to build and run the first rubber factory in northern Romania. His achievement by age twenty-seven testifies to both the unleashed energies of modern Jewish youth in interwar Europe and the obstacles they had to overcome.

Leibl, as he was known to family and friends, had learned politics the hard way. He was born the year of the so-called abortive Russian revolution, 1905, in Bialystok, which was still under tsarist rule. The tsar almost immediately scuttled the promised reforms for an elected government, setting off anti-Jewish pogroms, some spontaneous, some authorized. There began for the family a period of turmoil that lasted until the end of the First World War. The younger children were sent with their mother and younger cousins into the quieter interior while their father, David, and his older sons tried to adapt their textile business to the rapidly changing conditions.

At the dawn of the 1917 revolution, the family was reunited in Moscow, where the *muzinik*, the youngest of five children, four of them boys, celebrated his bar mitzvah. Leibl's modest Jewish ceremony on a Thursday morning was overshadowed by his far greater excitement hearing Leon Trotsky enthrall the crowds in Red Square. The Bolshevik takeover of industry and commerce propelled the family breadwinners back to Bialystok, but once there, Leo declined to follow the prescribed *yeshiva* education of his three older brothers, and at fifteen he left his traditional Jewish home in Bialystok to attend high school in a neighboring city. On his own thereafter, he continued on to Vilna University—renamed for Polish monarch Stefan Batory after the reunification of Poland in 1919.

The Polish Republic under Prime Minister Jozef Pilsudski was formally committed to minority rights, yet it also left the door open to nativist parties that wanted their region cleared of those minorities—Ukrainians and Germans and especially Jews—the latter of whom constituted a third of the population of Vilna. Student members of the nationalist party, the *Endecja*, once approached Leibl on the street and told him to get off the sidewalk, threatening him with a revolver. He opened his shirt and said, "Go ahead and shoot!" and then walked on, never mentioning this incident until almost the end of his life. In him and his friends, anti-Jewish hostility induced a correspondingly strong national resistance. Whereas Jewish youth elsewhere adopted the local language—in America, English, in the Soviet Union, Russian—most of the youth of Vilna spoke Yiddish, like its elders.

Two contrastive political pressures—discriminatory features of Polish nationalism on one hand and Britain's 1917 Balfour Declaration supporting "a national home for the Jewish people in Palestine" on the other—greatly enlivened Zionist sentiment and fueled the Zionist movement among the Jewish youth of Poland. Vilna soon had groups of Labor-Zionists, religious Zionists, Hebraist-Zionists, and Revisionists who focused on self-defense. Vilna was on the itinerary of every Zionist leader; representatives of the Yishuv, the Jewish community in Palestine, came to help organize emigration. In her Hebrew high school, Masza Welczer, soon to be Leibl's wife, sang the pioneering march, *Se'u tsiona nes vadegel*—Carry the flag to Zion! Leibl's decision to study agriculture, and when that proved impossible, chemistry, was predicated on his intention of emigrating to Palestine.

At the same time, like most of his student friends, Leibl started out on the Left, no doubt still fondly recalling the revolutionary firebrand he had heard in Moscow. Many Jews felt an affinity for Trotsky as a fellow Jew, and on his account gave Bolshevism the benefit of the doubt when it claimed to be furthering international brotherhood and egalitarian justice. With a Jew at the head of the Red Army, how bad could it be? Communism said that it was historically determined anyway. That the Soviet Union officially outlawed discrimination against Jewish individuals helped to mask its suppression of Hebrew, Jewish study, religious observance, and Zionism.

Although Leibl was too invested in his Jewish identity and in his studies to ever join the communists, he was close enough that a Bialystok friend who wanted to cross over to Soviet Russia turned to him for help. The process was known as *shvartsn di grenets*, or "blacking the border," that is, getting smuggled across the frontier separating the newly reestablished Polish Republic from the newly founded Soviet Union. To help his friend Chaim reach *his* promised land, Leibl and a third friend raised the required sum and gave the smuggler half on account, the rest to be paid when he returned with the password given him by Chaim once he was safely deposited at his destination.

The plan was conceived in high spirits. The boys chose for their password the Hebrew-Yiddish word *c'mat*, meaning "almost," but when spelled differently becomes an acronym for *kush mir in tukhes*, kiss my ass. How clever they must have felt when the smuggler returned the naughty password for the balance of the cash! But Chaim was never heard from again. This was the fate of many idealists whom the Soviets caught and convicted of spying, which did not dampen local enthusiasm for the Soviet promise.

Leibl, however, was taught his lesson. Chaim's mother, a Bialystok neighbor, blamed him for the disappearance of her son and threatened to denounce him. Leibl's father kept a wad of money in the house in case of his son's arrest, assuming that the police would accept a handsome bribe. Thereafter, my father stayed clear of communists and remained skeptical about the Soviet Union.

STUDENT DAYS ENDED WITH THE 1920s. Leibl received his master's degree in chemistry for a thesis on the influence of nitrogen on yeast. His cousin and roommate Srolke (short for Isroel) married and emigrated with his wife to Palestine where he became a high school teacher of physics. Leibl, too, had intended to "make *aliyah*," but after his marriage to Masza he was offered and accepted a job in a rubber factory in the Polish industrial city of Krosno.

The owners of the Krosno factory Wudeta, though Jews themselves, typically employed Gentiles for production and Jews strictly for management and sales. Leo's older brother Enoch was duly hired for the sales office. But they made an exception for the newly graduated chemist and soon put Leo (he remained Leibl to his wife and family) in charge of production for their domestic and foreign markets, including neighboring Romania. His rise was impressive!

When Romania's King Carol II imposed restrictions on Polish imports as part of his nationalist policy to develop local industry, his employers sent Leo to establish a new rubber factory in Czernowitz. He oversaw the building of CAUROM (CAUchook ROMania), which became a hugely successful producer of rubber goods ranging from rainwear to rubber balls. Other Jewish manufacturers in Czernowitz at the time produced buttons, candies and chocolate, chemical products, dried milk and processed foods, furniture, printed materials, soap and candles, soda water, and of course textiles. My parents joined a circle of young engineers, industrialists, and professionals; they were wealthier in Czernowitz than they would be ever again.

With his brother Enoch in the front office as sales manager, my father worked hard at an industry he adored, and among his rewards was a medal from the king. Despite that, he knew that not all Romanians shared the royal's gratitude for his efforts. Hard nationalists called the Jews predators, while Marxists saw the rapacious capitalist behind every factory owner. Much as Leo appreciated his newfound prosperity, he did not mistake his success for security. He realized that, should the Soviets ever invade Romania, his chances of survival as director of a factory would be as slim as they would be if Hitler were to attack from the West. Stalin had by then unleashed the Great Terror, leaving no doubt about his murderous methods.

It is this awareness of political reality, his refusal to wish away whatever threatened our happiness, that I came to admire in my father and aspired to emulate.

CR

MOTHER'S ROLE IN OUR EXODUS was secondary to Father's but no less substantial, for had she resisted our departure, he would not have organized it. And her readiness to leave was the more admirable, since in following Leibl she had already been twice uprooted.

In truth, the best part of my parents' lives would always remain Vilna where they met in the early 1920s and married at the end of the decade. The city famed since the eighteenth century as the Talmudic stronghold of the

Vilna Gaon—the genius Elijah ben Solomon—had lost none of its cultural preeminence in the process of modernization.

When German-trained scholars, including my later teacher Max Weinreich, wanted to establish an advanced institute for social studies, they chose Vilna as the site for their YIVO Institute for Jewish Research. The Vilna Jewish Teachers Seminary trained educators for the evolving network of Jewish schools in Poland. The Strashun Library was crammed with observant Jews studying Talmudic commentaries alongside aspiring modern Yiddish and Hebrew poets and writers. Vilna had five Yiddish dailies and over one hundred philanthropic organizations for a population of about sixty-five thousand Jews. I grew up believing that nowhere in the universe had there been a Jewish cultural center as dynamic as interwar Vilna.

My parents' stories of Vilna were sunny even when their subject was grim. They recalled mountain hikes or nocturnal walks in the forest as members of Vilna's Jewish student sporting club, hanging out with local actors and actresses of the Jewish theater and cabaret (Masza), public debates in the student union (Leibl), and an endless flow of friends, some of whom would later figure in my literary studies. Though Masza had lost both her parents by age nineteen, she did not experience all the usual consequences of orphancy. Several of the many half-sisters and brothers of her mother's first marriage lived in the vicinity and kept half an eye on her. Their parents had owned the local Matz Publishing House that specialized in Yiddish publications, both religious and secular. This brought her a trickle of income, but more importantly, she felt herself a prominent part of her native community that she considered the jewel of the Jewish Diaspora.

The young Jews of my parents' circle yielded to no one in their appreciation of the local landscape and as much of Polish culture as they were allowed to share. At the same time, they demonstratively spoke Yiddish and championed Zionism's reclamation of Jewish autonomy in the Land of Israel. They loved singing, and one of their favorite songs mocked their assimilating contemporaries who were trying to pass as Poles but were ultimately betrayed by their Jewish noses. The epithalamion a friend wrote for their nuptials warned Leibl that his wife would cook him a song for his supper.

Of course, the undercurrent of threat was always there, and the songs reflected that as well. In 1919, Polish Legionnaires celebrated newly proclaimed Polish independence with a pogrom against the Jews whose first casualty was the Yiddish writer-playwright A. Vayter (pen name of I. M. Devenishski). Vayter's girlfriend, shot trying to shield him with her body, was a friend of Masza's older sister. The Jews of Vilna were shaken to the core and turned his funeral into a public manifestation. The poet Avrom Reisen composed a Yiddish dirge to the music of Mendelsohn that Jewish schoolteachers taught their students. Thirteen-year-old Masza sang this with her class as they accompanied the body to burial:

Di shenste lid gezangen, the loveliest songs,
Sing them not in good times, but in dread time like this.
Ring out, sounds of glory, though the spring is gone,
Though the sun has set, though the poet is dead.
Khotsh der dikhter iz shoyn toyt.

She called this her hymn, and my brother David led us in singing it at the unveiling of her tombstone at the end of the century. The vast Vilna song repertoire of our parents included lullaby, lament, and everything in between.

By the time I took up Yiddish studies, some forty years after that dramatic moment in my mother's life, only elderly Jews were speaking the language. My attraction to it was the opposite. Parents made us feel that there would never be a happier place for youth than Vilna in the 1920s. Once, when I was a teenager, my parents visited a family that had just arrived from Poland with a daughter my age. Father made me as envious as I have ever been when he reported hearing her laugh with her friend and said, "I haven't heard laughter like that since I left Vilna."

It follows that despite its professional advantage, my parents' move to Krosno after their marriage was a rude jolt. Masza left adoring friends for a factory town with no Jewish society at all. The birth of Benjamin the following year, welcome as it was, increased her isolation as a young mother.

She knew nothing about infants and had no family or friends in Krosno to advise her, not even about the need to burp a baby as part of its feeding.

The second relocation to Czernowitz was therefore far more welcome. She and Leibl joined a Jewish society more acculturated than Vilna's, but strongly Zionist and openly Jewish. For the first time their wealth allowed Masza to support Yiddish writers and institutions as well as needier members of her family.

ଔ

ACCORDING TO THE 1936 CITY register of Czernowitz—then in Romania, presently Ukraine—Rut, female of the Mosaic faith, was born May 13 to Leib Rojskiss engineer (age thirty) and Masza Welczer housewife (age twenty-nine) residing at 43 Yarnic Street. Mother enjoyed telling me about my birth and it was one of her few stories that I could not get enough of. On a lovely day in May, she was standing by the window of her bedroom looking out into the garden where the landlord, Mr. Vinovic, was trimming the bushes. When he caught sight of her at the open window, he asked if she would like some flowers. She said yes, thank you, and then went into labor so quickly that I was born by the time he arrived with a bouquet.

I always thought of myself as born on a bed of roses (minus the thorns) in a sunny bedroom with a cheerful midwife tending to a joyful mother. Apart from Mr. Vinovic and the midwife, no one else featured in Mother's account of that sunny day, not my father or my older brother, Benjamin, who had just turned five and must have been more than usually concerned about the arrival of this little sister. In addition to the usual reasons for fearing the arrival of a new sibling, Ben had lost another younger sister before me—Odele, who died of meningitis at age two. Mother told us of being so distraught in the last stages of Odele's illness that she couldn't enter the sickroom to sit beside her dying child. She thought to spare Ben by never telling him that his sister was dead, hoping he would accept their explanation that she had "gone away" and stop asking about her, as he eventually did (possibly to spare the adults). When I then arrived two years later, he would surely have wondered how long I intended to stay around.

The truer story of my birth I learned quite accidentally in 1985 thanks to Alexandra Tulcea, who was born in Romania a year before me and grew up there under the communist regime. She was then the wife of Saul Bellow, and she and I got to talking at a reception for her husband celebrating his seventieth birthday in Montreal, his native city. Alexandra said her parents had close friends in Czernowitz, the Zalojeckis, both doctors, and she wondered whether my parents might have known the wife, Rosa, who was Jewish. From what I knew of our life in Romania, I said it was unlikely, but the next morning, I put the question to Mother: had she known a Rosa Zalojecki in Czernowitz?

"Of course," Mother said. "Rosa Samet."

"Zalojecki," I corrected. "She was an obstetrician and gynecologist."

Mother then corrected *me*: Rosa was a Jewish girl from Poland whose maiden name was Samet. She was married to a Ukrainian, Zalojecki— also a doctor.

"Of course I knew her. She gave you your name. When you were born, you came out so suddenly that I began to hemorrhage, and the midwife was afraid for my life, so she called in Rosa Samet and told her it was an emergency. Rosa was known as the best obstetrician in the city. She came right over and stopped the bleeding."

So much for the storied ease of my birth! Because Rosa was afraid of complications, she stayed with Mother for a while and during that interval asked what she intended to name me. Mother said, "Tamara," after a girl with lovely braids who had lived in their Vilna courtyard. (I was kept in braids for many years.) The good doctor strongly advised her against it, saying that she herself had suffered from being named Rosa and this was not a time to burden a Jewish child with a recognizably Jewish name. "She told me to call you Rut, a good Romanian name. I took her advice and told Father to register you as Rut." The Czernowitz registry had it right.

Mother recounted all this as though she had never imprinted in me the image of the child born on a bed of roses. It could be that she saw no contradiction between hemorrhage and bouquet, but had simply given me the happier version. My later attraction to literature over other forms of knowing had something in common with this realization that truth was not reducible to any single interpretation of the known facts. The sunny memory of my coming into the world was merely complicated, but not overshadowed for Mother by the accompanying hazards of my delivery. Compared to what preceded and what followed my birth, I can see why she wished to carry a cheerful image, like the golden locket she wore with my childhood picture in it.

Though no one ever compared me explicitly with Odele, her death hugely affected my life. Whether because Mother no longer trusted herself to raise a child or because it hurt too much to be reminded of the missing one, when I was born, she hired a nanny who then stayed on as my governess. This *guvernantke* slept in my room, saw to my needs, and relinquished me to the rest of the family at appropriate times, so that I readily identify with children of royalty who are raised from birth with expectations of disciplined behavior and high performance in return for the unlimited care and comfort they receive. Royals are required to prove themselves worthy of the benefits bestowed upon them. I was raised to be flawless, which then meant behaving like a self-controlled adult.

℞

Czernowitz when my parents arrived there from Poland in 1932 was known as "Little Vienna," and in Jewish circles as "Jerusalem on the Prut" thanks to the conspicuous presence of some forty-two thousand Jews, more than one-third of the population. The city had been part of the multiethnic Austro-Hungarian empire and stayed polyglot when it became incorporated into Romania after World War I. Its character was thus very different from that of more homogenous and nationalistic southern sections of the country. Multinational Austro-Hungary had conferred on every minority "an inviolable right to the preservation and use of its own nationality and language," which allowed Jews as one of those minorities to develop their culture in Hebrew and Yiddish. This had made Czernowitz the logical site of the 1908 founding International Conference on Yiddish, and the city's ongoing association with the language was one of the reasons my mother was so pleased to move there.

Czernowitz stayed polyglot when it was incorporated into Romania after the First World War. Still, no one pretended that its various languages enjoyed equal status. German remained the tongue of distinction as in Prague, another multilingual city of East Central Europe. Jews adapted linguistically in order to function economically and survive politically. If the Czernowitz elite spoke German, so did its Jews; and since our parents became part of the Czernowitz Jewish elite, they prepared us to enter its ranks. Ben attended a Romanian elementary school where I would certainly have joined him had we stayed in the city. My parents spoke Yiddish at home and German (or their version of it) in their social and professional affairs. They also knew Russian and Polish, and Mother had a working command of French.

Thanks to my nanny Peppi, a German-speaking Jew from Czernowitz, I spoke German impeccably. Heads were said to turn in the street when people overheard me conversing with her. When a visiting friend of Mother's tried to stop me from following her into the bathroom, I assured her that women need not feel ashamed in one another's presence—"*Frauen zu frauen dürfen sich nicht schämen.*" Stories about children often feature such cheekiness.

In his *Memoirs of an Anti-Semite*—the title's admission of bigotry is meant to enlist our trust—the German novelist Gregor von Rezzori gives us his impression of one of his Jewish mistresses:

> But her language, as I was saying: her sing-song, the flattened vowels, the peculiar syntax of people who, although having known an idiom since childhood (in her case, Romanian), remain alien to it, and then the Yiddish expressions interjected all over the place— these things betrayed her the instant she opened her mouth. . .

Rezzori engages us as a fellow native of Czernowitz and one of those amazingly multifaceted, cosmopolitan East Central Europeans that one often associates with Jews, but with the advantage—for him—of not being a

Jew, though his life was difficult enough. A well-born Austrian, he became a Romanian then a Soviet citizen as national boundaries kept shifting, without having moved. Like the Nobel laureate Elias Canetti, he wrote in German while commanding many other languages (in his case, Romanian, Italian, Polish, Ukrainian, French, English, and Yiddish), while being anything but German in cultural affinity. He was dazzlingly prolific in many genres, a self-advertised romancer of women, and a fearless observer of social under-currents at a time when people dissembled to save their lives.

Thus, if this is how Rezzori writes about a lover, we can imagine how the Jewish "sing-song" affected his less kindly disposed countrymen. Romania was reputed to be the most anti-Semitic country on the continent, yet I feel certain that had he encountered me with Peppi on one of our walks, my German chatter would have aroused in him no such revulsion. Indeed, he might have smiled and stopped to chat with the articulate four-year-old; I had curly blond hair, and Shirley Temple was then all the rage.

Of course, nothing turned out as intended. *Der mentsh trakht un got lakht.* English makes the point smartly—man proposes, God disposes—but in Yiddish God *laughs*, mocking our best efforts to control our fate. Intended to ready me for a lifetime in Europe, my mastery of German would prove its true value during our escape from Europe.

In Czernowitz, Masza's association with Yiddish was no longer in har-mony with the surroundings as it had been in Vilna and became instead the ambiguous distinction that it remained for the rest of her life. *Ambiguous* because the friends she made were all German-speaking, removed enough from the Jewish heartland to have traded in Yiddish for the language of Goethe and Schiller. Yet, just as Kafka was excited when he discovered the Yiddish theater, they were drawn to culture that felt more authenti-cally Jewish, particularly as the surrounding population grew colder and openly hostile.

Masza sometimes performed in Yiddish at the Zionist club, Masada, which she and Leo joined. The inscribed songbook by Mordecai Gebirtig, praising her renditions of his songs—the book she forgot in the haste of depar-ture—speaks to her success in bringing Yiddish culture into Czernowitz's

Jewish high society. The songs, many of them in the manner of folk ballads, were eerily nostalgic about the life still being lived, as if trying to capture its fading traces.

Ambiguous also because whereas Yiddish was associated with poverty and want, there were servants, a chauffeur for Father, a housemaid in addition to Peppi, and the means to help others back in Poland. My parents may have given up most other Jewish practices, but they both religiously observed the obligation of helping those in need, family members and friends first and foremost, but also the community at large. Back in Poland, two of Masza's siblings ran orphanages and children's summer colonies. The more they had, the more they felt obliged to provide for others.

Nonetheless, Mother did not fully trust their prosperity any more than Father could. One of the songs she learned during a visit from her older sister Anna Warshavski acknowledged this distrust: *Zol es geyn, zol es geyn vi es geyt, vayl dos redl fun lebn zikh dreyt.* "Let things go as they must, the wheel of fortune spins, today in my direction, tomorrow in yours." The song's plaintive tones, so at odds with Masza's temperament, seemed to foretell a reversal of fortune. As anti-Semitism hardened in Central Europe, its acculturating, upwardly mobile Jews recognized in the fundamental insecurity of Yiddish culture something hauntingly and prophetically familiar. Masza's songs were that augury.

In later years Mother was sometimes angry, even unforgiving, of those trapped in Europe by the war whom she suspected of having let their possessions weaken their powers of self-preservation: "She wouldn't leave her *carpets!*" Her annoyance may have masked guilt over having failed to rescue her beloved sister Annushka, murdered with her husband and family with the extermination of the Kovno Ghetto. Anna was a singer on the radio, a woman of wealth, and by 1940 was eager to leave Poland. But unlike Masza's husband, hers could not secure the necessary papers.

Gratuitous guilt would cling not only to most survivors but to those like my parents who made it to safety. Though I thought Mother's astringent way of dealing with it terribly unfair, I preferred it to Father's self-reproach.

A couple of years after I was born in 1936, Mother became pregnant again. Her mother had borne a dozen children, and she wanted more than two. Her obstetrician was a member of the Masada circle. When she went to confirm her pregnancy, the doctor told her to ready herself for an abortion: he would end the pregnancy then and there. Masza protested, but the doctor overrode her objections, insisting that this was no time to be having a Jewish child.

He may have been right. I doubt that our parents would have undertaken so uncertain a journey or managed it so adroitly if they'd had a new infant in tow. Owing our lives to this unborn child as we do, I cannot absolutely oppose abortion, though for the same reason I also believe in having more than just a replacement level of Jewish children. We are a people who naturally, like the forest after a fire, feels the need to regrow its ravaged part. The threat of extinction that forced Mother to abort the child she wanted later inspired her to bear two more once they had established a new home.

Peppi accompanied us to the train, but no farther; she stayed behind to take care of other children. As I have no memory of our parting, I can only record that we left Czernowitz on the same day in June 1940 that we received direct news of the Soviet invasion of Romania, and that I never saw Peppi again.

☙

MY PATERNAL GRANDFATHER, DAVID, WAS blind for the last forty of his eighty years. For the Passover seder of April 3, 1939, the entire Rojskiss family gathered at the patriarch's home in Bialystok—all except our branch because Ben and I had come down with scarlet fever. It was apparently at this gathering that *Zeyde*, who had instructed the family to buy a textile factory in Canada—textiles being the longstanding family business—now told the son and grandson whom he considered the sharpest businessmen to leave at once and arrange for others to follow.

Paternal grandparents David Roskies (1860–1943) and Odel Nay Roskies (1863–1932) in Bialystok. He was blind for his last decades.

One of my cousins believes that the two men had already been in Canada several months earlier to finalize the purchase of a woolen mill in Huntingdon, Quebec. Grandfather must have learned about the depressed state of Canada's textile industry and assumed that the government's concern over the production of woolen goods might outweigh its aversion to Jews. Or perhaps he did not know that Canada and especially Quebec were more opposed to Jewish immigration than any other Western country. The historians Irving Abella and Harold Troper called their book on Canada's wartime Jewish immigration policy *None is Too Many*. In our case, the officials evidently put economic interests first, helped by the large sum the family deposited for the privilege of entry.

Thanks to Grandfather's foresight, all four of his sons made it out of Europe, though one daughter-in-law and two granddaughters did not reach Canada until 1945. Doomed in Bialystok were Aunt Perele, the sister who stayed behind to care for our grandfather, along with her husband and two children, and the blind visionary himself. What he saw in his blindness was the black heart of Europe.

CR

BY 1940, FATHER REALIZED THAT we were doomed if we stayed in Czernowitz, and independently made contingency plans for our eventual departure. There were few routes of escape. The story circulated of the Jew who goes to a travel agent looking for somewhere he can move to. Palestine? The agent regretfully informs him the British had closed it to Jewish immigration. America? A restrictive quota. Italy? Spain? Dangerously fascist. After unsuccessfully going through one option after another, the Jew says, "Don't you have another globe?"

Happily, thanks to his expertise in rubber production, Leo had secured visas for South America. But he was not enthusiastic about moving to a place where he had learned there were only rich and poor. He preferred the freer democracies of North America, and since his brothers were already in Canada, he undoubtedly wanted to be near them.

When Paris fell to the Germans on June 14, the Romanian-Jewish writer Mihail Sebastian, who had maintained close connections with his fascist intellectual friends, filled his journal with despair over the appeasement he anticipated. "There will be newspapers, declarations, and political parties that present Hitler as a friend and sincere protector of France. When that time comes, all the panic and all the resentments will find release in one long pogrom."

Indeed, fascist-inspired disturbances were then raging around Bucharest as Father tried to arrange our travel. Thanks to that medal from King Carol II, the Romanian officials granted us exit permits—with no right of return. We left Romania as stateless persons, heading for Athens by train, hoping that somewhere along the way we would receive entry permits to Canada, secured by the family members already there. In Athens the precious documents reached us so that by the time we boarded the ship at Piraeus, headed for Lisbon, we could say that Montreal was our final destination.

We were refugees masquerading as tourists. My white shoes that Mother remembered to take with us when we left Czernowitz figure in a group photo taken in front of the Parthenon, where we are all in stylish

attire. Mother would later tell me that during our travels they took to calling me *Fräulein Hoffentlich* for the way I spiced my sentences with the word
"hopefully." They placed me in front when we came to checkpoints, trusting
that my confidence and cheeky German would render us passable.

By the time we reached Lisbon in September, France had fallen, touching off a "stampede" of refugees to the city, many of them similarly in transit. We were among approximately eighty thousand Jews who found temporary asylum in what had once been the launching pad of the Portuguese
Inquisition.

Family visiting the Acropolis during stop in Athens—refugees masquerading as tourists.
Masza prided herself on having remembered to pack Ruth's white shoes as well as her own.

Anyone who got to Lisbon had already run the gauntlet of officialdom.
This included border guards at ports in Italy and Gibraltar, who reserved
the right to sequester improperly documented persons. The Italians did not
remove any passengers from the ship, but the British did, and though they
spared us, the thoughtless cruelty of those officers impeding refugee flight
forever complicated our thinking about the British.

Father had secured us passage on the *Nea Hellas*, a Greek ship that was
to depart Lisbon on October 4 and dock in New York nine days later. From
there we were to travel to Montreal with our recently issued Canadian
papers. However, we needed transit visas for the few days between land-

ing in the United States and boarding the train to Montreal, and these the American consulate would not issue without medical tests that included an ophthalmologist's assessment of Father, who wore thick glasses.

When Leo went to the appointed medical office, he was informed that the doctor was on vacation and would not return until after our scheduled departure. Back we all went for a referral to another doctor, but now the consul denied Father's request and said he would have to wait for the authorized doctor's return.

Father exploded: "You are a crazy man! Our ship sails this week! Will you throw away the lives of these children? Give me the name of another doctor or I will kill you!"

Did he really say that? As I do not recall Father ever raising his voice to us, I like to imagine him shouting in his recently acquired English. In any case, his eruption had its effect. The consul said that I reminded him of his own daughter and issued us the visas. End of episode.

I was the adorable mascot, Ben, a potential security threat. Everything was discussed in our hearing, and he was under strict orders never to say anything unless directly spoken to, and never to reveal anything he knew. He spoke only Yiddish and Romanian and was just learning English. Already semiadult at age nine, he listened to Hitler's radio broadcasts and understood the menace in those ravings.

While I never lost the sense of security imbued in me since infancy, I don't think Ben ever regained the sense of security he lost during those desperate months. Families with the best laid plans were betrayed and doomed after successfully hiding for years. The bravest ghetto fighters fled through the sewers and emerged in open air only to be executed by tipped-off storm-troopers. Survivors returning to their native towns were axed and stoned by former neighbors. In the American consular office, Father almost cost us the lives he was working so hard to save. Yet his outburst parted the sea for us.

Author with parents, September 1940. Masza wrote on the back, "In Lisbon on the way to Canada."

We set sail for New York on the second day of Rosh Hashanah 1940 and arrived in Montreal on October 19. All that I remember from that period is a little green leather purse that Father bought me at an outdoor stand in Lisbon. It was square with a clasp at the top and a leather strap. I still had it in Montreal when we moved the first time, but then it disappeared, and I mourned its loss. Everyone has had dreams of the kind I dreamed about losing that purse. Maybe I had to lose it, as a stand-in for all the things that I did not remember parting with.

2

FREEDOM

After their flight from Egypt, the children of Israel are doomed to spend forty years in the desert: it takes that long for the whining and backsliding rabble to begin its transformation into a liberated people. The Bible seems to mock their trek from one watering hole to another as they set out from Rameses to camp at Succoth, from there to Etham, then on to Pihahiroth...and so on for forty-four verses.

Thanks to our parents, it took us just four months to reach our destination, and we never looked back. Still, it took much longer to adjust to Canada, the "true north" (as the national anthem has it), "strong and free."

Whereas our father had brought us out of bondage, it was Mother who set the terms for where and how we were to live.

Montreal, an island city on the Saint Lawrence River, is built around the eponymous Mont Royal that still more or less separates the French from the English, each community further stratified by how high it sits on the slopes.

Canada was not, like the United States, a homogenizing society with a single national history. Rather, it was the political union of two peoples, French and English, each dedicated to maintaining its separate religion, language, and identity. In this respect, Montreal resembled multiethnic cities like Vilna and Czernowitz. Jews were under no great pressure to assimilate where others were maintaining their separateness. I thought it symptomatic that Robert Allen Zimmerman of Duluth, Minnesota became Bob Dylan, but Leonard Cohen from Montreal remained Leonard Cohen.

Though the first Jews had arrived in Canada in the mid-eighteenth century, it was not until the United States severely restricted European immigration after the First World War that the Jewish population quickly grew. That lasted until the effects of the Depression and local animus against foreigners hardened Canadian immigration policy so that we were among only several hundred Jewish immigrants admitted in 1940. By then local Jews had already established a national Jewish congress headquartered in Montreal, a YM-YWHA, two Yiddish newspapers, the Jewish General Hospital, a federation of social services, a Jewish library, and a network of Jewish day schools.

Uncle Enoch and Aunt Mandy had rented us an upper duplex across the street from theirs at the outskirts of Westmount, the most affluent section of the city, where they and the rest of the family soon established themselves. The location also offered the most convenient route to Huntingdon Woolen Mills, sixty miles from Montreal, where Leo would join his three brothers. The husbands spent most of their time at work while the women handled everything else. Children were expected to stay out of trouble.

Ben and I were immediately registered in the elementary school within walking distance of our flat. My brother would take me by the hand to Herbert Symonds School, where I was placed in kindergarten and he in fourth grade. This lasted at most a couple of weeks, as I vomited every day until our parents allowed me to stay home. No one thought to notify the school when I stopped attending.

Fortunately for all of us, Mother felt uncomfortable in the western section of Montreal, and within a year she moved us to Outremont—the other side of the mountain. The lower sections of Outremont, largely French, also contained the Jewish immigrant area, so we were now closer to the Jewish Public Library and to several Jewish elementary schools. It was a less prestigious neighborhood, but Mother did not relocate because she preferred poverty. She had swept us away to be among Yiddish-speaking Jews and French Canadians. There we lived as well as we could afford in an upper-story duplex, eventually moving higher up the mountain to the street where both the Trudeau and Bourassa families, later to produce two prime ministers, had their homes. On that street, our parents would buy the first and only home they ever owned.

I don't know whether Father was equally keen to move away from the rest of his family or simply gave in to his wife. Each of his three brothers carved out his own cultural territory: Shiye, the eldest, remained religiously observant, Isaac joined a Jewish social club where he enjoyed playing cards, and Enoch, who had briefly directed a Hebrew school in Poland, became active in the cultural program of Westmount's imposing Shaar Hashomayim Synagogue. Our father, youngest of the four, joined the board of our Jewish school and supported Mother's involvement in Yiddish institutions.

Due to the long commute, made even longer by our move across the city, Father spent two nights a week at the Huntingdon Chateau where he shared a room with Enoch. With its marble entrance and imposing dining hall, the Chateau had been built during Prohibition conveniently close to the border as an oasis for thirsty Americans, but by the 1940s it stood mostly empty. There the two brothers planned the rescue of their father and sister from Bialystok, but by 1943 they knew they had failed.

ଔ

THE JEWISH PEOPLE'S SCHOOL OR *FOLK SHULE* THAT Ben and I began attending in 1942 stood in the heart of the Jewish immigrant district, a fifteen-minute streetcar ride from our home on Pratt Avenue, which then still bordered on farmland. Sometimes we had to run a gauntlet of Gentile boys shouting invectives at the Jewish kids, but they never physically attacked us and I don't recall being very afraid.

Our school days were divided into three-hour morning sessions and two-hour afternoon sessions, with an hour and a half for lunch. Although most of the other students lived around the school, Ben and I spent most of our lunchtime traveling to and from home. This prevented us from forming the sort of neighborhood friendships I imagined the other pupils enjoyed, but soon many of their families were also moving in our direction, and by seventh grade quite a few were living nearby.

Unlike the United States, Quebec had no public schools. Education was divided along confessional lines into Catholic and Protestant school systems; for these purposes, Jews were designated Protestant. As a result, Jews who were being mainstreamed into English society invited resentment from the French who might not have welcomed Jews into their Catholic schools but were offended by their affiliation with the English. This seemingly discriminatory system produced the most robust Jewish school network in the northern hemisphere; some saw a chance to establish Jewish elementary schools like those that had existed in Poland.

Despite the absence of European-style Jewish political parties, the Jews of Montreal managed to replicate their spectrum of diversity within their educational establishment, ranging from the Morris Winchevsky School (communist) to the Jewish Peretz schools (left-of-center Labor Zionist), the Jewish People's School (right-of-center Labor Zionist), the United Talmud Torah (Hebraist-Zionist), and Adath Israel (Orthodox-Zionist). There was also a socialist afternoon school as well as a sprouting of more orthodox schools that would multiply after the war. All of these institutions, serving over half the Jewish children in the city, were in Outremont.

Our Jewish People's School stood for a holistic, indivisible, and inclusive Jewish people. Without conforming to any of the formal divisions within the Zionist movement, it was politically centrist, ideologically close to both David Ben-Gurion, who became Israel's first prime minister, and his sometime rival Chaim Weizmann, its first president. As against Ben-Gurion's aggressive effort to replace Yiddish with Hebrew as the unifying national language of Israel, our school conducted some classes in Yiddish, the vernacular of our homes, while the Bible was read in Hebrew. This followed the natural functions of the two languages, Yiddish as the everyday spoken language of most Jews before the war while Hebrew stayed the eternal Jewish medium through time and space.

The Yiddish of our school was not the vehicle of "Yiddishism" or "Bundism"—ideologies committed respectively to the Jewish Diaspora and Jewish socialism—but the repository of Jewish literature and culture, of Sholem Aleichem and Y. L. Peretz. It was as though the school had emerged from the Jewish enlightenment of the nineteenth century without the factionalism that splintered Jewish communities—and many Jewish families—in Europe. This was also the culture of our home. The same poem by Avrom Reisen that we learned in school, about father's ashen face lighting up as he blesses the Hanukkah candles, Mother sang accompanying herself on the piano when we gathered to light the Hanukkah candles in our living room.

The teachers did not coddle us. Who could forget Peretz's story of "The Three Gifts?" A soul that has earned neither heaven nor hell is condemned to limbo unless it can find three gifts that will be acceptable to the guardians of heaven. Behavior on earth is so disappointing that it takes the soul eons to find them, which it can only do one at a time. The first: a Jew is robbed at knifepoint and slain when he does not let the robbers take a little sack—containing not the jewels they anticipate but earth from the Land of Israel. The second: a Jewess condemned to death requests pins to pin her skirt to her flesh so that when she is dragged through the streets by her hair tied to the tail of a horse, her modesty will be protected. The third: a Jew is made to run the gauntlet and has almost made it through to safety when a whip sweeps the skullcap from his head; he goes back to retrieve it and does not survive. The guardians of heaven accept the "beautiful" gifts: a grain of that earth, one of those pins, and the skullcap. We discussed what each of them represented in Jewish nationhood, morality, and faith. Only years later, reading the story as an adult, did I catch the complicating irony of those blood-stained presents and the Jewish heaven's questionable standard of martyrdom in accepting them. How gutsy of teachers in the upper grades to trust us with such modern folk tales. The Peretz of elementary school prepared me for the Peretz I later studied and taught.

The school's idea of Jewishness was conveyed indirectly. Ours was not a kosher home, but the subject never came up, inside or outside the classroom. Did my classmates and teachers attend synagogue? Ben and I accompanied Father on the High Holy Days, and on Simchat Torah we children paraded around with flags and apples, but the school did not prepare the boys for their bar mitzvahs or give us any kind of religious instruction.

At the same time, no one ever spoke disrespectfully of God or religious observance. Why would they, in a Jewish people's school? The holidays we prepared for with greatest enthusiasm were the same ones we celebrated at home: Hanukkah and Passover, with an emphasis on their historical-national significance. Purim, the feast day commemorating the political success of Queen Esther in ancient Persia, was the carnival day best suited for children. But during the early 1940s its celebration was subdued. Lessons in both history and literature reinforced the idea of a people who had survived, morally intact under varied conditions, and were about to recover the Land of Israel that had been under foreign domination since Roman times. We learned about the Roman sacking of Jerusalem, read stories about Jewish adaptation to life outside the Land of Israel, and sang songs about the pioneers who were rebuilding the homeland.

Our general studies curriculum reflected the same inclusiveness, most of it taught in English, and we prepared for full citizenship by learning French. No one pretended that by graduation we would be fluent in all four languages, but there were four valedictorians to vouch for the intention.

Spoken Hebrew was additionally helpful, should any of us choose to live in Erets Yisroel, aka Palestine, where the principal's son and several recent graduates were already members of *kibbutzim*. If the school had an unarticulated ideal it would have been the Israeli *kibbutz*. The Jewish pioneers had formed these collective settlements as a response to the challenges of transforming urban dwellers into an agricultural people, a dispersed minority into a unified nation, and endangered Jews into a potential army. Nowhere else in the world has the experiment in communal living been tested in greater freedom or variety. The absence of coercion allowed these settlements to change and eventually dissolve almost as readily as they had formed. But in those early postwar years they were an inspiring alternative to the ashes of Europe.

Our attachment to the Land of Israel was reinforced by what we learned, like the Zionide of twelfth century Spanish-Jewish philosopher poet Yehuda Halevi, whose own journey to the Land inspired generations of Jews:

My heart is in the East
But the rest of me far in the West—
How can I savor this life, even taste what I eat?
How, in the chains of the Moor,
Zion bound to the Cross,
Can I do what I've vowed to and must?
Gladly I'd leave
All the best of grand Spain
For one glimpse of Jerusalem's dust.

We sang this poem not in its original Hebrew, here translated by Hillel
Halkin, but in the Hebrew poet Chaim Nahman Bialik's Yiddish rendi-
tion, *Kh'hob fargesen ale libste*: "I've abandoned all my loved ones/ Left behind
my cherished nest./ I've given myself over to the sea:/ Bring me, sea, to
mother's breast." We learned that Bialik was our great national poet despite
his reluctance to assume that title. Mother in childhood had sung his song of
the bird from the Land of Israel that comes calling at his window—our version of Poe's "Raven." Bialik's poem of rage, "In the City of Slaughter," written in response to the 1903 pogrom in Kishinev, had roused Jews to undertake stronger self-defense. Eight centuries after Halevi set out for Jerusalem,
Bialik quit his native Russia to settle in Tel Aviv, the first modern Jewish
city. Our bilingual teachers found it natural that the poet had transposed
a Hebrew poem into his native Yiddish so that it could be sung by Jewish
schoolchildren in *their* native tongue. Zionist multilingualism, like Zionism
itself, was taken for granted.

Every year we were given little booklets of the kind used for lotteries or
raffles, in denominations from twenty-five cents to one dollar. Selling these
tickets, which bore pictures of youngsters in shorts against a background
suggestive of a kibbutz, was a highlight of my year. Many years later I
learned that the proceeds went to the Histadrut, the General Organization of
Workers. This was not exactly a scam: as one of the most powerful institutions in Palestine, the Histadrut was virtually synonymous with the Jewish
government-in-waiting. Through its conglomerates it employed more than

three-quarters of the workforce and ran the country's largest bank and health organization.

This association of Israel with socialism would hold firm until the Labor party suffered its first electoral defeat in 1977. But our school did not feel ideologically Marxist, and I suspect that in local elections most of our teachers, along with most Canadian Jews, tended liberal rather than socialist.

I took the sale of those Histadrut tickets as seriously as Girl Guides conducted their cookie sales and went far beyond my neighborhood looking for *mezuzahs* on the doorposts of approachable homes. I could not have told you that in those skinny little cases was parchment containing verses from Deuteronomy, but what they told *me* was that the families behind those doors were comfortable being canvassed by a fellow Jew. As it happened, I did best in the dense immigrant area where people were less wary, though it was always Father who contributed most by buying up all the tickets I was left with. This assignment, a form of conscription, inducted me into the Jewish people more effectively than any classroom instruction.

In contrast to Herbert Symonds School, the Folkshule felt like home. In the upper grades, my favorite teacher, Miss Schechter, taught us to parse sentences with diagrams that dangled clauses from sentences, phrases from clauses, and adjectives below them like ripe detachable fruit. But her moods fluctuated, and once, when I must have truly annoyed her, she slapped me hard, causing my nose to bleed. It never occurred to me to complain about this, nor did I feel her reprimand lessened her affection for me, since Mother, too, sometimes struck me when she was on edge.

One memorable day our seventh-grade teacher, Mrs. Mauer, became so irritated by the ignorant and vulgar graffiti of the boys entering puberty that she consecrated a morning period to a discussion in which, from her answers to our unsigned questions that she pulled out of a hat, I learned almost everything I had wanted to know about sex but did not wish to ask Mother and could not ask Ben—like the meaning of "cherry" or why Kotex sanitary napkins came in three strengths and why some children were born twins. The nervous tension broke when Mrs. Mauer, a great hockey fan, pulled out a question asking whether she thought the Canadiens would win the Stanley Cup.

Only once did home and school come into conflict. In seventh grade I was summoned to the office of the principal, Shloime Wiseman. Since my grades were stellar, I foresaw no problem. He asked me what *lerer* Kh. had taught us in yesterday's Bible class. (We called our Jewish studies instructors by the Yiddish term for "teacher.") I went over the lesson as well as I could. He asked whether anything derogatory had been said about our *bobbes* and *zeydes*. But we were studying Bible and I had no grandparents. Suddenly, I realized that this interrogation must involve my mother, who often found insult where none was intended.

When I protested that I had uttered no word that could have been construed as a complaint against our teacher, Wiseman believed me. He knew Mother well, and Father sat on the school's board of directors. He told me that in the future I should come to him and no one else with criticism, implying that I would have to speak more circumspectly at home.

I believe it was in June of 1943 that Principal Wiseman assembled the entire school in the auditorium to tell us what was happening to our people overseas. He said, "If each of you took one of your notebooks and wrote on every line of every page the name of a child and if we then collected all the notebooks in this auditorium, it would still not equal the number of Jewish children who have just been killed in Europe." Two of those names could have been Ben's and mine. I wanted to tear out at least a page or two from my notebook to save some of those children. I felt closer to them than to the ones around me in the hall.

Wiseman then told us about Shmuel Zygielbojm, the Jewish leader who had been rescued from the Warsaw Ghetto and sent to London to represent the Jews as a member of the Polish government-in-exile. There, he had tried in vain to alert the Allies to the mass murder of the Jews, which included his wife and child, and, unable to do it in any other way, committed suicide, leaving behind an accusation and appeal. Maybe because those children had just become my responsibility, the effect of this information on me was different from our principal's intention: I was infuriated by Zygielbojm's martyrdom—how dare he give Hitler yet another victim, instead of staying on to fight in Europe or Palestine!

Decades later, when the Montreal suburb of Côte Saint-Luc decided to dedicate a park to Zygielbojm's memory, I did not attend the ceremony. My anger lasted until the night before the signing of the Oslo Accords in 1993, when I finally understood what could have driven Zygielbojm to the breaking point—a story that will have to wait for a later chapter.

Ever since his arrival in Montreal in 1913 as a boy of fourteen, Principal Wiseman had supported himself by teaching, which had been his father's calling in Ukraine. Whereas others tried to replicate or adapt the traditional religious *cheder* instruction of the Old Country, he developed a new model that would prepare informed Jewish citizens for Canadian life. All that I took for granted in the Folkshule—the equilibrium of Jewish and general studies; the concept of a religiously inspired, self-reliant Jewish people; the familial warmth balanced by respectful teacher-student relations; a political centrism so natural it seemed synonymous with Jewishness—all of this was thoughtfully designed by Wiseman and the instructors he hired.

One or two generations earlier, they might have become rabbis, and a generation later, college professors. But in that first immigrant generation, supported by a community that shared their need for modern Jewish education, they bestowed their wisdom on us.

We had arrived in Montreal *af alem fartikn*, everything ready-made for our benefit. The solid school building that was overflowing by the time I graduated had been erected the year of our arrival and had only then received the formal accreditation that allowed us to continue to Protestant high school. In the upper grades and the advanced supplementary school classes I attended through most of high school, the faculty was supplemented by survivors of the war. How could these men and women, who had lost their own families, reenter classrooms to teach Jewish subjects to Jewish children? Their nerve impressed me more than what they taught.

ℭ℟

MOTHER'S ENERGY PROPELLED OUR RESETTLEMENT. She bore two new children in Canada. Our parents thought of calling the girl Victoria because her birth in November 1942 coincided with the start of General Montgomery's victory in North Africa. Instead, they named her Eva, used always in its diminutive form, *Evaleh*, just as I was *Ruteleh* and Benjamin (Binyomin) *Nyomeleh*. The youngest, Dovid Hirsh or David Gregory, born in 1948, was named for our paternal grandfather David, who perished in the Bialystok Ghetto, and for Mother's brother Grisha, murdered near Vilna. Mother was forty-two when she gave birth to *Dovidl*, and let it be known that she had not consulted Father in plotting his conception.

The author with her older brother Benjamin, Czernowitz, 1939. This was the great age of photography among Jews of East Central Europe. Thanks to Masza's priorities in taking her photo albums with her from Czernowitz, many such images survive.

Since I never visited other children in their homes, I had no idea that ours was unusual. Mother raised us with the same dedication to Yiddish language and culture that observant Jewish families had to the Commandments. Unlike in Czernowitz, where Ben and I had been taught Romanian and German, all that mattered to her in Canada was that we remained steadfastly in our own culture. She did not let on that she herself was picking up English, or that she functioned perfectly well in French; she even spoke Yiddish with Ksenia Gudzio, the Ukrainian girl who had spent the war as a slave laborer in Germany and whom Mother hired when she arrived in Canada as a seventeen-year-old refugee.

Jewish immigrants to North America were quicker than other ethnic groups to switch to English, since adaptation was a Jewish tradition of which Yiddish was itself a product—one of many such Jewish vernaculars that developed wherever Jews formed communities in other nations. Jewish parents urged their children to learn English as quickly and as well as possible so that they might benefit and benefit from their new home. Many had come to escape poverty, and Yiddish was associated with the poverty they wished to escape. They traded in their language to trade up economically, with no wish to escape their Jewishness. The exception to this pragmatism was those secular Jews, the Bundists and the Yiddishists, who had made Yiddish the repository of their Marxist "proletarian" culture. Yiddish was their substitute for religion and the vehicle of anticapitalism, their political creed.

Mother's insistence on Yiddish was not ideological. With nothing else left of Jewish Vilna, she held its language sacred. She bridled at being mistaken for a Bundist because her attachment to Yiddish had nothing in common with the Jewish Bund's Marxist assumptions, and she objected to the label Yiddishist, which implied opposition to Hebrew. People did not understand her distinctions. She scorned the nouveau riche flight from Yiddish, which was the mainstay of *her* Jewishness. Her Yiddish was marvelous: she never mixed it with other languages. As against the implied link between Yiddish and poverty, she insisted that everything about it must be sartorially elegant—*Yidish muz geyn sheyn ongeton.* For that purpose, she herself frequented the finest dress shops for European imports. Her message must have sunk in, because when I began teaching Yiddish literature at McGill in the late 1960s, I visited the Carriage Shop boutique in the best downtown store to buy the most fashionable outfits I ever owned.

No doubt there was some vanity in this spirit of *noblesse oblige*, but our mission was to endow Yiddish with dignity. When in my thirties I read for the first time the great Hebrew writer S. Y. Agnon's novel, *A Guest for the Night*, I recognized his comparable summons to nobility.

In 1930, Agnon, by then settled in Jerusalem, returned for a visit to his native city Buczacz—formerly Austria, then Poland, nowadays Ukraine. Its once robust Jewish community had been devastated by the First World War and from his Palestinian perspective it was already beyond recovery. He spun the actual week of his visit into the fictional year of the novel, describing the poverty, suffering, and political chaos in such evocative detail that by the time he completed it in the late 1930s, the book augured the coming world war as much as it registered the effects of the previous one. But while he is in Buczacz, Agnon's narrator reminds the demoralized Jews that they are the people of the God of Israel, Lord of the Universe, the King of Kings:

> Does the king refrain from putting the crown on his head because it is heavy? On the contrary, he puts it on his head and delights in it. . . .What good does this do the king? That I do not know. Why? Because I am not a king. But if I am not a king, I am a king's son, and I ought to know.

Speaking in the parabolic manner of Jewish *midrash*, Agnon suggests that if God Himself continues to wear His crown, that is, to guide Jewish history, the chosen people should bear His image with dignity. In that divine analog I recognized Mother's regard for the language of Jewish Vilna. To be born a Jew was a rare honor that required moral confidence—aristocracy of the spirit. Though I would later dispute the idea that Yiddish culture was a reliable conduit for Jewish faith, she, for her part, considered her Jewishness more authentic than that of many Orthodox Jews whom she suspected of using religion to conceal their misdeeds. While most Jewish immigrants to Canada wanted their children to acculturate as quickly as possible to take advantage of the free society, Mother took advantage of the free society to ensure that her children possessed and valued the best of their inheritance.

Like Agnon's narrator, Masza experienced her life in the form of stories. She attributed her decision to move us to a Jewish neighborhood to an incident at the first Canadian wedding she and Leo attended in 1941 at the Shaar Hashomayim Synagogue. As the procession started down the aisle, she heard the musicians playing her hymn, the song that had accompanied the funeral of the martyred poet A. Vayter in Vilna! Mother was musically literate enough to know that the same melody was also sung to Shaul Tchernikhovsky's Hebrew poem, "*Sakhki, sakhki al hakhalomoys*" ("You May Laugh at My Dreams"), composed in 1892 and recommended by some as an alternative to the Zionist hymn "Hatikvah." In other words, the music was as suitable for a wedding as for a funeral. But this was 1941, and in the throes of war, Mother seized on the purloined melody as evidence that the Westmount bourgeoisie was desecrating Jewish Vilna.

Mother's inverted snobbery, her concept of Jewish splendor, made us the only family I ever knew to move across the city from Westmount in order to be close to Yiddish institutions and Yiddish schools.

ଓଃ

SOON AFTER WE ARRIVED IN Montreal, Mother began promoting the work of local Yiddish authors and artists for whom the language was even more essential than it was for her. The North American marketplace for Yiddish books was never robust, leaving writers and poets dependent on the backing of patrons. Cultural patronage is a timeless practice, but with no government or institutions to sponsor them, Yiddish writers relied almost entirely on *metsenatn* to support their work. These Yiddish Maecenases, unlike more common patrons of the arts, were often shopkeepers, union members, and small factory owners and their wives who attended the lectures of visiting poets and writers and bought their books, sometimes supplementing their cost with discrete private contributions. All Yiddish writers held second jobs, the more fortunate in white-collar jobs as journalists or teachers.

Montreal was lucky to have several other prosperous supporters of Yiddish culture as well as our parents, and a Jewish public library that sponsored literary events.

In our early days in Montreal, I often accompanied my parents to the bookstore of Hertz Kalles, where we bought our prayer and Jewish school books as well as whatever new Yiddish books he recommended. By the 1950s, when the store moved westward, the Yiddish section was relegated to a back room. Father's favorite novel was actually *War and Peace*, which he read first in Russian, then in English. He was only half joking when he once apologized to me for not making me a coming out ball like Natasha's. Yet he was also an avid Yiddish reader when he could find the time, and the last novel he was reading when he died was Chava Rosenfarb's three-volume Yiddish epic *Dos boym fun lebn, The Tree of Life*, about Lodz and the Lodz Ghetto. Rosenfarb had settled in Montreal after the war and though my parents were not as friendly with her as they were with several other local writers, Father had bought the trilogy after hearing her speak and was deeply moved by her writing.

My parents subscribed to more Yiddish publications than they read. I don't think Father ever turned down a request for support. But Mother's truly creative effort was to sell customers preordered copies of books by local authors so that they could pay for their printing and publication. Fifty copies at ten dollars apiece would cover the advance to the publisher; some of her friends made additional contributions. Buyers then received their finished copies at a reception in our home where the authors read selections from their work and others praised it. It was this system of *prenumerantn*, prepublication subscriptions, that I later proposed to our teacher, Louis Dudek, when he needed funding to publish the work of a student named Leonard Cohen as the first book in a projected series of Young Canadian Poets.

With the support of Father's earnings, Mother became one of the most prominent local hostesses of Jewish literary gatherings. I grew up at the center of a lively literary world that imbued me with a reverence for writers and books, though I would have preferred to be on the writerly rather than commercial side of the exchange.

Leo Roskies, left, with Melekh Ravitch in the Laurentians, 1960s.

Masza's friendship with the Yiddish poet Melekh Ravitch was a particular boon to them both. Ravitch was one of the most unusual people I would
ever know, but this was not something I realized in childhood. Though he
lived very modestly, his employment at the Jewish Public Library was not
enough to sustain him, and Mother supplemented his income by various
strategies that included hiring him to teach us. He was a permanent guest
at our Passover seder and at every literary reception. As a vegetarian, he
required a special meal that caused more than the usual preparatory anxieties in the kitchen.

Ravitch had launched his literary career in Warsaw in the early 1920s
as part of a self-styled literary gang, the Khaliastre, and authored a book
provocatively entitled Naked Poems. Perhaps his qualms about being less
brilliant than the group's other members—the poets Peretz Markish and Uri
Zvi Greenberg and the novelist Israel Joshua Singer—made him assume the
added task of secretary of the Warsaw Yiddish Writers Association so that if
he could not stand at the pinnacle of Yiddish literature, he could be at its organizing center. He genuinely liked being in touch with the far-flung Yiddish
literary world, and had he not kept up his international correspondence and
scrupulously preserved it through all his travels, the National Library of

Israel would not have his most important archive in all of Yiddish letters. It is the more important because so much else of those years was destroyed.

In the 1930s, Ravitch undertook a journey around the globe, turning the anxious fate of the Jewish refugee into a voluntary adventure. In Australia he sought out the Aborigines, with the goal of bringing the culture of another scorned population to the attention of Yiddish readers. When he settled in Montreal shortly before we did, he continued in his role as secretary of the Yiddish literary community by corresponding with those authors who were still alive and inviting them to speak in Montreal. Thanks to him, we got to meet many of those luminaries, and Mother often organized gatherings in their honor.

Around our dining room table in 1951 I heard the poet Itzik Manger tell about the first time he got drunk by sipping wine through a straw from a hole in a barrel in the back of a horse-drawn wagon. (He happened to be drinking at the time of this recollection.) I later found the same account in Manger's writings and couldn't be sure whether it confirmed the truthfulness of his memory or the consistency of his storytelling.

Manger was born in my native Czernowitz and grew up in its atmosphere, but then in the late 1920s moved to the much larger Jewish center of Warsaw and there oversaw the performances of his popular mock biblical operettas. He played the *enfant terrible* of Yiddish letters, using inebriation as a screen for bad behavior. He mistreated those who tried to help him, including Ravitch, and much more shamefully, his former lover Rachel Auerbach who had rescued some of his writings in Warsaw during the war. Yet none of this misconduct affected the affection his poetry inspired.

This poem was everyone's favorite:

There is a tree that stands.
And bends beside the road
All its birds have flown away,
Leaving not a bird.

Seeing the abandoned tree naked before the storm, the boy in the poem tells his mother that he intends to become a bird and climb into its branches to sing it sweet comfort. But the mother fears for her child. "Take a scarf," she says, "and galoshes. Your fleece-lined cap, your woolen underwear...."

I try to fly, but I can't move...
Too many, many things
My mother's piled on her weak bird
And loaded down my wings

I look into my mother's eyes
And sadly, there I see
The love that won't let me become
The bird I want to be.

In the Yiddish world, where the people's approval counted for more than copyright protection, this poem set to music acquired the status of a folksong. Devil-may-care troubadour best remembered as tethered son.

Of all the poets I got to meet, Manger came closest to fulfilling my romantic image of the artist. The permanently dangling cigarette at the side of his mouth had something to do with it, though as far as that goes, Rokhl Korn was the more dedicated smoker. She didn't remove the cigarette even when she was talking.

Rokhl arrived in Montreal with her daughter and son-in-law in 1949 and immediately became a special friend of the family. Her daughter Renia was our physician, her son-in-law our dentist, and Mother became godmother to one of their twin boys. It wasn't until I went off to graduate school that I began to appreciate how good her poems really were. She and Ravitch had known one another in Poland, and there were uncorroborated rumors about their more than literary friendship, though that, like the dangling cigarette, went with the bohemian images that the term "poetry" inspired.

Poet and writer Rokhl Korn, Montreal, undated, with her trademark cigarette.

Whatever associations with poverty Yiddish had for others, I have explained that in our home Yiddish was the fount of high culture. Yet I may have underestimated some of its creators because they seemed so ordinary. Avrom Reisen, the author of Mother's hymn, was already elderly, more grandfather than revolutionary when he paid Montreal a visit. Others like J. I. Segal, who taught in a local Jewish day school, were just too familiar to inspire. Segal was unprepossessing, a family man with two daughters, struggling to make a living, transmuting domestic joys and sorrows into modern verse. It was years before I came to appreciate how consistently and remarkably his poetry could illumine the ordinary, exalt everyday life.

In truth, the most intriguing celebrity in our cultural orbit was not one of the poets but Hertz Grosbard, the actor, or rather, *diseur* who performed their works. He was in a different league from the local amateur Yiddish theater and from the touring professional companies that regularly performed in Montreal. The theatrical equivalent of a virtuoso, he had veered away from the Yiddish theater in 1927 with a solo literary recital based on the work of Itzik Manger and the fabulist Eliezer Shteynbarg, both residents of Czernowitz, where Grosbard was living at the time. (I began to notice how prominently my birthplace figured in Yiddish letters.)

Festive school banquet, Montreal 1950s. From left, seated, Leo and Masza Roskies, Leib and Sonia Tencer, Yechiel and Libe Shainblum. Standing, Sorke and Jacob Zipper, Chana and Shloime Wiseman. All except the Roskies were directly involved in education: Leib Tencer was vice-principal and Jacob Zipper, principal of the Jewish Peretz Schools where Sorke Zipper taught; Shloime Wiseman was principal of the Jewish People's School where Chana Wiseman taught and where Yechiel Shainblum, an artist, was a favorite teacher.

Despite the serious mien of its subjects, the photo speaks to the warm relations between the two schools that were originally joined and would merge again in 1971. The author's parents were friends with educators in both institutions. The Tencers, from Vilna, were the only ones at the table who had survived the war in Europe and arrived in the 1940s.

The two poets already had a small local following by the time Grosbard began performing their poems, but it was he who released the dramatic potential of Manger's ballads and the brilliant wit of Shteynbarg's fables as though he had been a partner to their creation. He kept these poets at the heart of his repertoire, carefully selecting works that showed off their distinction. Happily, recordings of his readings survive, though there are no films of his word concerts.

From the time Grosbard moved to Montreal in 1951, we attended all his local performances. Once I went with Mother to help set up the reception that was to follow his recital and saw him arrange the stage—bare but for a small table, chair, lamp, and book. Shunning all props and effects, he would not begin to speak until there was perfect silence in the hall, sometimes hard to achieve when the seats were moveable. His performances felt sacred, as if the slightest imperfection could profane the service, and though people laughed at the funny parts and cried when they were touched, I mostly held my breath. I sensed he was a genius, but I was afraid we could not meet his expectations, for he seemed to demand as much of the audience as of himself.

These evenings were the antithesis of the schmaltzy Yiddish theater that I also attended with my parents, where the audience applauded the rhetorical flourishes. Grosbard considered himself not part of, but a contrast to the popular Yiddish stage, and I think he must have formed my taste for understatement and artistic containment.

ૡ

As MOTHER SANCTIFIED YIDDISH, FATHER readopted some forms of observance that he had discontinued in adolescence, joining the nearest synagogue that he attended on the High Holy Days. Whatever our parents did was done without irony or the apologetic demurral that moderns often display when they participate in traditional rites. We took our parents' form of Jewish observance to be the regular practice of Judaism—but I remember one evening, around dinnertime, when Mother just happened to be serving an omelet with *shinke*, Yiddish for ham. The doorbell rang, and there on the front step stood our only religiously observant aunt, come on a surprise visit. Somehow, we felt that she had caught Mother in a sin and knew we had to keep Aunt from the kitchen. But how did we intuit this, when our parents had never even pretended to be "Orthodox"? I suppose that despite taking our Jewish practice as the national standard, we recognized that we were not in full compliance.

Mother's criticism of the hypocrisy and insincerity of Orthodox Jews did not extend to the God of Abraham. Her nonattendance at synagogue was not antinomian protest but a jealous wish to commune with God intimately in the privacy of her home. Neither of our parents ever mentioned their murdered families and communities in connection with God or prayer, leaving us to weigh that association for ourselves. We never used any other term for their erasure but *khurbn*, the same word that denotes the destructions of the Temple in Jerusalem. For the record, my siblings and I all keep the kosher home that our parents did not, and all the grandchildren attended Jewish day schools.

The most important feature of our Jewish observance was that both parents celebrated Passover with a strictness that belied our usual practice. We did not have separate dishes for dairy and meat, but on Pesach, Mother changed the tableware and allowed not a shred of prohibited *homets* in the house. On the two designated nights of the seder, Father conducted the reading of the Haggadah in the chant and reading style—the *nusah*—that he had absorbed from his father. We children accepted the anomalous meticulousness of this holiday, and to this day I would no sooner eat unleavened products on the eight days of Passover than I would boil a kid in its mother's milk. Indeed, Passover might have been invented so that our family could reenact our own flight "from a tyrant far worse than the Pharaoh who oppressed our ancestors in Egypt."

That phrase is from an insert to the Passover Haggadah circulated by the Canadian Jewish Congress right after the war to commemorate the Warsaw Ghetto uprising that had been launched on the first night of Passover 1943. We included this tribute to Jewish martyrdom and resistance just before the point in the seder when we asked God to pour out His wrath—for once!—on the nations that "*knew You not.*" The alignment of our experience with that of our ancestors was no doubt one of the reasons our parents observed Passover so religiously. When we recited, "In every generation let each man look upon himself as if he came forth out of Egypt," there was no "as if" about it.

Seders marked the passage of our years. I was often impatient when Father repeated something he had said the year before, but by adolescence

I regretted when he skipped any of his usual commentaries. As a child I resented the presence of guests who sat next to Father at the head of the table, but by adolescence I looked forward to their melodies and interpolations. Normally modest to a fault, Father conducted the seder with decisive authority, always pausing on the passage, "*And the Lord brought us forth out of Egypt*—not by the hands of an angel, and not by the hands of a seraph, and not by the hands of a messenger, but the Holy One, blessed be He, Himself, in His own glory and in His own person." Remember, he would caution, even God did not delegate authority when it came to anything important. I secretly hoped he was taking credit for the initiative he had shown in bringing us to Canada.

The wages of freedom is gratitude. At the seder we "thank, praise, laud, glorify, exalt, honor, bless, extol, and adore Him who…brought us forth from slavery to freedom, from sorrow to joy, from mourning to holiday, from darkness to light, and from bondage to redemption." Mother lit memorial candles more often than Sabbath candles, but this festival of spring we felt we were celebrating also on behalf of the dead. To the miracle of Passover, I added the miracle that in the midst of the war and the destruction of their formative world, our parents chose to observe the festival fully. With their broken hearts, I don't know how they did it.

3

RESPONSIBILITY

*B*en's bar mitzvah in May 1944 is the first day of my first eight years that I remember almost in its entirety. The ceremony took place after the liquidations of the ghettos of Vilna, Bialystok, and Kovno, and a year after the Russians fought off the Germans at Stalingrad. Domestic anxieties must also have been running high that morning because Mother, who had brought me by the hand to the synagogue, forgot about me after the service. I hadn't been told about the congregational *kiddush*, and when the synagogue emptied, with no one to ask where everyone else was, I walked back home alone. It turned out that no one had noticed my absence.

Whenever Mother referred to Ben's bar mitzvah, she would bring up the incident that ruined it for her. One of Father's three brothers had been unable to bring his family to Canada before the war. His wife and daughters remained in Poland until it was too late to help them escape. Although they would ultimately survive, their fate was then still uncertain. This uncle skipped the synagogue service and that afternoon arrived late at the small gathering in our home to berate Mother for celebrating while his family was in Nazi hands.

It was at this gathering of family and friends that Ben gave his bar mitzvah speech, parts of which I once could have quoted by heart. He spoke about *The Forgotten Ally*, a 1943 book by the Dutch-Canadian journalist Pierre Van Paassen which no one else in the room was likely to have read. Van Paassen had begun reporting from Palestine under the British Mandate in the mid-1920s, and he covered the large-scale Arab anti-Jewish riots of 1929. Impressed by the Jews and by the righteousness of their cause, he could not fathom why Britain favored Arab marauders over proven Jewish allies. He grew angrier about this injustice after the outbreak of the war when the Yishuv, the Jewish community of Palestine, gave massive help to the British while most pro-Axis Arab leaders betrayed them.

Ben praised this feisty Gentile who spoke up for Jews not out of sympathy for Hitler's victims but in appreciation of their contribution to the common cause. How bravely this journalist wrote in defense of the battling Jewish community of Palestine! How much sharper than a serpent's tooth was British ingratitude!

Although Ben had learned English only after we'd left Romania four years earlier, no one in the room spoke it so well. He had conceived of and written the talk without adult supervision, having learned more about the political situation from his shortwave radio than our parents or teachers did from their newspapers. Imagining our home as a lighthouse, I can see him rotating its beam from Europe to the Middle East, shifting our attention from the past to the future, from the war we hoped would soon end to the work that lay ahead of us. By age thirteen his responsibilities extended beyond the family to the Jewish people as a whole.

☙

My own rite of passage four years later at age twelve was spectacularly different. By then the war was over, but bat mitzvahs were then still unknown and it would not have occurred to me to want one. Not to say that we girls were neglected. Following the example of prosperous local Jewish families, I would have been entitled to a sweet sixteen. But since we never celebrated birthdays, I had no expectation of marking that occasion either.

Nonetheless, I was granted the greatest coming-of-age any Jewish child ever experienced. I turned twelve on May 13, 1948. Given the seven-hour time difference between Montreal and Tel Aviv, my assumption of Jewish responsibility coincided with the fifth day of Iyar 5708, when David Ben-

Gurion declared the independence of the Jewish state. Two days later my parents and I were among the estimated 20,000 Jews who poured into the stands of the Montreal Forum for a celebration grander than the one for the Montreal Canadiens when they won the Stanley Cup in 1946. Our principal, Shloime Wiseman, was among the speakers, and representatives from the newly founded Jewish state brought us greetings. When I later saw film clips of Jews dancing in the streets of Tel Aviv, I thought our excitement had outdone theirs.

In the preceding years, my parents had taken me along to commemorative evenings for the annihilated ghettos of Warsaw and Vilna. These were held early in the spring when the audience in heavy overcoats made the crowded halls feel like communities under siege. This mid-May public celebration of Israel's independence was open and joyous. On our way into the Forum, I caught sight of my older brother. All over the lobby, clusters of young people from the various youth organizations were holding large Israeli and Canadian flags the way firemen hold up rescue nets, urging us to throw in money, and there was Ben with his group, lifting the corner of a flag that already seemed heavy enough to assure the Jewish future in Israel.

The members of Ben's Zionist youth group were called Habonim, the Builders, and they intended to join the pioneers of Israel. Whenever they went, Ben would be going with them. Jewish youth groups often branched out from political movements, and even when they functioned independently, as this one did, they represented a certain faction of the Jewish polity. To the left of Habonim was Hashomer Hatzair, often aligned with the communists, while to the right, Young Judea was mainstream Zionist without any socialist connotation. I think that Ben signed up with Habonim more because of people he already knew in the group than on account of its socialist ideology, but on this occasion the groups were not competing as much as joining in celebration. These teenagers had just missed being conscripted into the Canadian armed forces to fight the Nazis or, as in Ben's case, being their victims.

As part of the ceremony, we recited the solemn remembrance prayer for the murdered Jews of Europe. It could not dull the thrill of "Hatikvah," the Zionist anthem confirming that *the hope* had been realized—"our hope of two thousand years, to be a free nation in our land, in the land of Zion and Jerusalem." Our knowledge that the country was under attack from surrounding Arab armies only served to raise the stakes for us: we would now have to do more, much more, in order to secure our Jewish homeland, raising funds for arms and the absorption of refugees, going to join the fight, and adding a new prayer to ask God's blessing for the state of Israel, "the first flowering of our redemption."

On the eve of World War II, the Canadian Jewish Congress had hired the Montreal poet A. M. Klein to help its president Samuel Bronfman with speechwriting. Bronfman was the founder of the Seagram's whiskey fortune, and for two decades the unlikely team of Bronfman & Klein, distiller and poet, rallied Canadian support for Jews in Europe and Palestine.

Bronfman had exploited the prohibition of alcohol in the United States to expand his firm into Canada's largest distillery, and when Canadian Jews were looking for someone to represent their interests, they persuaded their wealthiest Jew to take the position. Klein had trained as a lawyer but was far better known as a poet and intellectual writer. Among Quebec's English-language poets, he was the first to take a personal and literary interest in French-Canadian culture, and among his fellow Jewish writers he was both uniquely learned and uniquely responsive to events in Europe and Palestine.

The devotion of both these men to their fellow Jews distinguished them from their counterparts south of the border, who usually made their mark in society and culture by staying clear of the Jewish community. Jewish writers and intellectuals penetrating American culture in the 1940s were woefully deaf to Jewish needs when it counted most. Klein asked, "Where are the keepers of the world's conscience?" and in 1944 published a satiric epic, *The Hitleriad,* to destroy in poetry the man who was destroying his people.

Happier would I be with other themes—
(Who rallies nightmares when he could have dreams?)
With other themes, and subjects more august—
Adolf I sing but only since I must.

I must! Shall I continue the sweet words
That praise the blossoming flowers, the blossoming birds,
While, afar off, I hear the stampeding herds?
Shall I, within my ivory tower, sit
And play the solitaire of rhyme and wit,
While Indignation pounds upon the door,
And Pity sobs, until she sobs no more,
And, in the woods, there yelp the hounds of war?

This imitation of Pope's *Dunciad* ranks with Charlie Chaplin's "Great Dictator" as a hopeless attempt to mock Hitler off the stage of history. Still, I honor Klein's impossible project more than some artistically finer works of his morally somnambulant contemporaries.

After the war, the urgency of response to the Jewish crisis increased as the small community of Jews in Israel began rescuing the European refugees. In 1949, the CJC sent Klein to Israel to document and describe the "ingathering of exiles." He reported, newspaper-style, on his findings and then did what Chaim Nahman Bialik had done after filing the report of *his* fact-finding mission to Kishinev after the terrifying 1903 pogrom; the Jewish intellectuals of Odessa, shaken by the violence and its portent for Russian Jewry and for their own community, less than a hundred miles away, had sent Bialik to investigate and document the carnage. This he dutifully did, then sequestered himself to compose the epic poem *"Be'ir Ha-hareygah"*, "In the City of Slaughter," in which, rather than accuse the marauders, he adapted the tone and posture of the Hebrew prophets to excoriate his fellow Jews, and by inference their Judaism, for their passivity.

Then wilt thou flee to a yard, observe its mound.
Upon the mound lie two, and both are headless—
A Jew and his hound.
The self-same axe struck both, and both were flung
Unto the self-same heap where the swine seek dung;
Tomorrow the rain will wash their mingled blood
Into the runnels, and it will be lost

In rubbish heap, in stagnant pool, in mud.
Its cry will not be heard.

Even less predictable than Bialik's denigration of the victims was the effect this poem had in shaming Russian Jewish youth into political action. Klein, who was by then also the foremost English translator of Yiddish and Hebrew verse, reached for the sonority of the King James Bible in translating this poem just as Bialik had channeled the Hebrew Bible's prophetic force. Klein may then have followed Bialik's example when sent to cover the rebirth of Israel. The resurrection of the Jewish state was surely as momentous as the pogrom in Kishinev, and if Bialik's excoriation could call Jews to their duty, perhaps Klein could spark their national pride.

Klein's *The Second Scroll* cherishes the liberation of the Jews from twentieth-century Europe as reenactment of their liberation from Egypt. When I first read this book in college, I especially loved the part where the narrator compares his childhood fantasy about the coming of the Messiah with the actual experience of May 14, 1948:

> When as a young boy, the consolations and prophecies of Isaiah before me, I dreamed in the dingy Hebrew school the apocalyptic dream of a renewed Zion, always I imagined it as coming to pass thus: first I heard the roar and thunder of the battle of Gog and Magog; then, as silence fell, I saw through my mind's eye a great black aftermath cloud filling the heavens across the whole length of the humped horizon. The cloud then began to scatter, to be diminished, to subside, until revealed there shone the glory of a burnished dome—Hierosolyma the golden! [*Yerushalayim shel zahav*] Then lower it descended and lower, a mere breeze dispersed it, and clear was the horizon and before me there extended an undulating sunlit landscape.

In marvelous crescendo Klein then shows that the actual recovery of Israel far exceeded this dream in its splendor. How I wish I could have written like that!

Nowhere, not even in the sweep of Jewish history with its accounts of the Exodus and the kingdoms of David and Solomon, was there anything to rival the accomplishment of Jews who lost one-third of their numbers and in the same decade of the 1940s recovered their sovereignty. One might have expected hosannas, epic novels, blockbuster films, heroic symphonies—outpourings of joy and pride to mark the passage from slavery to freedom. *Less than Slaves* was what Benjamin Ferencz, one of the prosecuting team at the Nuremberg Trials, called his book about the Nazi treatment of Jews, suggesting that the modern Jewish road to liberation was even steeper than the biblical one. Yet until I came across Klein's novel, I found nothing to match my sense of grandeur.

There is no triumphalism in the Zionist canon. The Hebrew songs from Israel were muted. The musical ensembles of the Israel Defense Forces did not produce Sousa marches, much less any heroic songs like those of the Red Army Chorus whose records we continued to play after the war. Israelis were Jews, reluctant fighters and low-key victors. For grandeur I had to make do with Klein's rhetorical ascent from Gog and Magog to Jerusalem the Golden.

I COULD NOT HAVE FRAMED these thoughts so clearly in childhood, yet we produced our own version of Klein's script. In 1949, my graduating class of the Folkshule wrote and staged a school play without any starring roles. Act 1 was a series of tableaux: broken refugees on the ground rise to defy the British blockade, reach their homeland, and are last seen kissing its ground. In act 2 the oldest child in a Canadian family tells his parents he is going overseas to help secure and build Eretz Israel. Act 3, which required the most research, reenacted the debate at the United Nations that resulted in the General Assembly partition resolution of November 29, 1947. The final act showed young Jews in one of the settlements, possibly Kfar Etzion, trying to hold off the Arab armies in Israel's War of Independence. Our class spontaneously grasped the collective essence of the national drama.

Whenever Mother heard of someone from Vilna or Czernowitz who had survived and made it to some known address, she would comb through the photograph albums she had brought from Europe—her most precious possessions—and send them copies of any pictures she found of their relatives. When I visited one of those survivors in Israel in 1957, he showed me the photograph of his sister that Mother had sent him, his one and only memento of the past. Masza filled the house with glassware and tablecloths she bought from new immigrants who were getting a toehold as peddler-importers. Father found jobs for whom he could.

Not all of life was on this lofty level. I read comic books, Nancy Drew and Judy Bolton mysteries, *A Tree Grows in Brooklyn,* and in my first year of high school, the racier *Knock on Any Door.* I took elocution lessons and acted in popular children's theater productions. My greatest thrill was hanging out with my older brother and his best friend Seymour "Simmy" Berish. One day the two boys invited me to join them to see their high school's production of *A Date with Judy.* I was excited and asked for sartorial guidance: "I don't know what to wear." Simmy said, "If you had only one thing in the cupboard, you'd know exactly what to wear." I felt I had earned the rebuke, but then why were we seeing such a frivolous play?

ᘉ

EVERYONE KNEW THAT THE CREATION of Israel demanded something of us—but what? The winter of 1948, members of Habonim's Canadian contingent gathered at our home to plan their next step. Ben let me sit in a corner of the living room on condition that I keep quiet. Listening to their arguments, I found my brother the wisest in the group, the communist the handsomest, and the pacifist the most articulate. Barred from the discussion, I tried to figure out what I could from the materials being circulated.

The group intended the summer of 1949 to be their first step toward aliyah, their "ascent" to the homeland, and since the concept of moving to Israel was then still inseparable from the idea of collective settlement, they intended to move there together as the formative kernel of a new or existing kibbutz. Their immediate destination was Ein Hashofet, named by its American founders for the Zionist leader and U.S. Supreme Court justice (*shofet*) Louis D. Brandeis, and chosen by them for its proximate alignment with the moderate socialism of Habonim. For some in the group, the summer in Israel was to be just a college experience, like summer camp abroad, while for others it was the only practical way to get to Israel. But their discussion when they got together, based on articles and books, replicated the debates of the Zionist and socialist thinkers who tried to establish the theory behind their impulse to restore the Jewish people to its land.

The few arguments that I was able to follow were sparked by members who did not consider this particular kibbutz radical enough. Communist kibbutzim imposed greater restrictions on private ownership and required ideological loyalty to the Soviet Union. The group argued as if their lives were at stake—yet much as I admired their dedication, I wondered how they intended to stay together if they were already in such fierce disagreement. I still have in my possession their mimeographed "requirements for admission" (my explanations in square brackets):

> The purely social compatibility of the *haver* [comrade or member] will inevitably be influenced to a large degree by his net success in integrating himself into the totality of group activity. We must however guard against the tendency to set up as the social ideal either the versatile and accomplished mingler on the one extreme, or the ultra-efficient worker on the other. In general, compatibility entails not so much the ability to undertake intimate relations with all the *hevre* [group] (although a degree of this is greatly to be desired), but rather that, having made a few close friends, his temperament be such that it will not continuously clash with that of the majority.

And so forth. Even at age twelve, I had my doubts about their scheme, if not yet their grammar. Why, for instance, if they intended to settle in Israel, did they plan to return to Canada at the end of the summer? I did not want to lose my brother, but if *I* were going to help build the country I would take off for good, the way we had left Romania. Besides, every year when Ben and I packed for summer camp, we had a checklist of equipment: where was theirs? And wouldn't it make more sense to think about what they could bring to the new country, like hoes and shovels, or how they could contribute professionally to its welfare, rather than argue over principles of cooperation?

Ben was later to say that they would have been better off had they considered immigrating just as they were—ambitious youngsters looking to replicate the same urban life they enjoyed in Canada. But people don't normally move from better conditions to worse without some compelling recompense, and going all for one and one for all to rebuild the Land of Israel propelled them just as it had the earlier *halutzim* of Russia and Poland. Kibbutzim suited that early phase of pioneering. Indeed, socialism may never have had a better tryout than it did in those Israeli settlements where members could establish their own boundaries and rules.

Some early settlements were determinedly secular, shunning every Jewish practice including marriage, while others were founded as religiously observant egalitarian communities. Some hired outside labor, for example during harvest, while others insisted on complete self-sufficiency. Some kibbutzim, like Yad Mordechai or the kibbutz of Ghetto Fighters—*lohamey hagetaot*—were established by survivors of the war with a special mission to commemorate their comrades and their history. During the years of rationing and fighting off Arab attacks, habits of shared responsibility had the same importance as in the military.

Because members of Ben's Habonim group were still young and single they did not face questions that later broke up the collectives. Communal children's homes were tolerable as long as the economic and military situation required it, but once conditions improved, parents wanted to raise their own children, even if that meant making their own mistakes. It was only after Israel had won its independence and enhanced its security that its citizens craved personal autonomy as well, preferring the risks of a mixed capitalist economy to a central committee's enforced egalitarianism, and individual initiative to communal control.

Transit visa of Benjamin Roskies on way to Israel, May 1949.

The contribution of the kibbutzim would forever grace the annals of Israeli history even as the settlements themselves evolved into privatized villages and their collective children's homes gave way to single-family dwellings. The collective of the nation gradually grew independent of the kibbutz, which happened to be the only part of Israel I disliked. I shared the group's sense of responsibility for Israel but found their debates more silly than serious. Much as I would have wanted to go with Ben that summer, I would not willingly have submitted to the authority of that group or any other. Being second in a family of four (my younger brother David had just been born) was cooperative discipline enough.

CR

No DOUBT MY JAUNDICED VIEW of collective living was the result of attendance at summer camp from ages five to nineteen, the year before I married. At first, I was not given any say in the matter, and then going to camp in the summer became as habitual as attending school the rest of the year. Father was afraid Ben and I would contract polio if we stayed in the city, and who knows what Mother's state of mind was that summer of 1941 when the Germans took Vilna and began murdering its Jews even before they forced them into ghettos. I had learned not to put up a fight when both parents were in agreement. We were probably better off at camp.

Jewish summer camps remain a distinctive feature of Jewish life in North America, some run by organizations and others by private individuals or families. The same Zionist and leftist movements that sponsored youth groups also subsidized summer camps, and Jewish federations provided mainstream camping for children from poorer and immigrant families. Jewish content in the private camps varied according to the inclination of their owners, who were sometimes no less idealistic than the staff affiliated with the political movements.

Pripstein's Camp was located in the foothills of the Laurentian Mountains thirty miles north of Montreal. The place smelled of fresh cow's milk and hay and sometimes skunks; the camp's kitchen carried the more enticing aroma of the onion rolls that Mrs. Pripstein baked for visitors or anyone sick in the infirmary. Chaim Pripstein had left his job as an elementary school teacher to run, with his wife Pearl ("the daughter of a rabbi," my mother would emphasize), a modest country hotel catering to families like ours, she in the kitchen, he handling all the rest. The presence of children among their guests gave Chaim the idea of turning the hotel into a camp where he could pursue his educational vocation in healthier surroundings. Eventually, he would move the camp to a handsome lakeside property farther in the mountains. As of this writing, it still runs, taken over by some of its former campers.

The author at Pripstein's Camp, Summer, 1956. With Norman Samuels, right (later University Professor and provost at Rutgers University, Newark) and Stanley Wohl (later physician in California).

Having met Mr. and Mrs. Pripstein, my parents were justifiably confident that we would be safe under their care. Chaim, affectionately known as C. P., was always nailing down a loose shingle on one of the roofs or checking the cabins after lights out. Once a summer he appeared at the waterfront to beguile an audience of children and counselors by floating on his back while reading a newspaper and smoking a cigarette. Mainly, he encouraged children to get along with each other and hired counselors for their maturity rather than for any special talents or athletic skills. The camp's reputation for forbearance attracted parents with children who needed special care, and the ranks of its counselors would produce more psychologists, psychiatrists, social workers, and educators than many a school of higher learning.

C. P. took some risks in admitting campers. Donny (I have changed his name) sometimes roamed the campgrounds alone. At first I was a little afraid of his erratic behavior, but I grew accustomed to his fitful speech, his swaying back and forth like a devout Jew at prayer, and his unnerving habit of asking you where you lived, by which he meant at what numerical address, which is how he preferred to identify us. He confirmed C. P.'s expectation that children can learn to respect even someone radically idiosyncratic. Of all the Jewish values the camp transmitted through Sabbath services or Zionist songs, by far the most emphasized was mutual responsibility, enshrined in the Talmudic teaching *Kol Yisrael arevim zeh lazeh*, all Jews are responsible for one another. At Pripstein's, campers and counselors were to look out for the welfare of everyone else in the group.

I tried to do as well at camp as in school. The camp was unregimented but disciplined. We were expected to rise and shine, swiftly make a neat bed with hospital corners, strain to do well at swimming, hiking, sports, arts and crafts, and drama, show consideration to fellow campers and politeness to instructors, and write letters home during rest period. Except for drama, I did these things mostly out of a sense of duty. More than anything, I wanted to be alone, to read and daydream and be subject to no one else's expectations. My reading of books like *Heidi* and *Anne of Green Gables* assured me that I was not the first child to feel out of place.

No one who knew me at Pripstein's would have suspected my reluctance to be there, except possibly C. P., who understood a great deal about each of us. But when it came to one feature of camp, I positively rebelled. Blue and White Week, known elsewhere as Color War, divided campers and counselors into competing teams and scored all activities as contests between the two sides. The teams produced competing plays, art projects, and songs, giving no respite from rivalry, even at mealtime. Everyone but me seemed to enjoy the stimulation and the camaraderie of competition. But the normal pressure of having to perform at my best was now linked to securing victory for half the camp, and I could neither play at war nor understand why any-one would want to. Contending to win seemed the antithesis of cooperation. The year the program was introduced, I demanded to be excused, and every subsequent summer I had my parents submit a letter that exempted me from the contest.

Both Ben and I went on to become junior, then senior counselors, he naturally first, paving the way. One day, when I was eleven and he already a counselor at sixteen, I experienced real fear for the first time. Campers and counselors traded places for a day—an inversion I did not enjoy and from which I absented myself so as not to have to participate in any "entertain-ment" at our counselor's expense. Suddenly I saw my brother being chased by his whooping campers through the field that bordered one side of the camp property. He was running through high corn and the campers were bound to catch up with him. Of course, it was a game, and I must have known it. But at that moment I knew with certainty that Ben would be killed. Whether they captured him or he died trying to escape, his life would be over. I was struck with terror.

What was this about? Ben flourished at Pripstein's. He hung out with counselors who were all a few years older than he. At the end of one sea-son he took a camping trip with them, which is probably when he lost his virginity (knowledge I gained posthumously from reading his diary). At some point he became the camp bugler who roused us with "Reveille" in the morning and put us to sleep in the evening with "Taps." He also brought his BB gun to camp and was called in when there was a mouse to be shot. He composed the camp hymn and a delightful operetta, *Solomon and the Bee*, performed at the annual camp concert. Obviously, I was not alone in adoring and admiring him.

Why, then, was I so afraid for him, and why did the memory of that chase through the cornfield alarm me after Ben was long since dead? I like to think of myself as having been fearless, but it seems this was not quite accurate—rather than fear for myself I grew afraid for Ben and for the Jews trying to escape their pursuers. Whatever sanctuary others may have found in a camp or kibbutz—or, come to think of it, in a family—membership only increased my sense of duty. *Alone*, on my own, I could teach myself to be unafraid. Beginning in my early teens I would return home alone on dark winter evenings from afternoon classes or drama rehearsals and walk, not run, repeating, "We have nothing to fear but fear itself," the only English sentence, courtesy of President Roosevelt, that Mother included among her habitual Yiddish sayings. In my midteens I took to hitchhiking, once having to roll out of a car in motion when the driver started reaching for me in the passenger seat.

Alone, I considered myself invulnerable. But I could not bear threats to others and especially not to Ben, who was saddled with responsibility for more than he should have been expected to bear—some of it, unfairly, for me. Perhaps, then, my terror arose from the realization that, rather than expecting my brother always to protect me, I should have been protecting him. Those mimeographed Habonim instructions went on to say that the individual should be able "to find his place in the social structure of the group so that his basic social and gregarious needs are satisfied." I found no comfort in that social structure and harbored no illusion about them satisfying my needs. I wasn't sure I had the power to keep us all safe.

౫

I CAME TO REALIZE HOW much Pripstein's influenced my sense of collective responsibility when I read Leonard Cohen's first novel. I will say more about him in describing our college years when he was two years ahead of me, a senior to my sophomore. In 1963 when his book appeared, we were well past college and though he was already a published poet, I was thrilled when he told me he was writing a novel. Unlike him, I had always preferred fiction to verse and was eager to read about people like us. Leonard's book turned out to be everything, or almost everything, I'd hoped for, along the lines of James Joyce's *Portrait of the Artist* with the budding writer transposed to Montreal. I read *The Favorite Game* from cover to cover the day I bought it.

Depending on how well you knew Leonard, you could identify the landmarks and people that he was recasting in his autobiographical fiction.

The author was recognizable in the protagonist Lawrence Breavman, who like him grew up in Westmount, lost his father, experienced young love, wrote poetry, and hung out with his friend Krantz, Leonard's real-life buddy Morton Rosengarten—the Rosen*krantz* to his Guildenstern, or Hamlet. The novel ends with the poet Breavman serving briefly as a staff member at a camp, just as Leonard actually did at Pripstein's in the summer of 1957.

That summer, I was absent on my honeymoon in Israel—the subject of a later chapter—but I heard all about it from friends who had been my fellow counselors. In their eagerness to have Leonard join them at camp, they had persuaded C. P. to hire him despite the camp director's misgivings about employing "stars" who might be too caught up in their own lives to do the nurturing expected from the staff. Whereas parts of Leonard's description may have been based on other summer camps he had attended, one unmistakable human presence in the novel marked this camp as Pripstein's:

"What's your favorite store?" asked Martin.

"What's yours?"

"Dionne's. What's your favorite parking lot?"

"I don't know. What's yours?"

"Dionne's Parking Lot."

The questions excited Martin because now he asked breathlessly,

"How many windows in the building Dionne's is in?"

Trust Leonard to transcribe such a conversation exactly as it would have gone, with "Martin" growing more and more agitated. The precision of this portrait made Leonard's handling of Donny/Martin's role in the novel and other aspects of that sequence all the more shocking to me. Leonard casts Breavman as Martin's protector, with other counselors either indifferent to or critical of the boy's erratic behavior. He makes the camp bourgeois and its staff lackluster. To spice up the conclusion and enhance his own role as the sensitive exception to their mediocrity, he then has Martin killed, "accidentally run over by a bulldozer which was clearing a marshy area," where Martin was presumably hiding. In sum, Leonard had inverted the values of the camp that went out of its way to protect Donny through all the years he grew from childhood into adolescence, when it was actually Leonard who came from the buttoned-up part of Montreal Jewish society, he alone among the counselors who had belonged to a fraternity, and Pripstein's the place that had taught us sensitivity.

Leonard had the chutzpah to make his own fictional stand-in the only authentic caregiver in a camp that, in real life, hadn't wanted to hire him for precisely the reason that an artist would be incapable of being part of a supportive and sustaining group. The fictional Breavman even uses Martin's death as an excuse to abandon the camp three weeks early. Leonard did in fact leave early, probably because he grew bored with the work, and the other counselors had to pick up the slack. This can't have made him popular after they had pushed to have him hired, but just as the Yiddish world forgave Itzik Manger his cruelty, everyone was prepared to treat Leonard tenderly. I did not like Leonard any less after this disappointment, but as my very first insider's view of how fiction distorts truth, it punctured some of my reverence for literature and for him.

No need to remind me of what artistic license permits. By the time I read Leonard's book, I had completed my formal credits for a doctorate in comparative literature and was well aware that the artist has every right to resolve the tension between the collective and the individual in the latter's favor. I adored Leonard's company and knew that he was the best writer our cohort would produce. But my sympathies leapt to the defense of the camp that had provided summers of refuge for Donny/Martin and so many more of us. In my own years as a counselor I dealt with children who were asthmatic and diabetic, a girl whose parents had just divorced, three teenaged bedwetters, and other youngsters like myself at their age who just wanted to be left alone.

The book surprised me not in its departure from reality but because the literary outcome of the artist's celebration of himself was so paltry compared with what C. P. had wrought. The romantic idea of the sensitive artist in a bourgeois society was so much less interesting than the camp the Pripsteins had built.

I need not have been disheartened by Leonard's irresponsibility. After just one more novel, he realized that he was meant to be a poet—an art form that affords greater license to bask in the first-person singular. Soon he went all out by turning songwriter and pioneering a new troubadour art. He was at his best when he did not go beyond himself.

I wished for Ben that he, too, could have continued composing and playing music while serving as devoted son, husband, father, employee and employer, Jew and Canadian, friend and brother; but that isn't the way life works.

4

ACCOMMODATION

*I*n September 1949, I registered at Montreal's Strathcona Academy, the high school that served our district of Outremont. Most of the incoming students came from the city's two large feeder Protestant schools, which is to say that most of them were Jews.

Earlier I explained how Quebec's confessional school system defined Jews as Protestants "for purposes of education." As it happened, the majority of my former classmates at the Jewish People's School were headed for a different Protestant high school named for Baron Byng, a World War I hero. Academic rivalry between Strathcona and Baron Byng, the two schools with the largest Jewish populations, was reinforced by a perceptible divide between the former's prosperous district and the latter's still-immigrant one.

The girls ahead of me in the registration line seemed to be at home with each other. I was glad to be anonymous. Since I would soon be wearing a school uniform, Mother had bought me no autumn clothes except a dark purple silk dress with puffed sleeves for the Jewish holidays. There was irony in those puffed sleeves. My beloved Anne Shirley of Green Gables had longed for such a dress—but for purposes of a party, not high school registration. To hide the sleeves, I wore a cardigan that not even the torture of late summer heat could make me remove.

Torture was anyway never far from my mind. Here I was in Canada, growing up in the calmest place on the planet, while my parallel fantasy track often featured a scenario of chase-and-entrapment in which I was heroically required to hold out and refuse to surrender in the face of war, persecution, and murder. Many of the stories being told at home and in Jewish school were about families in hiding or being discovered. I tried to imagine what I would have done if we had been trapped in Europe, whether I would have joined a group of fighters, or held out against the Nazis if captured.

Ben, who attended Strathcona before me, had racked up such an exemplary academic and civic reputation that I was accorded some of the respect earned by him. I was assigned to an experimental "mixed class" of boys and girls made up of the top-ranking students from all incoming schools. Thirty-odd students were now consigned to a single academic ladder where one wrong answer could hurl you down three or four rungs in class standing.

I was already accustomed to mixed classes, but Strathcona's rules of conduct were new to me. On the first day I found myself twice dispatched to the principal's office, first for answering a question without waiting to be called upon and then for correcting the teacher who had misheard my reply: "But that's what I said!" Jewish school had not required the same degree of decorum—and had I been a boy, I might have been not just reprimanded but strapped. In the following years, the worst part of high school was the sound from the boys' section down the hall of the strap coming down on someone's hands. The Jew in Peretz's story running the gauntlet was my image of corporal punishment, and it was unbearable to imagine even a fraction of it meted out to the boys I knew. This was one of several ways I learned that it was better to be a girl.

On the whole, the girls did better at things that teachers cared about: neatness, clear handwriting, memorization, and anticipating teachers' expectations by being attuned less to the subject than to how they taught it. Though none of this came naturally to me, I figured out how to give them what they wanted, and as a result learned too little during my four years of high school even as I maintained suitably high grades. What I mostly mastered were the arts of adaptation.

CR

ANY OUTSIDE OBSERVER MIGHT HAVE mistaken our school for a thoroughly Christian institution. All our teachers were required to be Protestant, and our Jewish tax-paying parents were excluded from the school board. That Jews constituted over 90 percent of the student body went unmentioned before the High Holy Days, when none of us attended class, or at the annual Christmas assemblies at which all of us were present. The school day itself began with the Episcopal version of the Lord's Prayer: "Our Father who art in heaven, hallowed be thy name..." The absence of the name of Jesus meant we could recite it in good conscience.

We and our teachers thus formed a temporary coalition, like shipmates forced to cooperate during a voyage. The teachers expected us to "lead the province" in the matriculation exams at the end of senior year, and the fact that they would be judged by *our* success made us allies in a common cause.

Only once did I resent being in a Christian school. We were studying the Book of Esther, which may have been chosen as the book of the Bible most appropriate for us. But rather than highlight Mordecai's cleverness or Esther's courage or even Haman's cruelty, our teacher reproached the Jews in the story for taking bloodthirsty revenge. Towards the end of chapter nine, the Jews of Shushan kill three hundred of their foes and the Jews in the provinces who had been targeted for extinction kill seventy-five thousand. But in each case, "They did not lay their hand on the spoil." In Jewish school, we had celebrated the escape of Jews from Haman's murderous decree and commended them for killing their antagonists—*without looting*. Our teacher's emphasis on the killing seemed unfairly misplaced, but I sensed no malice in it, only lack of understanding.

Our mixed class was discontinued after that first year, apparently written off as a failed experiment, and I was relegated to far less lively all-girl classes. My bright and friendly new classmates did not seem interested in what interested me. Perhaps for that reason, I put greater effort into extra-curricular activities. In junior year I bought a large teddy bear and appointed myself mascot carrier for the boys' basketball team. No one objected to my ruse, which got me excused from class on afternoons when our team traveled to another school. Male sweat remains one of my favorite colognes.

The next target of my ambition was the student council, of which, by the end of junior year, I was elected president on the wry slogan, "Don't let the students' council be Ruthless." I thereupon made good on my campaign promises: to acquire a new backboard for the baseball diamond and to eliminate strapping. I accomplished the latter by proposing to our principal, Miss Hay, that she suspend physical punishment for a period of months and if behavior did not worsen or perhaps even improved, prohibit the practice thereafter. She agreed with alacrity and I don't think strapping was ever reinstated. The school must have been ready for this change.

I even found a creative use for the reversal-of-roles gimmick of "camper-counselor day" that I had dreaded at camp. My suggestion: that upperclass students contemplating a career in education be permitted on a certain day to take over as teachers of the junior grades. Anticipating favorable publicity, Miss Hay invited the press to cover the event; there I was in the next day's paper, shown teaching one of the lower grades.

Do you find this girl insufferable? I, too, had begun to tire of her ambition. In elementary school I had started lessons in elocution and acting in productions of the local children's theater. After hitting my prime at fifteen as Jo in *Little Women*, I was certain I had found my profession. The following season, disappointed to be cast as stand-in for the female lead, I got to play the part after all when the assigned actress broke her ankle. Spooked by the thought that I might inadvertently have wished for her accident, I quit the program at the end of the year. Even worse than my fear of failure was the thought that success had to come at someone else's expense.

It would seem that everything came easily to me in high school except feeling at ease. When I later read sociologist David Riesman's distinction between the inner-directed or outer-directed personality it made little sense to me because my inner-directed self was habitually intent on proving itself useful to others. No one I knew was more independent than I, freer of parental supervision, more outspoken, or less afraid of authority. At the same time, where would I have drawn the line between the girl who wanted to be school president and her hopes of saving the boys from strapping? I couldn't have asked my classmates to vote for me unless I thought I was doing it to improve the school for them. Two years after my birth Jerry Siegel and Joe Shuster had created Clark Kent with a similar cast of mind—someone who wanted to protect good from forces of evil, including those in himself.

Part of this inflated sense of my obligation no doubt had to do with the burden of privilege impressed on me since earliest childhood by Peppi, who taught me adult behavior, by Mother's moral aversion to throwing out even a crust of bread when others were starving, by Father's writing checks for myriad charities on Saturday mornings when other Jews were in synagogue. Poverty and injustice, the preoccupation of Yiddish and also of English literature (as I was learning from Charles Dickens), made special demands on those fortunate to have escaped hardship. Jewish good fortune levied nondischargeable debts.

CR

BY THE UPPER GRADES IN high school, the same unease about advantage and competition made me begin to worry whether doing well in class also made it harder to be liked, and my anxiety increased once I wanted to be liked by the boys with whom I was competing. There was no one to talk to about any of these things. Ben was out of the house by then, and I had never gone to my parents with problems. I was attracted to boys who had Ben's qualities of intelligence, kindness, strength of character, and—this occurred to me only much later—vulnerability; they were never from well-to-do families.

As senior year approached, the mathematics teacher, Mr. Russell, announced that he would offer early morning classes for Latin-track students who wanted to take an additional set of matriculation exams in mathematics, where it was easier to score a perfect grade. Math was my worst subject and I had no intention of mastering trigonometry. But I was pursuing a boy who was taking the class and so became one of only two girls to accept Mr. Russell's challenge. I spent most of the class time exchanging notes with the object of my affections. When I earned a mark of sixteen out of one hundred on the first test, Mr. Russell took me aside and gently asked me to drop the class, lest I lower the school average. Luckily, the boy in question had already asked me out.

I told everyone about my disastrous grade, thinking it would enhance my standing as an average kid. Arriving home in a state of euphoria, I flounced into the kitchen proclaiming, "I failed my math test!" Oblivious of the true nature of my accomplishment, Mother slapped me—I think for the last time.

Two generations earlier, my parents would have already been arranging my marriage. But we were required to find our own mates, with no adult guidance beyond my father's telling me not to let the moon be my matchmaker, a line he might have picked up from a Russian novel. About this time, I realized that attracting someone I liked involved a different set of skills from those that won me the high grades.

At one school assembly, standing on the stage beside Miss Hay for the singing of "God Save the Queen"—Canada was then still part of the British Commonwealth—I was shocked to see two seniors, Jerry Pearl and Herbie Greenwald, demonstratively seated amid all the students on their feet. The three of us were aware that England had prevented Jewish immigration to Palestine during the most critical years of the war and that it had unfairly continued to side with the Arabs right up to Israel's War of Independence. I realized my friends were acting in political solidarity with Israel, but I was fairly certain that Miss Hay did not understand the point of their dissent. Had she said anything I would have explained that their protest against Britain's injustice intended no disloyalty to Canada or the Queen. I was very proud of them and terribly worried for them, my inflated sense of danger seeing them threatened with expulsion (though I was sober enough to realize that this sort of infraction was not punishable by strapping). As the principal said nothing, I was left ashamed that the obligation to be on good behavior had overtaken my stand for justice.

That junior year of high school I knew that I had another reason to be ashamed. Two girls had joined our class, a frizzy blond and a bobbed brunette. Both were Jewish refugees who had survived the war in France. The teacher introduced them only by name, Ida and Monique. Though curiosity and duty prompted me to befriend these newcomers, and though I sensed that we had much in common, I preferred to be among the popular girls in the class. I was never rude to the pair, yet I felt shabby neglecting them. Had they made any appeal to me, I would eagerly have responded, but I did not make the first move. This failure to welcome them doubtless haunted me more than it had troubled them. As it happens, some of my closest adult friends turned out to be refugees.

CR

HAD MY EDUCATION BEEN CONFINED to my Protestant high school I would have been left, like most of my classmates, with very little Jewish knowledge. Happily—if sometimes a little reluctantly—I attended *mitl-shule*, the extension classes of the Jewish People's School that met twice a week and on Sunday mornings. The few of us who continued with this program had the benefit of fine teachers and an advanced curriculum in Jewish literature and history. Given the ongoing need to stand up for the Jews, I was lucky to learn more about what I was defending.

When I once tried to summarize what we had been taught, I called it our inclusive Jewish heritage "from the Tanach to the Palmach," that is, from the Hebrew Bible to the underground Jewish army in Palestine, unaware that David Ben-Gurion, Israel's first prime minister, had used the same phrase to *overleap* the millennia between the loss of Jewish sovereignty and its recovery. He wanted modern Zionism to return as much as possible to its biblical source and to renounce the alleged passivity of the intervening centuries. Whatever his thinking, we who would probably be staying in Canada needed to know how Jews had managed abroad between the Maccabees and the present.

I later made these comments at a festive dinner thanking the teachers of the Folkshule for having given us the security to move out as Jews into the North American mainstream. The guest speaker at that event was the well-known American Jewish social philosopher Horace Kallen, who had come from New York to honor Shloime Wiseman as a distinguished educator and personal friend. Their comradeship must have grown from shared ideas about Jewish citizenship that Wiseman incorporated in our school and Kallen developed in books like *Cultural Pluralism and the American Idea.* As a cultural pluralist—a concept he developed—Kallen resisted the idea of assimilation represented by the homogenizing image of the melting pot. The finest American, or in our case, Canadian, would be the one who experienced citizenship as a confident Jew.

The assimilationist idea of America had been championed by Israel Zangwill's 1908 play, *The Melting Pot,* in which the marriage between a Jew and the daughter of a Russian pogromist is the template for the American future. Zangwill had pivoted away from his early Zionism to an ideal of Anglo-American identity and his play became its eponymous illustration. The only way forward, as he saw it, was for all immigrants to give up the differences that elsewhere led to bloodshed. Kallen championed the opposite ideal and pointed out that our Canadian multiculturalism already showed that ethnic minorities could coexist within a heterogeneous democracy. For this to happen, children like us would have to be educated in their own traditions and languages. Whereas exclusive Protestant school education would have fostered deracination, our additional Jewish instruction reinforced the Jewish tiles in the Canadian mosaic. Complimenting me for anticipating his prepared remarks, Kallen said we would serve our countries best by maintaining the *pluribus* in the phrase *e pluribus unum.*

This was true as far as it went, but in my experience, camping was at least as decisive in forging Kallen's concept of Jewish identity. Teenagers tend to bridle at directions imposed from above, whereas camping inspires them to exceed goals they set for themselves. Counselors in training (CITs) and junior counselors learn to guide activities in which they were once trained by others.

After junior year of high school (our ninth grade), when I had already worked as a junior counselor at Pripstein's, a boy who had just transferred to Strathcona urged me to join him and his friends at their Hebrew-speaking Camp Massad. He blew off my objection that I knew almost no Hebrew, saying I would pick it up like an immigrant—sink or swim—and indeed, the first Hebrew word I added to my vocabulary that summer was *yitushim*, mosquitoes. Ashamed to know less than the others, I quickly memorized all of the traditional daily blessings and the lyrics of Hebrew songs, along the way picking up the meaning of announcements over the loudspeaker (*ramkol*) about the dining room (*khadar okhel*) and canteen (*tsurkaniya*). At Folkshule we had never learned the traditional blessings and this memorization proved a true blessing in all the years since.

The adjustment from Pripstein's, where I had been a camper since the age of five, was almost as severe as the shift had been from Jewish to Protestant school. Pripstein's exuded familial generosity; the administration of Massad, founded in 1947 by a consortium of Zionist educators, tried to keep costs down and amenities to a minimum. Whereas Pripstein's conveyed most of its Jewishness informally, Massad's requirement that we speak only Hebrew, though not strictly enforced, reflected at once a stronger national purpose and a greater degree of religious observance. All my fellow counselors had come from schools where Hebrew was taught as the sole national language as part of that Zionist-Hebraist amalgam. I was no less Zionist, but I had lacked the language.

At Massad we learned Israeli songs and dances, and as CITs, we were also taught songs and games for children. A member of the Habima Theater in Tel Aviv directed us in a contemporary Israeli play set during Israel's War of Independence; I played a mother whose son is killed in battle. In a very small way, my struggle to master the language felt like part of Israel's fight to secure the future of the Jewish people.

I felt no disloyalty to Yiddish in going to a Hebrew-speaking camp. In fact, my parents were very pleased when they drove up for the performance of the play. It seemed obvious without saying—*muvan me'eylav*—that in the fulfilment of Zionism, the integration of Jews from myriad countries and cultures in a single sovereign state required common use of our only unifying language.

At Camp Massad, playing baseball in Hebrew or taking evening walks speaking Hebrew took on a national aspect in just the way that Yiddish did for Mother, who readily accepted Hebrew as its complement. She had studied both languages in her Jewish school in Vilna. There were still ideologues on both sides of the language wars, but thankfully I never felt I had to choose, like the Yiddish-Hebrew writer Mendele Mocher Sforim, who said that writing in both languages was like breathing through two nostrils. This writer, unknown to me at the time, was to become one of my literary heroes.

The only doubts about this new direction in my life arose during my second summer at Massad, the year of transition from high school to college, when I was promised a visit from Ben, by then the editor of the student publication of the International Zionist Federation of America (IZFA) that was both a house organ and a forum for the kind of political discussion I had witnessed among his friends. Ben was by then a student of textile engineering in Philadelphia with the intention of bringing his professional training to Israel. On my first solo trip to New York that spring, Ben, who had driven in from Philadelphia, took me to the Sabra nightclub where we heard the great Israeli singer Shoshana Damari.

Shoshana Damari had come to Israel as a child from Yemen and represented a new style of Israeli culture that seemed more authentic because it was from the Middle East. Thanks to Massad, I knew most of the songs she sang that night and could have danced to the music of one of them, "*El ginat egoz*"—lyrics courtesy of *Song of Songs* ("I went down to the nut grove/ To see the budding of the vale") and choreography of the Yemenite dance company Inbal. Damari's signature songs, composed by one of Israel's leading poets, Warsaw-born Natan Alterman, had been set to Eastern-sounding music in the kind of fusion between its European and Middle Eastern cultures that the country was beginning to cultivate. When she sang the ballad "Kalanyot," about the red anemones that are native to Israel, the whole nightclub joined in the chorus. The North Americans felt special pride in knowing Israel's popular repertoire.

Naturally, I expected Ben to like Massad. Yet when I proudly showed him around, I realized that he was not as enthusiastic as I'd anticipated. I tried guessing the reason, but just as I had never admitted to him my reservations about the collectivist ideology of his Habonim group, he may not have wanted to express his discomfort with the camp's religious Hebraism. While to my fellow counselors I remained a slightly alien import from the secular-Yiddish sector, Ben was slightly put off by Massad's "bourgeois" centrism that had a heavier component of religious observance than we practiced at home. Within the same solidly Zionist orbit and its shared idea of the Jewish people, it seemed that we were pulling in subtly different directions.

Or else I may just have begun to notice that he and I were really separate people and that I would have to go through life on my own, with or without his all-important approval. By then, I was surer of myself than I had been on the day of high school registration. Our parents had bought a house two doors up from Strathcona that literally narrowed the distance between home and school. By senior year I was as familiar with the school's culture as I had been at Folkshule, on good terms with the principal and with dozens of students. I glided easily between the hymns at Christmas assemblies and Mother's Hanukkah songs at our annual family celebration.

Our Quebec society was anyway quickly evolving. Three years after I graduated, the Strathcona building was sold and replaced by Outremont High School, part of the nondenominational school system that had replaced the earlier confessional schools. My younger siblings Eva and David both attended the new high school. On my few visits to it when Mother asked me to stand in for her at parent-teacher meetings, I would no more think back to my own adolescence than a butterfly does to the caterpillar it once was.

It was painful to realize that Ben and I could differ. He had been my guardian and substitute parent when needed. My taste in music was formed by the contempt he showed for the Johnnie Ray record I once brought home, and by seeing him blissfully absorbed when he listened to Bach's *St. Matthew Passion*. He didn't recommend books to me, but picking up whatever he brought home, I one day found in a little paperback called *Discovery* (1954) a story by Saul Bellow, "The Gonzaga Manuscripts," about an American researcher in Spain who reminded me of Ben. Bellow had taken up the familiar theme of naïve American in malevolent Europe, and despite the absence of anything explicitly Jewish about the story, it combined humor with moral seriousness in a way that felt very familiar. Bellow became and thereafter remained my favorite writer.

Oddly enough, I think I first realized my self-sufficiency on that trip to New York at Ben's invitation. He met me at Grand Central Station, drove me to Philadelphia where I first saw television in his landlady's living room, showed me around the Textile Institute where he was studying, then took me back to New York the next day for that splendid evening at the Sabra. Even better than the grown-up time with him was traveling coach there and back on the night train, where the conductors who boarded to check our passports at the Canadian-US border were the only interruption to my solitary fantasies and thoughts. Nowhere before, at home, school, or camp, had I been as private as I needed to be. When I got a room of my own at thirteen, I could still hear my little brother on the other side of the wall and feel the comings and goings in the household with antennae that readied me for motherhood but thwarted my adolescent wish to be alone. Those train rides through the night, surrounded by strangers who would remain strangers, let me taste the autonomy I then wanted, or thought I wanted, more than anything in the world.

I began taking lone trips to New York. I contrived the second one the following year as an alternative to the obligatory sweet sixteen. I asked my father for $250, less than the cost of a party, and more than enough to cover the train, two nights at the Victoria Hotel, a Broadway show or movie around Times Square, and a day roaming around Greenwich Village bookstores and coffee houses. After that, at least once a year, I asked for a small sum to supplement what I earned teaching Sunday school. Twice I invited friends to go with me, but other girls were rarely given permission and though sharing the trip was pleasant it was never as thrilling as going by myself.

New York was a magnet, the place where it happened. Montreal had Her Majesty's Theater where I often attended theater and ballet, and Plateau Hall on Calixa-Lavallée, a street with a name as marvelous as the music one heard there. But they could not compare with the excitement of the Broadway scene and the cultural intensity of off Broadway that I discovered in my college years. I saw Jason Robards as Hickey Hickman in *The Iceman Cometh* at some place in the Village, which is the actual setting of Eugene O'Neill's play.

Watching this pitchman challenge a cast of drinkers to translate their pipe dreams into action, and then seeing them, one by one, describe their failures seemed to me the ultimate statement about human experience. How much more so when Hickey reveals the crime that *he* has been concealing! Had any grown up then advised me that the playwright might be an untrustworthy peddler of doom, I would not have listened. Four hours of humorless pessimism was to me in my teens the noblest unmasking of truth. Let's just say that Ben's taste in music proved sounder than mine in theater.

5

DISCOVERY

*W*hen I entered college in the fall of 1953, I was as free as I would ever be. By then, McGill University had done away with measures restricting the number of Jewish undergraduates and was admitting any local student who had scored well in Quebec's provincial examinations. There was still a quota on Jews in certain professional faculties like medicine or architecture but those restrictions, too, were being relaxed. The influx of European refugees was making Montreal more cosmopolitan and the McGill campus that stands at the center of the city soon offered its students their choice of neighborhood Hungarian coffee shops as well as French-Canadian cuisine.

The fifties—later denigrated as an age of stifling conformism—were for us the most fortunate adolescence imaginable. The worst lay behind us and the best lay ahead: we could not imagine repetition of the horrors that had just been perpetrated in Europe. By then, those horrors were familiar not only from newsreels and books like John Hersey's *The Wall*, based on actual events of the Warsaw Ghetto, but from reports of survivors who kept bringing my parents corroboration of what they had hoped never to hear. We knew we had special reason to count our blessings. It did not occur to me that in Canada anything could stop me from becoming whatever I wanted to be. I had only to figure out what that was.

Intellectual adventure was what I really craved when I entered McGill, but my high expectations were quickly dampened by freshman requirements of more Latin and math and by professors drawn from the same dour Scottish and English stock as our teachers in high school. As for elective courses, I foolishly chose the history of philosophy, which opened with lectures on Heraclitus. One step into his hypothetical river and I knew I couldn't care less if it was the same or different from the one I had stepped into the day before. By sophomore year I had registered for the Honors English program, figuring it would somehow lead me to a career.

The real benefit of McGill's undergraduate program proved to be its lack of oversight. In classes where no one took attendance, I could be absent for weeks at a time and still handily complete the course by reading the assigned texts and acing the final exam. Together with Lionel Tiger, the future eminent anthropologist, I also won release from the compulsory composition class. I had met Lionel in high school, when he was at Baron Byng, and the success of our joint petition for discharge from our writing instructor, Miss Fricker, sealed a lasting friendship.

More congenial instruction was available in the basement offices of the McGill *Daily*, whose mostly male editors would teach me journalism from the ground up. Having grown up in a family that prized literacy, in a household of books, with parents who supported writers and a community that revered the best of them, I not surprisingly thought of myself as a potential writer and responded to the *Daily*'s first call for new freshmen staffers. I began putting in about forty hours a week, learning about concision, verification, and the preference for verbs over adjectives—not to mention the art of composing headlines. The news editor drilled us on avoiding editorial comment with a description of a "red-necked" police officer, asking how the reporter could possibly have *known* that detail.

My early news assignments fell largely in the realm of culture. I covered talks by the poets Stephen Spender and Dylan Thomas, the mountaineer Sir Edmund Hillary, and the composer Gian Carlo Menotti. By sophomore year, I was made features editor. There, too, I tried to maintain a standard of objectivity by offering competing views on contentious issues. Our model for debate was "may the better-articulated argument win."

Nonetheless, I deserved to be called sophomoric for emblazoning my section's pages with Bertrand Russell's dictum, "Men fear thought more than they fear death." I ought to have asked whether the philosopher included himself in this fatuous statement of contempt for "ordinary" humans. My own views were conventional—reactionary conservatives bad, progressive liberals good—no doubt because I, too, feared to think.

Conformism in my liberal-trending Jewish society, which often felt audacious in then-conservative Quebec, was conformist nonetheless. I remember the shock of hearing an American journalist explain his support for Dwight D. Eisenhower over Adlai Stevenson in the presidential campaign of 1956 and being moved from, "How can he possibly be saying this?" to, "Wow! I had better give this more thought!" He contrasted the candidates to show the advantages of the man who was practiced in action over the liberal intellectual. I had not been exposed to such a possibility. More difficult was then trying to explain the point to those who had not attended the talk.

Journalism was how I was becoming educated, and when daytime hours did not suffice, I volunteered to put the paper to bed, taking copy down to the Montreal *Gazette* where I would watch the typesetters block the pages and run off trial sheets to proofread. When I was done, a taxi was called that never brought me home before 2:00 in the morning. My parents became so accustomed to this that they stopped waiting up for me.

It later occurred to me that my intellectual models, the New York cohort of writer-critics who attended City College in the 1930s, had likewise spent their college years under the unsupervised regimen of harried immigrant parents. With so porous a safety net at home, we had to make sure we did not fall through. Our parents had to trust us, and we had no choice but to earn that trust. None of us got drunk or took drugs or failed to graduate.

Counterintuitively, however, living at home also gave us greater freedom to spend our days in smoky debate, to join and quit political associations, and to risk offending teachers. We meant it when we sang, "Our thoughts are free. No hunter can trap them/ no scholar can map them/ no man can deny/ *Die gedanken sind frei!*"

In those days, very few French Canadians attended McGill, the English university; nor did the subject of race figure for us as it did in the United States. The only dark-skinned people I knew at college were from the British West Indies. One was elected Carnival Queen. Another became editor of the *Daily*, which was where you congregated to get away from ethno-religious compartmentalization. For despite the general whiteness of the student body, such compartmentalization was very much a reality. Just as in high school, I moved every day between a Jewish home and an essentially Protestant school where the distinction between Jew and Gentile was still crystal clear.

Though I did not consider joining the Jewish sorority, I was briefly active at the campus Hillel and in my junior year cochaired the youth division of Montreal's Combined Jewish Appeal. One day I was sitting among the Jewish sorority crowd when a girl came by carrying a large box from a downtown store. Everyone asked, "What did you buy?" She took out and modeled a winter coat. Incredulity all around: *our* families were mainly connected with the clothing industry, also known as the *shmatteh* business, and none of us had ever bought a coat in a retail store.

Montreal's ethnic and economic divisions did not exactly overlap but just as it took no special talent to recognize Gentiles from Jews, we Jews could further situate one another by our feeder high schools. In Outremont there were Strathcona and Baron Byng, corresponding roughly to upper middle class and lower middle class plus immigrants; but now we were also together with contemporaries from Westmount, the domain of longer-established and often wealthier families, where Jews were a minority. I was eager to explore what was as yet unfamiliar.

By sophomore year, as well as choosing a concentration, I had found or, rather, was discovered by, a Gentile girl determined to escape her family's Anglo-Saxon chauvinism. No such friendship would have happened by chance; these were elective affinities. Ann Powell said she picked me out when she noticed that we were both in Honors English and members of McGill's Scarlet Key honors society.

Newly elected members McGill Red Wing Society 1956–57, counterpart of the male honors Scarlet Key Society; they hosted public events, welcomed visitors and foreign students. Ann Powell (Coulson) is at left, author, second from right. (Coronet Studio photo)

She had much to teach me. The first time we played tennis—I had never taken lessons or developed a reliable backhand—I told her that I only rallied but did not play. She said, "Like hell you don't!" and served into my side of the court when I wasn't there to return it, calling, "Fifteen-love!" and forcing me into a competition that would continue for decades until she left Montreal. I don't think I ever won a set from her, not only because she was the far better player but also because she would not allow herself to be beaten, whereas I, who otherwise liked to excel, did not like making anyone lose.

My reluctance did not quite extend to schoolwork, however. "Can you imagine?" she said after we had both aced a class, "Sally accused me of having *studied* for the exam as though it were a crime to want to come first!" To befriend the person with whom you compete and to compete with a good friend were as foreign to me as eggnog at Christmas, which I likewise learned to enjoy thanks to Christians on the *Daily*.

Ann and her brothers had attended a private school that lay entirely outside my ken. Clearly, we both enjoyed our friendship as much for what separated us as for what we had in common. Yet we did not really mingle socially or get to know one another's circle. On a rare visit to her Westmount home, I was baffled to see how old-fashioned the bathroom was; it had never been remodeled. This was the kind of sociological detail that fed comedy about the conspicuous consumption of Jews and the ascetic habits of WASPs. A stereotype could occasionally be inferred or confirmed from evidence.

CR

WHEN IT CAME TO MY fellow Jews, the boys from Baron Byng seemed to me more substantial and bolder than those from Strathcona, and it was thanks to my friendship with them that I learned about communism up close. Though not communists themselves, they knew members of the Student Labor Progressive Party Club, founded at McGill in the 1940s and active even after the Soviet tyrant Joseph Stalin died in March 1953. The families of the LPP members belonged to the United Jewish Peoples' Order—more sect than movement, and essentially subversive in its constant denial that it was unequivocally obedient to the Soviet regime.

Indeed, UJPO families were the most *observant* Jews I knew in college. They served their competing religion with priestly devotion: the USSR was their Zion, the Comintern their rabbinic authority, Yiddish their proletarian culture, and loyalty what they owed to the Soviet people. Their class enemies were Jews like me whose family owned a factory, and college was where they trolled for us "undeserving rich."

If you moved among Jews and aspiring intellectuals, you could hardly avoid communists, who by the mid-1950s would face a crisis greater than the one of 1939 when the nonaggression pact between Hitler and Stalin had demolished the claim that the Soviet Union was the Jews' last hope against fascism. The Nazi-Soviet alliance split apart kibbutzim in Palestine and Jewish families in Montreal; a boy I knew had to stop fraternizing with his cousins. But once Germany attacked the Soviet Union in the summer of 1941, communism regained the moral high ground as the Russians became American allies, fought off the German invaders at Stalingrad, and liberated some of the concentration camps. That same year Stalin established a Jewish Anti-Fascist Committee, two of whose best-known members, actor-director Shloime Mikhoels and poet Itzik Feffer, were sent to America to rally support for the Lend-Lease Act that provided Russia with money and supplies. The Soviets had always used American Jewish party members to propagandize and recruited some of them for espionage when that was deemed useful.

With the end of the war, there came another betrayal. Stalin launched an anti-Jewish campaign that members of UJPO could not ignore. Given that Yiddish was their medium of communication with fellow Jews in the Soviet Union, they were the first to learn of the "fatal accidents" and "mysterious disappearances" of prominent Jewish cultural figures, including Mikhoels and Feffer. The great American baritone Paul Robeson, who epitomized the Left's black-Jewish alliance, was asked by his American Jewish comrades to meet with Feffer on his trip to the Soviet Union to see why he had stopped communicating. He then dutifully reassured the Jews back home of Feffer's well-being, though the poet—brought straight from prison for the interview—had given him signs of the torture he was enduring. From outside the communist camp, the Montreal poet A. M. Klein pronounced their ideology "a saying of grace before poison."

There was also the issue of communist infiltration in Canada, resembling the case of Julius and Ethel Rosenberg in the United States. In 1945 the Soviet spy Igor Gouzenko defected to Canada and exposed Fred Rose, né Fishel Rosenberg (no relative), as a fellow spy. Rose was a member of parliament from the immigrant Cartier district where UJPO had its headquarters. Convicted of espionage, but not executed like the American Rosenbergs, he was released into voluntary exile in his native Poland, where I would later visit him.

It was hard for members of UJPO to wrench themselves free of their tight community of faith. Only with Nikita Khrushchev's "secret" 1956 speech officially revealing Stalin's crimes, and after a couple of UJPO members traveled to Russia to confirm his postwar purge of the Jewish Anti-Fascist Committee, did the organization begin to unravel. But its last phase, which saw McGill's LPP Club morphing into the Folk Music Society, was also its most influential. As a beneficiary of this metamorphosis, I can attest to how effectively it repackaged the movement's message.

Folk music became part of my life. I attended UJPO-sponsored concerts of Pete Seeger and The Weavers, Jean Ritchie and Betty Sanders. I took up the guitar and learned the repertoire of *Sing Out!*, the folk-music magazine founded in 1950 to "create, promote, and distribute songs of labor and the American people." The songs told me to go down and join the union because "ain't nobody there can join it for you." The banks were made of marble with a guard at every door. Far and wide as the eye can wander, I fought with the German Peat Bog soldiers on the Republican side of the Spanish Civil War, singing "*Die Heimat ist weit,* the homeland is distant. *Doch wir sind bereit.* But we are ready. *Wir kämpfen und siegen für dich,* We fight to victory for you. *Freiheit,* Freedom!" Had the cold war been fought through folk music alone, American free enterprise would have long since crumbled.

Earlier there had even been a brief interval when the Soviets, hoping to displace British influence in the Middle East, sided with the then-infant state of Israel, and echoes of that temporary closeness lingered in the Weavers' repertoire:

> *Tzena, Tzena, Tzena, Tzena/*
> Can't you hear the music playing in the city square?
> Come where all our friends will find us with the dancers there.
> *Tzena, Tzena* join the celebration.
> There'll be people there from every nation.
> Dawn will find us laughing in the sun-
> light, dancing in the city square.

When the Weavers pushed "Tzena" onto the hit parade, I paid no attention at first to how they had also redacted the Hebrew version we'd sung at Camp Massad. Composed in 1941 by Yehiel Chagiz, a Polish immigrant to Palestine who was then serving in the Jewish Brigade, the Hebrew song urged the girls on a *moshav* (agricultural collective settlement) not to shy away from army men. Chagiz was ingeniously playing on *Tzena Ur'ena,* the title of a seventeenth-century Yiddish rendering of the Pentateuch that was intended for the use of women and became the most popular Yiddish book of all time. Turning this summons to Torah into a call for the young women of Palestine to shed their modesty and join the soldiers, he also updated the term *ben ḥayil*, "man of valor," to mean *ish tsava*, "an army man," for now Jews were required to evolve from a religious into a soldiering society.

The Weavers neutered the Israeli battle call into a hootenanny. Nevertheless, Pete Seeger's banjo drew me, for the only time in my life, to ideas I otherwise opposed. Let me not exaggerate: I didn't come close to joining a movement, but I was attracted enough by Soviet culture to overlook the murderous deeds that were just then coming to light.

Unlike other aspects of college life that pulled against the culture of my home, folk music was familiar. Mother's way of celebrating Hanukkah was to gather the family around the piano and guide us through a medley that began with the prescribed blessings but then included Yiddish songs from Vilna and Hebrew ones we learned in Jewish school. She made no distinctions either, when she and Father sang together during our long car trips, between the various languages of the songs—by far the majority in Yiddish— or their provenance. When my college friend Jack Novick discovered folk singer Martha Schlamme, I brought home her recording of Yiddish songs, and this forged a strong connection between the two kinds of singing. There was no political ideology in Mother's choice of repertoire and likewise, paying no attention to their sources, I drifted into "the International" just as its ideologues intended.

03

THE SUMMER OF 1956 WAS to be my last as a counselor at Pripstein's Camp. The head counselor was Jack Novick and together we resolved to shake the campers out of their bourgeois complacency by introducing them to a couple of foreign cultures. We chose India because the dance counselor wanted to teach Indian dances, and Russia for its complex mix of Jewish and communist associations. As ours was a Jewish camp, we also included a third unit on Israel, presenting the kibbutz as a miniature of the socialist ideal. We prepared for those weeks with stories, games, art and theater projects, and especially with songs from the Internationalist playbook. I did not think of it as leftism but as an antidote to our parochial and—have I mentioned— bourgeois complacency.

That summer the camp owners' daughter was being courted by a striking man of thirty-three who spoke with a foreign accent. Immanuel Braverman had fought in the Polish army; captured by the Russians, he'd spent most of the war in a Soviet prison camp. Upon his release at war's end, he volunteered in Israel's War of Independence and afterward came to join his father in Canada.

Immanuel visited the camp on weekends. Incensed to find us romancing the Soviet Union, he confronted us with the facts of communist brutality. I ascribed this hectoring to his unfortunate personal experience and felt no immediate need to alter our plans. Could we help it if the best folk music and highest egalitarian ideals happened to come under communist sponsorship? Was he not parochial to be raising political objections to our international cultural mission?

Immanuel was the first anticommunist I encountered in a Jewish community that leaned reflexively left. My father's opposition to communism was always tempered by loyalty to the boyhood friends who had devoted and sacrificed their lives to the Soviet experiment; hating the ideology, he felt obliged to honor those martyred in its cause. Immanuel tolerated no such sentimentality. Although his intervention did not make us change our program that summer, thanks largely to him I stopped flirting with communism and its folk-song outreach. He readied me for the revelations of Robert Conquest, Aleksandr Solzhenitsyn, and Nadezhda Mandelstam.

Eventually, in well-deserved comeuppance, I would be treated by the young to the same condescension I had showed Immanuel. Whenever I saw him in the years that followed, I thanked him for setting me straight.

CR

LEST I LEAVE THE MISTAKEN impression that *none* of my college learning occurred in the classroom, I must pay tribute to Louis Dudek, whose four-semester sequence on great writings of European literature I have described elsewhere as driving us "like sheep before a storm." Dudek was the only teacher I encountered in the English department who resembled my teachers in Jewish school in ways not clear to me at the time. He was a European, from a Polish Catholic family, and making his way through Columbia University to becoming a professor of English literature had been fraught with some of the same cultural anxieties experienced by Jews like Lionel Trilling. Like Trilling, too, he believed that ideas were the driving force of human affairs and distilled them from the literary works he chose to teach. He could not possibly have expected us to read in the week he assigned to each Voltaire's *Candide,* Rousseau's *Confessions, La Nouvelle Heloise*…all the way to *Buddenbrooks* and *Ulysses.* But he gave us the blueprint for what we had to master of modern Western civilization.

The class met three times a week in the late afternoon, when the waning of the day seemed to turn up the emotional heat. It was the only literature class with a majority of males. Not that Dudek appeared to notice sex differences among his students. From Rousseau's *Emile* he highlighted the sentences, "Educate [women] like men. . . .[N]ature means them to think, to will, to love, to cultivate their minds as well as their persons." I needed no assurance that I was as mentally agile as the boys in the class. They argued harder than the girls, and I enjoyed their argument at least as much as playing tennis with Ann.

In creating this course, Dudek repackaged the modern part of the core curriculum of Columbia University where he had done his graduate work. He would scrawl a quotation on the blackboard: "My friend! A man is a man; and whatever be the extent of his reasoning powers, they are of little avail when passion rages within, and he feels himself confined by the narrow limits of human nature."

This, from Goethe's *The Sorrows of Young Werther,* made me feverish the night I read it. A young man who spends spring and summer in a rural township falls in love with a woman already engaged to another. He cannot control his desire even after her marriage to his rival. Indeed, the presence of that stolid and considerate husband goads Werther into ever wilder excesses of feeling. His suicide seemed the ultimate expression of emotional authenticity over bland conformism.

It was one thing to read true love magazines and to daydream about falling in love and quite another to be stirred to desire as part of one's favorite college course. I was simultaneously studying the British Romantics, alternately dazzled by the poems and personalities of Shelley and Byron and dismissive of their exaggerated claims; I knew when I first heard it that poets were *not* the unacknowledged legislators of the world. Goethe's romantic novel, on the other hand, maybe because it is narrated by a sober editor, broke through my reserve.

Swept up by Werther's yearning, I was hardly surprised to learn that many young Germans had followed his example in taking their lives. My good behavior, my solid work schedule, the whole business of trying to meet expectations was called into question by this young man whose love knew no bounds. I did not so much think his actions admirable as *feel* the nobility of his passion.

But next day in class, to my surprise and horror, Dudek likened *Sturm und Drang,* the anarchy of passion, to the tantrum of a child who does not know what to do with the freedom it has won. Sounding like my parents, he warned that since our human wants cannot possibly be satisfied, it was dangerous to challenge the boundaries of human existence by striving for the infinite.

A student backed this up with the ingenious argument that Goethe was clearly warning against emotional excess, because he had his Werther reading the poet Ossian: a fake primitive invented by the Scottish poet James Macpherson. Goethe thus revealed Werther's inauthenticity by showing him to be in thrall to a bogus poet!

Upon hearing this, the tears came on so fast I had to flee to the ladies' room—tears of shame and remorse. How could I have so badly misunderstood the book by identifying with what I thought was the greater sincerity rather than recognizing it as a parable of emotive glut? I had given myself over to the romantic lover that Goethe was when he wrote the book; Dudek meant for us to realize that the adult Goethe had himself repudiated the passions he had unleashed.

I was more than ready to speak up when I disagreed, but this student, endorsed by the teacher, persuaded and humbled me utterly. This was the first time I was chastened in a matter of taste and it hurt much more than doing poorly in an exam. The intellectual adventure I craved had come—but not as I imagined.

Though the term *conservative* did not enter public discussion until decades later, I knew my lapse had something to do with rejecting adolescence. All these self-corrections were coming from the same direction. Immanuel's instruction on the failed Bolshevik revolution, the political advantage Eisenhower might have over Stevenson, the adult over the younger Goethe—these were as sobering as Edmund Burke's reflections on the revolution in France, elsewhere suggested as ancillary reading. The caring, protective stability of my home began to feel more attractive than Hemingway's Paris. At seventeen I was ready to say, with the aging William Butler Yeats, "Though leaves are many, the root is one;/ Through all the lying days of my youth/ I swayed my leaves and flowers in the sun;/ Now I may wither into the truth."

AND YET, AND YET…SOMETHING FELT missing even in Dudek's marvelously instructive class.

Jews, who constituted over a third of the McGill student body in arts and sciences, were nowhere present in the curriculum. A survey course of economic history included the Rothschilds, but without so much as mentioning the historical role of Jews in European trade and commerce. Hebrew, once a staple of the divinity school, had been eliminated in the 1930s and never reinstated. In Dudek's two-year survey of European literature I would have expected some mention of the Jews. He taught Kafka without revealing that he was Jewish, and Louis-Ferdinand Céline, author of the nihilist classic *Journey to the End of the Night*, ignoring its prominent anti-Semitism. As with our high school teachers, avoidance of the Jewish subject was probably due not to aversion but to the way you step around mud to stay on dry ground.

Hitler's erasure of the Jews of Europe had made them too toxic to mention. The Holocaust later became so sensationalized that Americans hallowed it as the symbol of evil, but that was years later, when everyone was inured to the horror. By then Hollywood was ready to make blockbuster films about it. Jewish comedienne Sarah Silverman joked about her young niece who reports she has just learned in school that sixty million Jews were killed. Sarah corrects her, "Six million." The child shrugs and says, "Whatever." No such lightness prevailed in that first postwar decade when teachers and the Gentiles around us did not yet know how to speak about the enormity. "In the house of the hanged, one does not talk about ropes," the German-Jewish wit Heinrich Heine once wrote in another context, and since we Jews were the hanged, how could one talk about our annihilation in our presence?

I was finally provoked to speak up in the Dudek class when we studied *Thus Spake Zarathustra*. William Blake had prepared me for Nietzsche's challenge to Judeo-Christianity, and I knew by heart some of the Devil's sayings from Blake's *The Marriage of Heaven and Hell*:

"Drive your cart and your plow over the bones of the dead."
"The road of excess leads to the palace of wisdom."
"Prudence is a rich ugly old maid courted by Incapacity."
And in particular: "One law for the lion and ox is Oppression."

Nor was I shocked when Nietzsche's anti-Moses descends from the mountain to announce (in italics) that "God is dead!" My parents and many Jews of their generation probably kept God alive only because there was no other framework mighty enough to contain their grief and protest. Jacob Glatstein, who became one of my favorite Yiddish poets, threatened the Almighty, "Without Jews there will be no Jewish God. / Should we, God forbid, leave this world, / the light of your poor tent would be extinguished." Truthfully, Nietzsche's death of God seemed childish compared to the grappling with God I saw going on in Jewish tradition.

What distressed me in Nietzsche was not any of the existential business, but rather the undeniable resemblance between his *Übermenschen* and

Nazi thugs. Zarathustra says, "Of all that is written, I love only what a person hath written with his blood. Write with blood, and thou wilt find that blood is spirit." But they had written with *our* blood and tried to prove their superiority by destroying *ours*.

For his part, Dudek presented a benign Nietzsche-as-liberator from the wreckage caused by Darwin's theory of human evolution. He said that in pronouncing the death of God, Zarathustra cancels the divine authority behind which lay the unrealistic Christian ethic of pity, of turning the other cheek—itself, in Nietzsche's view, an extension of Jewish morality.

Dudek discredited the belief that that Nazism arose because of these dark teachings and he argued the reverse—that the rise of Nazism proved the *need* for Nietzsche's philosophy of the superman. Nietzsche saw all around him a society that had already become essentially godless, secular, and despairing. It was to rescue humankind from this despair that he urged man to be honest about his true nature and affirm what he found best in himself. That best emphatically included the will to power, properly conceived.

It was dazzling to hear our teacher tease out the "humanistic" aspects of Zarathustra's warning against the Jewish morality on which I had been raised, which yoked the idea of freedom to a responsibility to help to free others. The judiciousness of Talmudic law arrived at through so many centuries of refinement was far removed from Zarathustra's peremptory tone and teachings. I realized that my teacher expected me to transcend my Jewishness, but at that point I balked. After class I asked him how he could ignore the noxious form that Nietzsche's Übermensch had assumed in German history. If philosophy was to be taken seriously, I said, it had to bear responsibility for its influence. Dudek listened patiently and then said, "Would you hold Jesus responsible for the Inquisition?"

I lacked the wit to retort, "Wouldn't you?" Instead, reduced to silence, I took the question home to discuss with my father. How could we distinguish between ideas and their consequences? In Father's chosen field of chemistry, elements could prove beneficial or harmful, depending on their dosage and application. Science determined how such elements worked through controlled experiments, but how were we to figure out the right equation in the uncontrolled conditions of life? I had the confidence not to accept Nietzsche as the savior of our morality, but for the moment I lacked the arguments to back myself up. And since I was no longer attending Jewish afternoon school, I did not have the academic ballast to counter this cumulative erasure of our culture.

CR

YET MY FIRST SIGN THAT a new Jewish culture was emerging from our ranks came thanks to Dudek. As well as teaching literature, Dudek was himself a poet, part of a circle of local poets who were taking over from the generation of A. M. Klein. The group included the much more flamboyant, manifestly Jewish Irving Layton, together with whom he published Canadian poetry magazines. Dudek's courses on modern poetry attracted a different kind of student from those in the European Literature course, and among them were several budding poets. I was a sophomore when our teacher decided to launch a McGill poetry series with a volume by his most talented senior, Leonard Cohen.

Leonard Cohen with fellow Canadian poet Irving Layton, Montreal 1997. Layton was the closest to a mentor that Leonard ever allowed himself. This mature photo registers their lasting friendship. (Gift to the author from photographer Ron Diamond)

I first came to know Leonard in the glancing way one became aware of certain upperclassmen: He was said to be the star pupil of novelist Hugh MacLennan. He played background music for the Drama Club's performance of Shakespeare. I was impressed by the rumor that he kept flunking his Latin. Through the *Daily* I was involved with all the literary projects on campus, so when Dudek began to organize his poetry series, he reasonably involved me in it, probably assuming that his two Jewish students already knew one another.

Louis would not have recognized the differences between Leonard from Westmount and me from the other side of the mountain where I attended UJPO concerts and Yiddish lectures at the Jewish Public Library. There was a bit of unspoken snobbery on both sides: Leonard was a fraternity boy, and were it not for his reputation as a poet, I would have paid him no attention.

My uncles, like his, belonged to the same Shaar Hashomayim Synagogue. But while his relatives were scions of the congregation, trustees in top hats, mine were latecomers with European accents. Also, he was a Kohen, member of the priesthood, a distinction that came into effect only when being called up first to the Torah but one that mattered to the young man who felt himself innately distinguished. Leonard's was the déclassé branch of the family thanks to his father's having married a Russian immigrant (named Masza, like my mother). But his father's death when he was only nine also wrapped him in the tragic mantle of orphancy. Our literary-cultural ambitions brought us together, while socially we belonged to different spheres.

Late one afternoon, Louis invited Leonard and me to join him at Joe's Steakhouse down the street from campus to figure out some of the details of publication. There were no tablecloths so everyone took notes on the table. It was agreed that Freda Guttman would design the cover, and that we would use the best quality paper. Louis needed money for the down payment. Following my mother's example of subsidizing Yiddish books through the system of advance sales known as prenumerantn, I proposed to begin selling advance copies for the agreed price of one dollar. I still have in my possession some of the orders for the 200 advance copies I sold, from Sonny (Mortimer)

Zuckerman, Rabbi Samuel Cass of Hillel, and Professor R. S. Walker, chair of the English department. I used all my *Daily* connections and the skills acquired from selling those Histadrut tickets in elementary school.

I was excited about the book. The working title, *Let Us Compare Mythologies*, placed Judaism into cultural contention without ceding its claim to preeminence. If all religious certainties were being demoted to the status of myths, thanks to anthropological books like James Frazer's *The Golden Bough* or the inchoate transnational ideas of the poet Ezra Pound whom Louis Dudek adored, at least Leonard was including Judaism among them. Yet I was never completely satisfied with the way he treated his Jewishness. After all, I was the daughter of Masza Roskies, who had moved us away from Westmount's veneer of acculturation into a much more profound way of life that included Jewish languages and learning and responsibility for one's fellow Jews. But at a minimum, Leonard spoke as a Jew, even taking pride in being a true Kohen.

Of the many poets I came to know personally, Leonard was the first of my generation. He combined the courtliness of Klein with the sensuousness of Layton, the two best-known Canadian Jewish poets. Leonard discussed with Layton the possibility of setting their poems to music, so as to break out of the confines of "Canadian poetry" into the mass market. But when Leonard did break out, he did it solo, accompanying himself on guitar on the second floor of Dunn's Delicatessen on Sainte-Catherine Street. Suddenly the action was no longer just in New York.

Leonard's later celebrity so overshadowed the rest of that buoyant time that later, in writing about those years, I could say that I remembered him more vividly than I remembered myself. Individual talent needed fertile soil, and many others were painting and sculpting and studying architecture— and also writing. Adele Wiseman, who had moved to Montreal from her native Winnipeg, won the Governor General's Award for Fiction in 1956 for *The Sacrifice,* a novel modeled on the biblical story of Abraham and Isaac. We had our tragic poet, too, in Steve Smith, the youngest to appear in the *McGill Poetry Series*, who died of bone cancer at twenty-two just as he was entering his final year of college. Dudek and I visited him together at the Jewish General Hospital after his leg had been amputated. An unfinished poem of his read: "he died like a pen running out of ink."

Mordecai Richler, a Baron Byng boy, had gone off to London to become a novelist as an earlier generation of expatriates had left small-town America for Europe, but his 1959 novel *The Apprenticeship of Duddy Kravitz* put his native Montreal on the map the way Philip Roth did Newark, New Jersey. Montreal Jews were bringing their fiction home, and now local poetry was springing up too.

Our time at college coincided with the relaxation of Catholic influence in Quebec that had affected us non-Catholics mostly through a law prohibiting anyone under the age of sixteen from attending the movies. The ban was not formally repealed until 1961, but it had stopped being enforced and we had, in any event, already won that freedom. The city had come alive. We attended superior French plays and movies as often as English. With some friends, I thought of establishing the kind of bookstore-cum-coffeeshop that we visited on our trips to New York's Greenwich Village. We never got beyond the planning stages, but others soon did.

Until then it had seemed that we Jews were learning to fit into a society that kindly tolerated our presence. The emergence of local Jewish culture *in English* made the city ours as much as anyone's. In the States, movies and novels about Jewish ambition ended with Jews marrying Gentiles. We were in this respect a generation behind, or maybe the Canadian mosaic encouraged religious and ethnic coexistence, acculturation rather than assimilation. No one I knew dated across religious lines, though sports and culture brought us together.

∽

As we graduated and moved out into the world, each of us knew we had to find a profession to pursue—and a partner who would see us through it. Young men generally waited to marry until they had, if not the means, then at least good prospects of supporting a wife and family. Young women looked over the field and were looked over in turn. More important for me than finding my profession was finding a husband and starting a family. I did not think myself conventional, but it was obvious that my other ambitions could wait their biological turn.

6

DESTINY

The Yiddish term *bashert*—"destined" or "preordained"—conjures up the image of a divine matchmaking service in which, forty days before a child is born, a heavenly voice proclaims: "The daughter of so-and-so is intended for the son of thus-and-such." Commonly invoked by Jews looking for their partners in life—, this folk belief (with its source in the Talmud, no less) escorts the male *basherter* and female *basherte* to the marriage canopy under which they establish a new unit of the Jewish people.

And there's something more: to be identified in this scheme specifically as someone's daughter or son implies that even if the respective parents haven't been directly involved in locating the destined soulmate, they approve the match. Love results in a marriage ratified and sanctified by the community in fulfillment of God's plan.

The literature I studied at college inverted this scheme. In the famous medieval romance, the noble Tristan is sent by his uncle King Mark to Ireland to fetch his intended bride. Mindless monarch! On their long sea voyage, Tristan and Iseult are not merely drawn to one another like any two hot-blooded youngsters; they "inadvertently" drink the love potion intended to be shared by Iseult and the king at *their* wedding. As I read, I could hear my father's voice rendering his beloved passage of the Passover Haggadah: "'*And the Lord brought us forth out of Egypt*—not by the hands of an angel, and not by the hands of a seraph, and not by the hands of a messenger, but by the Holy One, blessed be He, Himself in His own glory and in His own person." The king's plan backfires because he failed to heed God's teaching: if you want something important done, you must do it yourself. Meanwhile I swooned to the pair who gave themselves up utterly to love, throwing caution to the winds along with duty, loyalty, and other traditional virtues.

When I went off to college, I realized that I was moving into Gentile society and was more or less ready for Shakespeare's Shylock, Dickens's Fagin, and other negative images of Jews in the work of authors I admired. Unpleasant as this was, I knew that the Jewish way of life owed no apology to the civilization that had given us Hitler and Stalin. But no one had warned me against attacks on conventional marriage and family that sustained the Jewish way of life.

That may be why, about a dozen years later, when I taught my first courses on Yiddish literature, I turned to Sholem Aleichem's story of Tevye the Dairyman, whose several daughters rebel against his authority and the tradition on which it rests. Tevye's daughters love their father, but they discover they can claim the right to choose their husbands without parental oversight. Sholem Aleichem, who was raising his own daughters, realized what this portended for the Jewish future. Tevye's oldest daughter merely falls in love with someone of a lower status than Tevye would have liked; the second marries a communist revolutionary; the third marries a Christian and converts to his religion. Each represents an ideological challenge greater than the one before, but underlying them all is the new code of Love. Every society tries to tame the lure of Eros and only those that succeed, survive.

Somehow, despite the combined influence of medieval romance and Flaubert's disdain for the tedium of married bourgeois life, I knew I had to accept the conjugal arrangement that Mother in one of her rotten moods called "a truss and a bedpan." In life, my parents fiercely supported each other—Father, often at the expense of his children who would have liked him to take their side. My parents held hands when visiting me at camp, and on our long car trips they sang songs of their youth. Their marriage granted us life and a steady home and a model to follow, so that whatever fantasies we might entertain about illicit love, we wouldn't pursue them at the expense of family. I learned early on that the Jewish people grows organically from the Jewish family.

ᢒᎧ

THAT MY OLDER BROTHER BEN was seriously looking for his intended I learned one morning when I saw him shaving in the bathroom with the door open and walked in to ask how his date had gone the night before.

"Fine."

"When are you going out with her again?"

"I'm not."

"Why not? You said it went well."

"Because I don't want to marry her."

(Incredulously) "You mean you're only going to date girls you want to marry?"

"Otherwise, what's the point?"

Several weeks later, at a weekend seminar with the religious philosopher Will Herberg, I introduced my brother to Louise, a junior I had met at a previous college event. He offered her a lift home. They were engaged in May and married in August.

That same semester, the sports editor of the McGill *Daily* asked me whether I might be interested in a summer job as a camp counselor. He said he was recruiting for a Jewish boys' camp. A *boys'* camp? Was I interested? Need you ask? The owners of Camp Leawood, Jules and Frances Leavitt, had a five-year-old daughter and were looking for a female counselor to take charge of the small group of girls they intended to create for her. In hiring me, Jules said I was welcome to hang out with the male counselors, but he hoped I would not become involved with any of them.

Turning up for the staff meeting at the owners' home a couple of weeks before camp opened, I found their daughter waiting on the doorstep—not for me but for a much-respected counselor who'd been at the camp the past few summers. When he arrived, I fell in love with him on sight. Once camp started, I invented an excuse to adjust my schedule so that at least one of my days off would coincide with Len's. On the first such day, he and I walked twenty miles and everything fell into place.

It turned out that Len had been sports editor of the *Daily* four years before I joined the paper. He was also a graduate of the same Jewish People's School that Ben and I attended, and had actually been present at Ben's bar mitzvah party in our home. How's that for *bashert*?

In the sweet year that followed, I concentrated happily on school, friends, work on the *Daily*, and classical and folk-music concerts. Len was studying law at the Université de Montréal, where I sometimes went to meet him in the library. The next summer we were back at Leawood, which was turning coed.

Yet what saith Lysander in *A Midsummer Night's Dream*? "The course of true love never did run smooth." First off, I learned that our families were not strangers. Len's mother had died when he was four; his father had then married the proverbial wicked stepmother, who sent him packing to his mother's sister Vera. Aunt Vera and Mother had been part of a local amateur Yiddish theater group, and it was during their abbreviated friendship that Mother had invited Len to Ben's bar mitzvah party. Then came a fatal quarrel, and the two women had not spoken since.

So I had found the only person in the city from whose surrogate parent my family was actually estranged. But this only added spice to our romance. Besides, both sides saw advantage in our union.

For me, the bigger hurdle was the aura of inevitability that made us so compatible. In my reading I'd come across the stifling marriages of Emma Bovary, Anna Karenina, even Lawrence's Lady Chatterley. Romantic literature encouraged me to take high risks even if they ended in tragedy and reminded me that I'd had no real adventures since my childhood flight from Europe. If I were now to pass from the parental nest to feathering my own, was I doomed to remain a dull, comic foil?

More afraid of entering into such a marriage than of remaining an old maid at eighteen, I told Len that I was not yet ready and that I was leaving for New York at the end of my junior year. It is hard to reconstruct what I thought I was doing.

The evening before my departure, my parents asked to have a word with me. I had given them no information about my plans because I had none to give. Two of my longtime high school buddies were driving to New York the next day and would give me a lift to an apartment where I could have a mattress until I found a place of my own.

One might have imagined Mother and Father frantic with worry. Did I intend to return for senior year? Was the breakup with Len irreversible? Showing remarkably little anxiety about my departure, they said only that they had not yet had a chance to advise me about life. This was technically true, since I never went to them with my personal problems and had in fact developed the unnecessary habit of lying to them in order to conceal my blameless activities. Now, more to set their minds at ease than to elicit their guidance, I said, very well, each of you can give me *one* piece of advice that I promise to follow.

Father said, "Don't drink when you are alone."

Mother said, "Don't play cards."

Until then I had not drunk anything more than the Manischewitz served on Sabbath and Passover and had never even owned a deck of cards. God only knows where they had picked up these notions of big-city debauchery. But these were the innocent 1950s, a wholesome interval in human affairs when the greatest threat to adolescents apparently came from medieval, Romantic, and antibourgeois literature.

I found a fifth-floor walkup on West 23rd Street and part-time work at the Gotham Book Mart on West 47th. When the owner Frances Steloff learned that I was from Montreal, she asked whether I could persuade A. M. Klein to attend the store's annual Bloomsday celebration. The Gotham was home to the James Joyce Society and Klein had published a "Talmudic" commentary on a chapter of *Ulysses*. Regretfully, I let her know that her esteemed Joycean had ceased to write due to a severe depression.

New York enchanted me. With my friend Jack Novick I walked the streets, once until dawn. A musician friend of Jack's made me a present of Bach's orchestral suites that became my favorite record. When Jack acquired a girlfriend, the three of us would go to the movies together—usually some French *nouvelle vague* import—and then argue about the film for hours.

I didn't get beyond a couple of pages in the novel I had vaguely intended to write—enough to persuade me that I was better suited for marriage than bohemia. After about a month I also realized that my modest savings were running out. Even if working at Miss Steloff's could have become a regular job, I wouldn't have wanted it on a permanent basis and didn't know what else I could do that might sustain me. I liked being on my own just enough to know that I wouldn't like it for much longer. So I returned to Montreal for my senior year at McGill, and Len and I married the following March, just before my graduation and Len's from law school.

It had been a risible rebellion, but I was in for a surprise. The morning after our wedding, I awoke to find almost everything unchanged. Len was asleep beside me and that was comforting, though I could not imagine anyone sleeping after dawn. But I had not expected to be having the same thoughts and facing the same questions that I thought marriage would resolve. Exams faced me the following month, then graduation, then the summer of honeymoon travel we had planned. But once that was over? I had still to decide what to "do" with my life.

Marriage of Leonard Wisse and Ruth Roskies, March 17, 1957. Right to left, Benjamin and Louise Roskies, bride's parents, about-to-be-wedded couple, Len's aunt Vera Slatkin and son Daniel Slatkin. Seated, Eva and David Roskies, Len's sister Natalie Wisse. Portrait of grandfather David Roskies looks on.

Original plans for a simple home wedding grew to include meal for extended family followed by successive receptions for family friends and friends of the couple. The inappropriately elaborate gown was urged on Masza by her dressmaker who had sewn it for a cancelled wedding. Masza tripped on the train following the bride down the stairs but recovered her balance without injury.

To be sure, marriage involved the happy prospect of moving from my parents' house into our own apartment, and I was not under the same pressure as my brother or husband to support a family. But I knew I would have to go to work.

CR

WHEN I LEFT COLLEGE, I didn't expect to see the inside of a classroom ever again. In junior year I had won a scholarship from the Canadian Women's Press Club, so upon returning from our honeymoon I approached it for help in finding a job in journalism, offering as credentials my multiyear experience on the McGill *Daily*. Rather than a placement on one of Montreal's several English newspapers, the Press Club's women directed me to a position as press officer of the Canadian Jewish Congress.

Though somewhat dismayed at being pigeonholed, I was nevertheless glad to find employment in an institution conveniently located just a few blocks from our downtown apartment. For sixty-five dollars a week I was expected to put out the monthly *Bulletin*, arrange the annual CJC conference, prepare press releases, and "fill in" wherever I was needed.

Founded in the wake of World War I as the national organization of Canadian Jewry, the CJC had acquired great urgency in the 1930s when anti-Semitism demanded coordinated action both at home and abroad. Samuel Bronfman, the wealthiest Jew in the country (and the employer of A. M. Klein), was persuaded to assume its presidency. Perhaps to offset Bronfman's reputation as a former bootlegger, the person chosen to head the organization was an elegant lawyer, Saul Hayes, whom no one would have taken for a Jew. He was the perfect public face of the still largely immigrant Jewish community, and also an excellent boss who trusted me to get things done.

Initially annoyed at being branded a Jew, I no sooner began working for a Jewish organization than I felt it was not Jewish *enough*. My first quarrel with Mr. Hayes, as I always referred to him, arose over his indifference to the prospect of government funding for Jewish day schools. I've described earlier how Quebec's confessional school system had prompted the establishment of separate Jewish schools sustained entirely through fees and private donations. In 1958, a group of Jewish parents formed to seek government support for the "secular" part of their children's schooling, arguing that their taxes should not subsidize Protestant schools without reimbursement for the universally mandated part of education to which all Canadian children were entitled.

The group wanted CJC to press its claim with the province, but the board members, almost none of whom sent their children to Jewish schools, were unwilling to challenge the government. I took the side of the parents. Things got so heated that at one community meeting a parent unplugged the microphone during a board member's speech. But the parents eventually prevailed, and, with a little extra pressure from the CJC, the provincial government granted their appeal. This has kept Jewish day school education in Quebec more equitable than it is in the United States.

The year 1959 had been designated the "Bicentenary of Canadian Jewry," and it was my job to help plan and publicize the celebratory events, of which the capstone was to be the dedication of a plaque to Aaron Philip Hart, one of those first Jewish settlers who prospered mightily in his new land. We invited Maurice Duplessis, Quebec's premier, to do the honors, and Mr. Hayes instructed me to place an ad in the local papers inviting all members of the Hart family to join us.

I hesitated, having read in B. G. Sacks's *History of the Jews in Canada* that Hart had enjoyed a version of the medieval *droit du seigneur*—a master's first right to girls on his estate on their wedding night. But we received several cheerful responses and no complaints from French-Canadian claimants to the family line. I looked forward to interviewing some of them, but it was not to be. Premier Duplessis, whose repressive reign was dubbed La Grande Noirceur—the Great Darkness—died days before our event, which we canceled as a result.

Duplessis's death ushered in a period of liberalization that rapidly transformed Quebec's fundamentally Catholic society. The birthrate dropped spectacularly. Nuns and priests disappeared from among us. Monasteries were transformed into music schools. But the Hart family legacy also made me realize that our province had always been more complicated than it seemed.

I tried to use the CJC *Bulletin* to promote Jewish writers and artists. One of the books that most excited me was Isaac Bashevis Singer's first collection of translated stories, *Gimpel the Fool*. Bashevis, as he was known in Yiddish, was not one of the writers we had read in Jewish school, and discovering him on my own made him that much more exciting—that and his roguish humor. Gimpel of the title story was a preposterously exaggerated version of the cuckold, whom I had first encountered as the butt of Geoffrey Chaucer's smutty "Miller's Tale." Jewish society of the *shtetl*, the East European town, was usually accused of repressed sexuality and confining sexual norms. What then was Bashevis doing with this character whom the town knowingly marries off to the local prostitute and mocks for "fathering" many children, none of whom is actually his? This writer was either deliberately perverse or he had found a new way of portraying evil through deceptively familiar storytelling.

The brilliance of this story had been heightened in the English translation by Saul Bellow, and some of the other stories of the collection were almost as good. Until this time, the literary spheres of Yiddish and English had been entirely separate and now the dominant culture seemed to be discovering that Yiddish had works on the same level of excellence. Bashevis's flirtation with nihilism made him the natural Yiddish writer to spearhead this transition: sin came through much spicier when served up by an old-style chronicler, retelling tales from the old country. This story collection also included one in the voice of a rookie demon who seduces a young wife through the mirror, appealing to her vanity ingeniously, entertainingly, and with perfect success.

Condescension to Yiddish on the part of the English literati had not been reciprocal. When I was studying with Melech Ravitch he was translating *The Old Man and the Sea,* and it was because of him that I read that Hemingway novel. Jacob Glatstein, the most brilliant and well-read of American Yiddish poets and intellectuals, said with no little bitterness that being a *Yiddish* writer, he had to know about W. H. Auden whereas Auden did not have to know about him. I concluded that Yiddish writers were the more worldly because, in fact, they *were* more worldly, just as I knew myself to be intellectually more mature than Leonard Cohen though he wrote more beautifully. We had experienced more of human history, and our Jewish concerns demanded that we pay close attention to political events in Europe, the Middle East, and all that affected the rest of the world. If the balance of fame tipped to the side of English rather than Yiddish writers it was because a review in the *New York Times Book Review* counted for more than one in the Yiddish *Forward* or our local *Keneder Adler,* the Canadian Eagle.

Author watching Saul Bellow being interviewed at reception in his honor, Jewish Public Library, Montreal, November 9, 1968. A minute later a man interrupted the interview to tell Saul that his grandfather had been a neighbor of the Bellows family in the 1940s. Saul instantly launched into so vivid a description of the gentleman that his grandson exclaimed, "You remember him better than I do!"

Yet Bashevis Singer's sudden popularity suggested that Yiddish high culture might be coming into its own. I coaxed Leonard Cohen into reviewing the book, thinking that one great writer (for so I considered Leonard) would know how to appreciate another. You need not bother looking this up. Rather than turning me down, Leonard kept delaying the submission. As the deadline for the issue approached, I called to say that I'd come by that evening to pick up the review, sure that this would force him to complete so simple a task. Instead, at his place on Stanley Street, we passed the hours in conversation until I finally realized there was nothing to be had. To fill the assigned space, I would have to write the piece myself.

Lest you think this diminished my affection or respect for Leonard, it was quite the opposite: in those days I respected him all the more for not writing solely out of obligation and continued to believe that he would have done the better job.

CR

JUST BEFORE I BEGAN WORKING at the Canadian Jewish Congress, Len and I spent the summer in Israel on our slightly postponed honeymoon, his first trip overseas and mine since coming to Canada. We had expected to spend a couple of weeks in Paris, but arrived during an exceptional heat wave, and were made additionally uncomfortable by some of the natives who mocked Len's Quebecois-accented French. I bought a half dozen novels—Jean Genet, Henry Miller, which were banned in Canada—and then we cut short our stay and eagerly set out for Tel Aviv. I didn't consider at the time that leaving Europe in a hurry replayed my childhood and made the Jewish homeland feel that much more welcoming.

In Israel we never felt like tourists. Taking in everything from the Tel Aviv beach to a school for children with Down syndrome, we visited European friends of my parents who had survived the Shoah and Father's cousins who had gone to Palestine in the 1930s. The packages and assistance parents had sent some of these people made them eager to "repay" that support. Thoughtless North American that I was, I did not realize that rationing had put a strain on our hosts' domestic economy; nor did we heed their warnings against visiting certain parts of the country. Youth seemed never-ending, and war something over and done with.

The week before leaving Montreal, as we were walking through McGill campus, Len and I had run into Stanley Cassin, whom we knew from Camp Leawood, and mentioned that we were about to leave for Israel. He asked that if we happened to visit Kibbutz Sasa, could we give his regards to Nahum and Aviva Ravel? On one excursion, we took the northernmost roundabout route to Haifa, not realizing that the road we were following was off limits. The police who stopped us urged us to drive straight on, making sure that we reached our destination before sundown. But I had seen Sasa on the map along the very road we were taking, and though we would not have gone out of our way there for that purpose, it seemed preposterous to be so close without fulfilling Stanley's request. Bending police orders, we turned off at the kibbutz that was in its earliest stages of development; the dirt road looked as if it had just been cleared of the rocks that were piled on both sides.

There was nothing resembling an office. We stopped the first person we saw and asked where we could find the Ravels. Nahum, she said, was in the field, but Aviva was probably in their *tsrif*, pointing to a nearby cabin. I knocked and a woman came to the door who answered to the name. I felt like that other Stanley in Africa and said with an adventurer's sense of accomplishment, "We have regards for you from Stanley Cassin." She said, "We are not talking to Stanley!" and shut the door.

A comic routine? Hardly. Ideological fervor was still at the high pitch of Ben's Habonim discussions, and Sasa was a kibbutz of the far-Left Hashomer Hatsa'ir, one of the most fired up—in Yiddish, *farbrent*—of the Zionist movements. Stanley Cassin had neglected to tell us that on returning to Montreal, ostensibly to further his studies, he had left the movement. Many years later when the Ravels were themselves back in Montreal, Aviva and I smiled over this episode, but we did not laugh. That fanatical devotion had meant something in its time and deserved no mockery once its urgency had been tempered.

In Tel Aviv we were staying with a family not far from the beach, where we spent many relaxed hours between sand and water. But elsewhere tension was sometimes palpable. One night after the theater and a snack Len and I walked back across the city and saw a small crowd of people at the corner of our street. It was 1:00 a.m. Two cars were facing one another at the intersection, not touching, but one had not turned wide enough and the other perhaps too wide, making it necessary for at least one of the drivers to back up so that both could then proceed. There matters stood. Neither driver would budge until the other did. Neighbors kept coming from the buildings as the argument heated up. It seemed evident to me that the two middle-aged men were relitigating some unrelated injustice. They looked as though they had been through a lot. I did not want to wait around for the outcome. By morning the intersection was clear, no broken glass. Children were on their way to school and parents to work.

Our close family friend and my sometime teacher, Melech Ravitch, had written ahead to his fellow poet Avrom Sutzkever in Tel Aviv to let him know we were coming. Beyond his literary fame, Sutzkever's biography had made him legendary. He had begun writing in his teens in Vilna, then one of the most culturally productive cities in the Jewish firmament, and published two books of poetry before he and his wife were incarcerated in the Vilna Ghetto in 1941. There he managed the seemingly impossible. With faith in the deathlessness of great poetry, and in himself as its creator, Sutzkever had continued writing even as he and his wife also worked in the underground resistance.

His assurance broke through his poetry's bleakest situations and moods. In a poem (dated December 30, 1941) addressed to a murdered "friend" at the barbed wire, the poet asks the dead man's forgiveness for eating the blood-stained food he had still been clutching to his heart. He tries to comfort this nameless man who is now intimately known to the poet through this act.

Silent comrade, / I absorb you and live.
Demand a reckoning from the world/ through my every thread.
Should I fall as you fell/ by the barbed wire
Let another swallow my word/ as I do your bread.

A poem on the death of his mother (dated October 1942) ends with the similar consolation that as long as he is there, she is there as well, "as the pit of the plum/ already contains the tree/ and the nest and the bird/ and all else besides." Poetry was a way of ingesting and forever preserving the actuality that was so cruelly being crushed.

In September 1943 Sutzkever and his wife escaped through the sewers to the forests to join a partisan group. A Lithuanian partisan leader and courier had delivered several of his poems to the Jewish Anti-Fascist Committee in the Soviet Union, which dispatched a small plane to a landing strip near the forests to airlift him and his wife to Moscow. His report on the Vilna Ghetto was the first news of the fate of Polish Jewry to be featured in the

Soviet media. After the war, he testified at the Nuremberg Trials, and was then repatriated to Poland with his wife and the daughter born to them in Moscow. From there they went to France, and with the intervention of Golda Meir (then Golda Meyerson), to British Mandate Palestine in 1947.

He arrived just before Israel declared its independence and undertook his own act of literary resurrection: in Tel Aviv he founded a Yiddish quarterly called *Di goldene keyt*, the Golden Chain, signifying the unbroken chain of Jewish tradition and his intention of maintaining Yiddish creativity in the Land of Israel.

Sutzkever seemed to personify Jewish history in the making. Though I was not yet familiar with much of his work, I would have wanted to contact him even without Ravitch's urging. His powers were immediately apparent. When I called, he asked us to meet him outside the printing plant where he was correcting page proofs. Of medium height and build, in his vigorous early forties, he emerged into the blazing sunlight in shirtsleeves and a peaked cap. Had I not recognized him from his pictures, I might have taken him for the plant foreman. Shaking hands, his grip was much stronger than I had expected and belied the world-wearier images I had formed of poets. He told us he had no time to spare just then but invited us to join him and his wife at a wedding the following evening. The children of his good friends were being married and would "surely welcome us among their guests"—a sentiment Len and I very much doubted. But Sutzkever's wish seemed everyone's command. When we showed up at the wedding, we were indeed treated as favored guests, and a couple of days later he suggested that we travel together to Ein Gedi, the oasis where David had hidden from King Saul.

The trip was a highlight of that summer. In Beer Sheva, we bunked overnight at an Arab house where Len and I, Sutzkever, his teenage daughter Rina, and Didi Frimerman—the son of our Tel Aviv hosts who had served in the army and was serving as our trusted guide—bedded down in five cots along the walls of a large empty room. From across the room, Sutzkever asked me what I thought of the dedication Ravitch had made in his most recent book of poems, *To Rokhl, for all my days*. "And what about their nights?" he laughed. Inhibited by his daughter's presence from answering in kind, I realized that though I had been thinking of them both as "Yiddish poets," he was a generation younger than Ravitch, and wanted me to know it.

With artists Yosl and Audrey Bergner in Tel Aviv, summer 1957. Yosl's father, Melech Ravitch, had asked his son and daughter-in-law to give us one of their paintings as a wedding gift. We remained their friends and devotees ever after.

The police in Beer Sheva told us not to proceed to the city of Sodom without armed escort but Sutzkever waved off the warning. As said, though I knew that Israel was under daily attack from Arab marauders, I did not take such dangers into account, least of all when traveling with Len and two experienced fighters. The owner of a gas pump in Sodom warned us not to drive on to Ein Gedi but when a hitchhiker volunteered to guide us there, Sutzkever did not have to urge us to take up the offer. We traveled along an unpaved desert road that could have disabled a tank. Taking risks seemed child's play in the company of this man who had "survived his *Akedah,*" quoting from a poem of his that I loved. He was Abraham whose infant son had been put to death at birth in the ghetto hospital on German orders. He was also the intended sacrifice who had been spared.

Our hitchhiker was a member of the kibbutz at Ein Gedi, which was even younger than Sasa. This one had been founded by an army unit of Nahal, acronym for *Noar Halutzi Lohem,* the pioneer youth units of Israel's military that trained simultaneously to establish permanent agricultural settlements. Had we not given him the ride our guide would have had to wait another two days for the next supply vehicle headed for his kibbutz. This outpost, very close to the Jordanian border, was still too poor to offer us more than that night's supper and cots under the open sky, but in turn for having delivered him, our guide treated us to a small tour that included a swim in the natural pool at the foot of "Saul's cave."

⋘

ONE EVEN MORE DRAMATIC EVENT awaited me before our departure. I had gone looking for a suitable present for Mother and entered the shop that might carry such an item without realizing that I wasn't appropriately dressed for a place that specialized in religious books. Seeing me in shorts and sleeveless blouse, the elderly bookseller assumed I was in the wrong place. To set him right, I asked, speaking Yiddish rather than Hebrew, whether he might have any book published by the Matz Press of Vilna, explaining that Fradl Matz was my grandmother. The old man removed his glasses and looked through me at something distant and dear. He said, "Your mother was the most beautiful woman in Vilna." He had skipped a generation, as Mother often did when she called us by one of her sibling's names, but then rather than speak more of her told me about his fellow book distributor Yisroel Welczer who was Fradl's second husband.

Had I wanted to write romances I could have done no better than to rehearse the improbable story of grandmother Fradl, married off at fifteen by *her* mother to the widower Yehuda Leib Matz, a man three times her age who had fallen in love with her and was prepared to give rather than receive the customary marriage dowry. Fradl was lured into the engagement thinking that she was being betrothed to his thirty-year old brother. I'll bet this is not what most readers imagine to be the religious decorum of "traditional Jews," yet perhaps it was not so indecorous after all, since Matz won over the frightened girl with his kindness, and they had a very fruitful union. He hired wet-nurses for the ten children she bore him and welcomed her partnership in running the Matz Press, Vilna's third largest Jewish publishing house. When she inherited the business after his death, she ran it under her own name. The printing presses were in the basement of the courtyard building where they lived on Zavalna Street, and the family apartment was on an upper story.

The second romance to which the bookseller now alluded had been even racier than her first. As a book distributor, Welczer must have encountered Fradl whenever he came to Vilna to pick up books on consignment that he would then sell in the provinces. Upon learning that Yehuda Leib Matz had died, he divorced his wife in Josefow and wooed Fradl as a widower. Was this really how it happened? Did Grandmother pretend to believe him or marry him knowing the truth? Had they fallen in love before Matz died—she with him as well as he with her? Once they married, to the intense annoyance of her older children, he joined Fradl in running the business. He and Fradl had two daughters of their own, of whom the younger, Gitl, died in infancy, leaving Mother the only lovechild of a much-resented stepfather. She later regretted having sided with her half siblings against the man who had won their mother's heart.

I left the store with a prayer book published by the Matz Press and confirmation of Mother's stories I had never expected to find. Fradl's picture had always hung over my parents' bed, but for the first time I realized that I really had a grandmother who had once been my age, and newly married. The time in Israel had connected me back to the Europe I came from.

In sum, I was still very much under the impression of that summer when I began working at the CJC, and, encouraged by correspondence with Sutzkever, one of the first things I proposed to Mr. Hayes was that we organize a Canadian speaking tour for the poet, with Montreal as his home base.

CR

Sutzkever's visit, his first to North America, was arranged for the spring of 1959. Several Jewish organizations in the United States had clamored for such a tour, but Sutzkever was denied an American visa despite valiant efforts by his fellow poet Judd Teller, who was well-connected in Washington. Both men traced the denial of a visa to his denunciation as a communist, a charge he angrily dismissed as a spiteful lie. They came to believe that the informer was the wife of the Yiddish poet and novelist Chaim Grade, then living in New York, who was notoriously jealous of her husband's reputation and tried to protect it by damaging his competitors.

Maternal grandmother, Fradl Polachek Matz Welczer of Vilna (1863–1921). Of the four grandparents (none of whom the author ever met), portraits of only the two epic figures, David and Fradl, hung in our home.

This was Grade's second wife, his first having been killed along with his mother and the rest of Vilna Jewry while he, who had thought the women would be safe, had made his way into the Soviet interior. (I may as well include this information since Inna Grade's denunciations, in an episode that can wait its turn, later tried to thwart my academic advancement at McGill and Harvard.) The two poets had been the young stars of Jewish literary Vilna before the war. Whatever their artistic and personal differences, they maintained cordial relations afterwards, but Inna Grade became the scourge of Yiddish literature. When the Nobel Prize in Literature was awarded to

Isaac Bashevis Singer, she gave interviews protesting that it should have gone to her husband.

However the tour had come about, America's loss was Canada's gain. At Sutzkever's first public evening in Montreal, crowds jammed the hall. Yiddish writers came from New York to meet this envoy from a vanished world. Though he was by inclination a lyrical poet, Sutzkever spoke as that envoy. He first described the occasion for each poem and then declaimed it, as though we were party to its creation. The best known of them told of the teacher Mira Bernstein who had directed one of the underground schools in the Vilna ghetto, tracking her efforts to keep the school intact and to inspire her students as their numbers steadily dropped from 130 to seven. Their hiding place is discovered as she is reading "the third gift" of Peretz's iconic story—the point where poetic invention takes over from history. Dated May 10, 1943, the poem ends with the image of Mira as a flower surrounded by her pupils, the bees. The flower is faded, "but in tomorrow's dew it will blossom anew." Sutzkever dated most poems he wrote in the ghetto to keep the actuality firm against the threat of his and the ghetto's obliteration.

I arranged with Sam Gesser, the local impresario, to record Sutzkever for the Folkways label. Bringing my worlds together, I took him to meet Louis Dudek and listened to the two men speaking in Polish about Polish poetry.

Sutzkever also asked me to arrange a meeting with A. M. Klein, who had translated reams of Yiddish and Hebrew poetry into English and whom I'd still not met. Once again, I explained that Klein's depression discouraged visitors. But here again, Sutzkever prevailed. When I called the Klein home to relay the request, the poet answered and cheerfully invited us over, and when we showed up on the appointed day, he betrayed no hint of gloom. The two men were about the same medium height, Klein looking very much the disciplined lawyer he had been for several decades. The home was modest. Bessie, his wife, appeared briefly in a housedress, but then excused herself and we did not see her again. There were no refreshments—nothing to interrupt the talk, some of it while standing. As the two Abrahams conversed in Yiddish, Sutzkever proved himself remarkably well-informed about Klein's translations into English, a language he presumably did not know. I was torn between wanting their conversation to continue forever and worrying about our host's alleged fragility.

Before the end of the visit, Klein invited us to see his study. It seemed an odd but touching courtesy at the conclusion of a wonderful meeting. I was therefore surprised when, afterward, a visibly troubled Sutzkever stopped at the first street corner to ask my impression.

"Are you serious?" I replied. "It was splendid! He was buoyed by your coming. I am so glad you and he got together!"

Sutzkever looked grim and said, "Didn't you see his desk? There was nothing on it. Not a pen or a shred of paper. When that happens, a writer is finished."

Was that what Klein had meant us to see, or had he hoped that Sutzkever's presence would inspire his return to work? As far as I know, he never did.

The most dramatic rendezvous I arranged for Sutzkever during his stay in Montreal was a secret meeting with Max Weinreich who was to fly in from New York for an overnight stay. The two men badly needed seclusion and shunned any public knowledge of their reunion. Sutzkever had been Weinreich's protégé in Vilna and now the balance had changed: Sutzkever was the one with hard-won knowledge of Jewish Vilna in its death-throes. As Len and I drove with Sutzkever in the car to pick up Weinreich at the airport and then straight to a hotel at the foothills of the Laurentians, I felt that I was setting up a historic tryst. We installed them there and returned late the next day to take Weinrich back to the airport. During the trips there and back they spoke in the back of the car with a respectful intimacy more intense than any love I had ever witnessed.

In addition to public readings and private meetings, Sutzkever was also feted in private homes, including my parents'. Most of the people invited that evening were from Vilna: one had been with him in the forests, several others were survivors, and some, like my parents, had left the city before the war. Leaning against the mantelpiece and slowly draining his tumbler of Scotch, Sutzkever spoke of *Yung Vilne* (Young Vilna), his pre-war literary circle of poets, writers, and artists, and quoted this disquieting poem by Leyzer Volf:

Why does a dog bark at the moon?
Because he thinks: it's a piece of red meat.
Why does a teacher beat the children?
Because *he* doesn't know the alphabet.

Why do the stars fall down?
Because it's lonely with God.
Why do they chop down the forests?
So the beasts should come into town.

After he had spoken about the major poets in the group, Sutzkever veered off into an odd reminiscence about a certain Moyshe-Itske Barg who alternated between bouts in a mental institution and spurts of creativity. There was an incident about Moyshe-Itske rescuing a dog from the dogcatcher, about stitching his poems on his girlfriend's sewing machine, and then about him bounding into Sutzkever's room to announce that he, Moyshe-Itske, was immortal: he was never going to die! Sutzkever fearing the worst tried to reason with him by pointing out that, of the three men his visitor most admired—Dostoevsky, Napoleon, and Moses—Dostoevsky had managed to cheat death but once, Napoleon had died in exile, and Moses was not even accorded entry into the Promised Land. This quieted the man for only a moment. Then he shouted, "Someone's got to break through!" Sutzkever raised his voice in imitation of this cry. And he was done.

From apparently artless rambling about a manic depressive there had emerged the power of a community driven beyond conceivable limits to affirm its eternity. Someone *had* broken through: Sutzkever now lived in the Promised Land that Moses never reached. One did not have to use a word like "miraculous" to invoke miracles. The otherworldly people casually smoking and drinking in our living room had just heard the lecture of a lifetime. The destruction of Jewish Vilna had been impressed on us until there was no further hope of its survival. I can't speak for others in the room; I suddenly felt Vilna come back alive.

As his departure neared, Sutzkever asked me what I intended to do in the coming years, implying that I was not destined to work at CJC forever. I said I might resume study of English literature.

"Why not Yiddish literature?" he asked.

I laughed and said, "And what would I do? Teach Sholem Aleichem?"

Before the words were out of my mouth, I wanted to retract this implied insult to Yiddish and the Yiddish master before me. I had been studying Yiddish literature for years, had attended lectures by Yiddish poets and writers, had met some of the greatest of them in our parents' home. I had just arranged the tour of one of the great poets of our time. How, then, could I have said what I said? The absence of Jewish subjects in the college curriculum had evidently suggested to me that that Jewish subjects did not *belong* in the college curriculum! To save face, I tried to explain that there was nowhere I could pursue such studies, but Sutzkever had apparently anticipated this and said that Professor Uriel Weinreich at Columbia University was offering scholarships to students of Yiddish language and literature, and I would surely be admitted to his program. Uriel was Max Weinreich's son and already a distinguished linguist in his own right. The next day I called, and began my studies at Columbia in the winter of 1960.

Parting with Avrom Sutzkever at the airport before his departure from Montreal, May 1959. Photo by Hertz Grosbard, who was a skilled photographer as well as diseur.

I was so used to charting my own path that I was sure marriage was no impediment to my plans and that Len would not object to my getting a graduate degree in this nonexistent field. I also failed to notice the agents of destiny's shaping hand. From the Sutzkever-Weinreich correspondence later published in *Di goldene keyt*, I would learn that during their retreat the two had talked about recruiting for his son's Columbia program and recognized in me a fish eager to take the bait. I had simply fallen in with *their* plan.

7

PERSEVERANCE

Graduate school was harder than I anticipated. I arrived in New York at the beginning of January 1960 armed with a friend's offer of temporary lodging, only to find the room so cold that I slept in my winter coat. Until I could register at Columbia University and make use of its facilities, I stayed warm in the main branch of the New York Public Library, plucking Yiddish books from the shelves of the Judaica reading room and hoping to get a head start in my studies. I read Sholem Aleichem and looked for the kind of historical overviews that were available for other European literatures. I did not really know what I was looking for. Though in the past I'd often chafed at the requirement to follow a prescribed syllabus at a set pace, now my random reading made me long for a teacher's guidance.

Most of the people in the reading room were elderly dozers; the most alert among them was a regular who kept long hours surrounded by an array of books. One day, browsing a shelf near his table to see what he was studying, I realized from the way he was turning the pages backward that he could read neither Hebrew nor English. Over the next few days, I became touched by his worshipful imitation of a scholar. I wondered whether I, too, might be something of a fake, more attracted by the ambition of scholarship than fully equipped to achieve it.

In attending McGill and getting married, I had been doing what I wanted but also what was expected of me. Now that I was cutting my own path, I had to persuade myself I was doing the right thing. Columbia did not make it easy. Uriel Weinreich, who had admitted me into the Yiddish program, chaired the university's Department of Linguistics, in which the other students of Yiddish were duly enrolled. To pursue studies in *literature* I had to register instead in the Department of English and Comparative Literature, which meant taking most of my courses in subjects other than Yiddish and passing language-proficiency exams not only in German but in French and Latin instead of one of the Slavic tongues closer to my field of interest.

I was thus at once the school's only literature student in Yiddish and the only Yiddish student in literature. Were it not for my weekly tutorial with Uriel's father, Max, I might have returned to Montreal.

ෆ

YIDDISH SAYS: *TSU SHLIMAZL DARF men oykh hobn mazl*—even bad luck needs its good luck. Uriel was on sabbatical the semester I arrived, so his father, Max, who was part-time professor of Yiddish at City College of New York, had taken over his seminar on Yiddish literature, with me as his only student. At sixty-six, he was the oldest of my teachers but decidedly the most adventurous in spirit and least constrained by bureaucratic or formal academic considerations.

Max Weinreich in the 1960s when he was writing his *History of the Yiddish Language.* One of the founders of the YIVO Institute for Jewish Research in 1925, he oversaw its transfer from Vilna to New York and remained its guiding force there.

Born in Latvia, Max Weinreich had studied in Russia and Germany, earning his PhD in philology from the University of Marburg before joining several others to found the YIVO Institute for Jewish Research in Vilna in 1925. The YIVO (a Yiddish acronym for Jewish Scientific Institute) was the closest European equivalent to the Hebrew University, which opened the same year in Jerusalem. Of its research branches—history, education, economics & social anthropology—Max Weinreich headed the fourth branch of language and literature, but his interests overlapped with all the others.

The German-trained founders of YIVO chose Vilna as the logical home for their Jewish center of learning and used Yiddish, then the vernacular of some ten million Jews, as their language of operations. As well as research and publication, Weinreich dedicated much of his energy to the education of local youth. He founded and became head scoutmaster of a youth organization, *Bin* (Bee), that combined Boy Scouts founder Robert Baden-Powell's healthful discipline with immersion in Jewish national culture. Sutzkever was one of its teenage members and published his first poem in its magazine. Clearly, the senior Weinreich liked being among younger people. From the moment we began our tutorial he made me feel he enjoyed it almost as much as I did.

It was agreed that we would devote our weekly sessions to the work of a single writer, Sholem Yankev Abramovitch, better known by his pen name Mendele Mokher Sforim or Mendele the Book Peddler. Max—as I thought of my teacher—was certain that Mendele—as he always referred to him—was so central to the development of modern Jewish literature that a strong knowledge of his work would provide a solid foundation for my further studies.

Abramovitch-Mendele, who was born 1835 in the Byelorussian town of Kapulye (Kopyl) and died 1917 in the port city Odessa, was almost certainly the greatest modern Jewish literary genius, credited with establishing—or "grandfathering"—modern literatures in both Yiddish and Hebrew. The reversals of his adolescence readied him for a lifetime of social observation. Carefully educated and nurtured until early teens in a household that he later lovingly memorialized, he was plummeted from security to destitution when his father died and his mother could no longer support him. He was sent to board at a yeshiva where his reputation as an outstanding student caught the attention of a traveling mendicant who intended to profit by brokering the boy's marriage to the daughter of a wealthy family. Such arrangements were common, and though his first arranged marriage ended badly, the second, arranged without nefarious intentions, brought him a decade of time to study and educate himself in European as well as Jewish sources. He wrote social and literary criticism, translated a major work of natural history, and was quickly recognized as a leading intellectual of the Haskalah, the Jewish Enlightenment, before turning to fiction under the pen name that subsumed his identity. Max was likewise a refined intellectual who chose to disseminate his teaching at a popular level—an affinity I must have sensed, though it has taken me until now to name it.

Each week, in chronological order, I would report on one of Mendele's works. Because Max had a special interest in the *process* of writing, and because Mendele was a compulsive reviser, my assigned task was to compare variants whenever they existed. In truth this exercise did not thrill me as much as it did my teacher, whose fascination with language excited his curiosity about every exchange of a Slavic-based term for one from German or Hebrew, or the slightest modification of a character's speech. For my part, dazzled by Mendele's intelligence and bruising candor, I wanted to understand how he had developed from an angry young critic of his society into its most incisive interpreter.

Studying Mendele in 1960 was complicated by the knowledge that the world he had tried to reform had been annihilated for none of the faults he had identified. His first Yiddish work of fiction, *The Little Man*, was a scathing portrait of the Jewish boy who learns to be "small," parasitic, by emulating the dishonest grownups around him. There was little subtlety in this satire of Jewish community corruption and of people who use the camouflage of piety to mask their cheating and outright theft. Models of hypocrisy were already there aplenty in Charles Dickens's *pecksniffery*, and in Russian writers like Gogol and Saltykov-Shchedrin. Mendele adapted their ridicule to his own society and added as a corrective the figure of an enlightened

Jew named Goodheart whose broad education, civic understanding, and upright behavior teach our misled little man how to behave more like a good European.

Mendele's satire soon grew more sophisticated, and so, too, his criticism. His novel *Fishke the Lame*, or in its Hebrew version, *Book of Beggars*, intertwines a sentimental plot with wholesale dissection of Jewish society. Into the frame story of Mendele and a fellow traveling book peddler comes the eponymous Fishke, who works as a bath attendant until the town marries him off to a blind beggarwoman. She draws him into an itinerant beggars' gang whose members advertise their deformities to prey on people's sympathies. Fishke falls in love with a hunchbacked girl, abandoned by her parents and forcibly conscripted by the gang's leader. This was territory into which young Abramovitch had himself been drawn as a teenager by the mendicant who exploited his innocence. Far from romanticizing the crippled crew, each with his or her own disability, Mendele presents all of Jewish society through the synecdoche of the beggar's pouch, including even the writers who peddle their books door to door. This was a more devastating indictment of Jewish weakness and depravity than any anti-Jewish writer could have produced.

Philip Roth's *Goodbye, Columbus* appeared at the time that I was studying Mendele. It was admittedly more fun reading this collection of stories about Newark Jews, written from a contemporary's perspective (Roth was three years older than I). These, too, were social satires, here of the American Jewish middle class that was a generation removed from its traditions and from Europe. The stories mocked Jewish suburbanites who are incensed by the prospect of an Orthodox yeshiva in their neighborhood, Jewish recruits in the military who try to use their Jewishness to escape army responsibilities, Jews who substitute material comfort and security for real culture and passion, and Jews who are afraid to question the premises of their faith. I shared some of this scorn and liked the book so much I wrote Roth the first and only fan letter I ever sent to a writer whom I didn't know personally. His later complaint that he was being censured by the Jewish community neglected to mention the far greater adoration that boosted his sales. When

Roth tried his hand at writing about Gentile America, he found he needed the Jews because he had no better subject and certainly no better market.

Despite my admiration, reading Roth in tandem with Mendele made me see that the decline in Jewish life was actually as evident in his fiction as in his subjects. Roth's coverage of Jewish life was necessarily skimpier than Mendele's, and his language thinner. Even the best writers can only work with the material they have at hand and few American Jewish writers inherited anything like the rich Jewishness of Eastern Europe. By richness I mean the cultural density of a God-inspired civilization cultivated through three millennia in multiple Jewish languages with sustained high levels of literacy. Weinreich's fascination with the intricacies of Mendele's Yiddish had no equivalent among American Jewish linguists, though Roth had a terrific ear and delivering dialogue was one of his specialties. But he was reduced to sex because his subjects no longer shared much of a culture. I found the Jewishness of Philip Roth more sterile than the faith of the Hadassah women he joked about, and neither then, nor later, was I ever tempted to exchange my focus on Yiddish for the expanding field of American Jewish letters.

The main difference as I saw it was that Mendele shared and felt responsible for the fate of his fellow Jews in a way that Roth did not. Mendele—as opposed to his creator Abramovitch—never pretends to be more perceptive than his subjects, whereas the Roth narrator assumes a moral superiority over the vulgar Jews. In the title story, "Goodbye, Columbus" (punning on Columbus, Ohio), the narrator, who holds a summer job in a library, takes special interest in a little "colored boy" and even bends the rules to encourage the child's interest in the art of Paul Gauguin. This was just the kind of self-enhancement that had offended me in Leonard Cohen's phony treatment of the boy at Pripstein's. The implied contrast between the pure sensitivity of the black child with the crassness of Jews—always excepting the writer himself—is a distortion into which Abramovitch at his angriest was not tempted.

To be honest, history had a hand in this. With the first Russian pogrom in Odessa in 1871, Abramovitch-Mendele realized that Jews were being attacked not for the "beggary" of which he accused them but rather for the little that they possessed. He feared that by drawing attention to the corruption in Jewish society he inadvertently may have stoked the anti-Jewish prejudice of Russian authorities. His original reformist platform had assumed that Jews needed to become worthier of acceptance into Russian society. The pogroms and discriminatory tsarist policies called that logic into question.

Turning against his former enlightened position, he wrote a novel, *The Mare*, in which Isrolik, a member of the Society for the Prevention of Cruelty to Animals, modeled on himself, sees a bedraggled mare being chased into a ditch by a gang of boys and yapping dogs. When Isrolik approaches the poor creature after they have finished sporting with her, he is surprised to hear her speak with a human voice. The allegorical creature is the Jewish people, once a prince, but metamorphosed into this hunted female prey when he/she was driven from their home. In feisty dialogue the mare exposes the hypocrisy of Isrolik's attempts to "help her" out of her misery by persuading her to make a better show of herself. She protests: "The dance cannot precede the food," which is to say that basic rights must be granted and cannot be earned. At the point of processing this idea, the young man is grabbed by the Devil who takes him for a flight above Europe where he sees the horror being done to the Jews and others across the continent.

Mendele had translated Jules Verne's *Five Weeks in a Balloon*, and here in place of the evils of Africa, Isrolik, in the grip of the Devil, looks down on the evils of Europe. This exposé of the Jewish condition and the potential harm Jewish reformers can do on an already hostile continent was the boldest, most incisive treatment of modern Jewish politics I had ever seen and it informed my subsequent understanding of the relations among Jews, their intellectual elites, and the enemies who are out to get them.

○३

MAX WEINREICH SPOKE OF VILNA as lovingly as my mother. Thanks to my mother's stories, I could trade anecdotes with him, like the one about Max's father-in-law, the prominent Vilna doctor Tsemach Szabad, who had cared for my grandmother Fradl Matz when she was dying of tuberculosis and on one of his last home visits had remarked, "You can't patch up silk." What he may have intended as a tribute to the patient's refinement, my then-teenage mother heard as a premature death sentence and never forgave him.

Had Hitler not intervened, I might have found myself in 1960 traveling to study with Max in Vilna and boarding there with my uncle Grisha, Mother's older brother, who lived about a fifteen-minute walk from the YIVO building. Murdered in 1942, Grisha had assisted Doctor Szabad in his work in local orphanages and clinics. By then, providentially, YIVO had established a branch in New York, which after World War II took over as its center. Max and his son Uriel were attending a conference in Denmark when the Germans invaded Poland, so they could not return and left for America instead. The other half of the family, Regina and their son Gabriel, reached America through Siberia and Japan.

After every class, Max treated me to dinner at a Chinese restaurant underneath the elevated subway platform at Broadway and 125th Street. Missing sight in one eye—courtesy of anti-Semitic hoodlums in pre-war Vilna—he had shown great bravery in championing his beliefs, which meant standing up to the Jewish Left as well as the Polish Right. Like Mendele, he, too, had undergone a political reorientation. Radicalized members of his youth movement *Bin*, cheered on by the Soviets, rebelled against its "bourgeois" and chauvinistic nationalism. He said he knew that politics had prevailed over scholarship when his Soviet-Yiddish counterparts began referring to him in the plural as "the Weinreichs." In still-communist-free Poland, he launched a contest to collect the autobiographies of Jewish teenagers, which remains one of the liveliest sources of information about East European Jewish youth in its prime.

Aspiring to be as bold as he, after our Chinese dinner I would insist on accompanying him to his subway stop at Lenox Avenue. This for me meant walking back alone in the dark along 125th Street in alert awareness of being the only white person on the street. If I got nervous, I would stop a man or woman to ask the time. Even a curt exchange relieved the tension and made me regret my lack of trust.

FREE AS A JEW

The following autumn, once Uriel returned from his sabbatical, I signed up for all his Yiddish courses and for the seminar given by the great Jewish historian Salo Baron, which met weekly in the professor's home. Uriel, Noam Chomsky's contemporary and, like him, a rising young star of linguistics, failed to inspire me with his love of theory, but I learned much from him about poetics. Baron was one of only three tenured professors of Jewish studies in America at the time, launched on his great project *The Social and Religious History of the Jews* that eventually ran to eighteen volumes. Though I had never taken his classes, he let me join the seminar that met around his dining table, with his wife Jeanette serving us tea and sweets. This seminar was a welcome break from the literature department's stiffer lectures. Baron did not wear his learning as lightly as Max Weinreich, but he, too, tried to put his students at ease.

To satisfy the Baron seminar's research requirement, I chose the topic of *Yung Vilna* ("Young Vilna"), the group of poets and writers about whom Sutzkever had rhapsodized in my parents' living room. Offered no guidance in going about a literary-historical project of this kind, I decided to read the entire 1930s run of the daily Vilna *Tog*, which sometimes published the group's work. In the YIVO library, then at the corner of Fifth Avenue and 86th Street (the future Neue Gallerie), I ordered up one year's folio at a time and lost myself in the news stories and advertisements while searching for anything relating to "my" writers. I was wildly excited whenever I came across the occasional poem or reference to a soccer game the group had played against another team.

The day I turned a page in the 1939 volume and suddenly found nothing beyond it, I was as unprepared as the young poets must have been on the day in Vilna when the Soviets swept in. For a while, I didn't know how to go on.

Though the members of *Yung Vilna* were about the same age as I was when reading about them, we did not have much in common. They were on the barricades and I was in a graduate program, living in a rented room in marital limbo. They were so consumed by political events and social problems that the nonconformists among them like Elkhanan Vogler and Sutzkever who wrote about nature were not invited to participate in their public readings. Sutzkever won local recognition only by sending his poems to the New York "Introspectivist" literary journal *Inzikh* and corresponding with its editor, Aaron Leyeles.

But digging deeper I found that the political stamp they put on their public appearances did not fully claim any one of them. Shimshon Cahan, an editor of the *Tog*, befriended and wrote about the Gypsies in nearby Trocki; Leyzer Volf tried to escape his provincialism by half-seriously imagining himself in Paris. Vilna their mother city—*ir v'eym*—was as sentimentally precious to them as the mothers who nursed them. Their fathers all seemed to be deceased, leaving them freer, more exposed and responsible than we ever needed to be.

How my other courses paled by comparison! Even the writings of Samuel Johnson with whom I felt the greatest affinity could not vie with the immediacy of my Jewish readings. One week, Baron canceled our seminar because he had flown to Israel to testify at the trial of Adolf Eichmann, whose proceedings I watched on television with my landlady every evening. He had been asked to provide an historical overview of events involving Eichmann because the defendant's deeds had to be understood in context and this was the only chance Jews would ever have to put Hitlerism on trial—even though such prosecution was absurdly inadequate, and justice unattainable.

By day I would be immersed in the animate community of Vilna's sixty-five thousand Jews, worrying that the government had confiscated *Yung Vilna's* little magazine and imprisoned its organizer Shmerke Kaczerginski, and in the evening I would watch the testimony of Shoah survivors and think again and again, how could what happened have happened? I was already familiar with much of the material Salo Baron was presenting. The shock came later with Hannah Arendt's report on the trial in the *New Yorker* and the publication of her book *Eichmann in Jerusalem: The Banality of Evil.* In the meantime, I was pursuing my graduate work.

CR

LEN AND I RENDEZVOUSED EVERY few weeks either in Montreal or in Albany, midway between our two cities, and Montreal friends sometimes dropped by to lure me from study. One evening I walked with Leonard Cohen to a double feature at a theater on 42nd Street that screened foreign films. As always, Leonard's responses to things never ceased to surprise me: he fell asleep during the obligatorily "meaningful" postwar film (Roberto Rossellini and Federico Fellini's *Open City,* if I'm remembering right) but was riveted by the histrionic Russian version of *Othello.* When the movies ended, we sat in a coffee shop for another couple of hours talking about the poetry of Wordsworth, he in praise of "Tintern Abbey" and I increasingly worried about the next day's assignment.

I made a few great friends in those classes. One of them, Bruce Ducker, turned up at the beginning of March in white shirt, slacks, and tennis shoes to declare, in F. Scott Fitzgerald mode, the start of gin and tonic season. In a course on American literature with Richard Chase, who was also a major literary critic and American thinker, my classmate Peter Shaw already seemed the professor's equal in sheer intellectual verve; he also beat me at ping-pong. Unlike at McGill, at Columbia I neither knew nor wondered who was or was not Jewish. My only connection with Jewish life was through my courses and when I went home for the holidays and for my younger brother David's bar mitzvah.

With Professor Chase I suffered my second lesson in taste after the one I had experienced with Dudek over *The Sorrows of Young Werther,* only this time it cost me the teacher's respect. Along with Philip Roth, the other American "Jewish" writer to win fame in those years was J. D. Salinger. His wildly popular *Catcher in the Rye* I associated with adolescence, preferring the Franny and Zooey stories that had appeared in the *New Yorker.* Like Roth, Salinger forswore the bourgeois middle-classism of the 1950s, less by satirizing the staid than by sentimentalizing the quirky Glass family. I had obtained two copies of the *New Yorker* with the most recent story in the Franny and Zooey series, "Seymour: An Introduction," about the brother whose suicide haunts the family, and in appreciation of Chase's lectures on

American literature, I cut and pasted the story into a fine notebook that I bought for that purpose.

The moment I presented it to him in his office, I realized I had made a terrible mistake. He thanked me so dryly it seemed he was exercising restraint by not handing back my gift. Too rattled to ask for an explanation—or if necessary, his forgiveness—I was left to figure out why he considered Salinger second rate. In our two subsequent seminars I never did cut through his reserve or get up the nerve to ask about this incident, feeling certain that he looked down on me for my schoolgirl taste. I don't think I ever submitted to anyone else's judgment, but these painful challenges to my early enthusiasms by teachers I respected made me think harder about quality, which is different from taste.

The judgment of those we respect forms part of our education. Chase's contempt for the *New York Times Book Review* editor J. Donald Adams, whom he referred to as "J. Donald Duck," and his fellow professor Fred Dupee's flaunted disdain for the *New Yorker* warned me against ever bowing before those two arbiters of culture—or any others. I came to trust Chase and Dupee and their intellectual cohort because, having already cast off their radicalism by the time I met them, they treated literature as an autonomous sphere—indeed, the sacred sphere that dare not be compromised. They had found a way of treating literature as a carrier of ideas without surrendering an independent standard of art, and *that* was the balance I wanted to acquire.

○প

By the spring of 1961 I had completed my MA and all requirements for the PhD except for comprehensive oral exams and a dissertation. Feeling the need to return to Montreal, I fully expected to cram for the exams and complete my degree from there. Uriel and I tentatively agreed on a dissertation topic: the question of whether Yiddish literature possessed a comic tradition independent of its towering master Sholem Aleichem. One special pleasure of my graduate studies had been returning to Yiddish authors like Sholem Aleichem and Y. L. Peretz whom I had read in elementary and high school and seeing how relatively little I had then understood or appreciated. I expected my thesis to bring these revelations to light.

None of this worked out as planned. Of the two professors who would have guided my work, Chase took his life in 1962 and Uriel Weinreich was diagnosed with cancer. I did not want to trouble him once I learned that he was ill, and by the time he succumbed in 1967, at an absurdly young age, I had long since let my Columbia affiliation lapse.

Before leaving Columbia, I had scheduled an obligatory meeting with the director of graduate studies to confirm the areas that would be covered in my comprehensive exams. Following guidelines, I presented my proposal to Professor N. My major field would be Yiddish literature, with two minors in Romantic and American literature and, for the fourth exam on a major writer I substituted for the set choice of either Chaucer, Shakespeare, or Milton, an exam on all three "classic" Yiddish masters, Mendele, Sholem Aleichem, *and* Peretz.

Professor N. refused altogether to accept any testing on Yiddish. I protested that I had been admitted on the understanding that Yiddish literature would be my main area of concentration. Very well, he conceded, I could use Yiddish as one of my two *minor* areas. But I would also have to pass an additional exam in Renaissance literature. Why, I asked? My program of study had its own requirements, and I was fully prepared to read in the areas related to it. Couldn't we design a set of exams with my priorities in mind?

From some of my fellow students, I knew that had I made a similar case for French or Russian, my modifications would have been accepted. Moreover, in my previous exchanges with officialdom both in New York and Montreal, I had absorbed the impression that if only I could explain things satisfactorily, a reasonable compromise would invariably ensue. But this man's position hardened with each explanation I offered.

I asked Uriel whether he could intercede on my behalf, but he demurred, suggesting I find another champion inside my department. By then, however, something in me had stiffened, and I refused that option. Professor N. was the department's head of graduate studies, and I'd be damned if I would give him another chance to turn me down.

Somewhat impulsively, I returned to Montreal with no plan in hand, and eventually let the deadline run out for registering with absentee status. Because I was provoked into leaving a degree program that I was on the path to completing, I would later have to redo all of my graduate work in a course of study even further from my goal.

I was baffled. Why should that elegant, well-mannered, and respected scholar seek to harm me as a Jew studying Jewish subjects? Only years later did I hear that he, too, was a Jew—and then suddenly I saw him as clearly as when mist lifts from the lake on a summer's dawn. He had expected Columbia to insulate him from the shabby Jewishness he thought he had escaped, and as an aspirant to high culture he must have felt the same disgust for Yiddish that Henry Adams recorded feeling for the jabbering Jews he saw descending on New York City at the turn of the twentieth century. Whatever the particular sources of N.'s contempt, I felt certain that were he not a Jew, he would have shown me greater academic respect.

If the entire course of my life had been determined in childhood by the war against the Jews in Europe, this was the first time that anti-Jewishness affected me as an adult. The incident left me dissatisfied with the reflexive term "Jewish self-hatred" when I found it applied by the sociologist Kurt Lewin to the sort of behavior I had witnessed. To me the term made little sense. The professor did not hate the squelched Jew in himself but rather the Jew still present in me. The psychological source of his aggression, implied in the concept of "*self*-hatred," was less relevant than its manifestation against another member of the tribe.

Anti-Jewishness in a Jew hurt because one had lost a potential familiar, and because, as Lewin explains, members of a social minority who want to be liked by everyone else may respond by trying even harder to repudiate their origins. After this I began to pay attention to the phenomenon of anti-Jewish Jews, or as I preferred to think of them, Jewish anti-Semites. I studied this subject in Yiddish literature and once new strains of anti-Jewish politics surfaced among anti-Zionists in the 1970s, I quickly recognized them as an aggravating feature of American Jewish life. In this way Columbia University taught me more than I had aspired to know.

Once back in Montreal, I applied for a teaching position at the local Jewish Teachers' Seminary, a small institution that had been established by the Canadian Jewish Congress to restock the thinning ranks of European-trained educators for the network of Canadian Jewish day schools. The administrator informed me that, alas, the seminary was being phased out, apparently on the assumption that teachers from Israel could begin to replace those no longer coming from Europe. But I was invited to deliver a public Yiddish lecture to an adult gathering at one of the local Jewish day schools.

Lectures had been the main entertainment of my parents' circle, and I had attended enough of them to know what was expected. At Columbia, Uriel had introduced me to the sonnets of the American Yiddish poet Mani Leib, whose "children's verse" I'd learned in elementary school—charming folk ballads about the prophet Elijah, about a fearless young scamp *Yingl Tsingl Khvat* whose magic ring can bring welcome snow to a muddy town, and about an eponymous Stranger with the power to right social wrongs.

Kalt un finster iz di nakht.
Tír un toyer tsugemakht;

Fenster blinde on a shayn
Shtarn in der nakht arayn.

In simple vocabulary and lulling rhythm this narrative poem conjures up a cold dark night when the Stranger sets out through the Ukrainian steppes of shuttered homes and pitch-black windows to bring nourishment and light wherever he is welcomed, that is, wherever these qualities are already present in spirit and have only to be rewarded materially. Mani Leib was our own Jewish *Child's Garden of Verses*. But I intended to speak, rather, about the poet's mature sonnets that he wrote during his sojourn in a tuberculosis sanatorium.

Mani Leib was one of dozens of young poets among the hundreds of thousands of Jews who came to New York at the beginning of the twentieth century. The Yiddish and Hebrew literary renaissance in Europe was sprouting offshoots in Palestine and America, both more inclined to poetry than prose, probably because there was as yet no solid social grounding for fiction. While some of the immigrant poets plunged right into the maelstrom, others like Mani Leib took the freedom to write a private, inward, and softening poetry as against the public protest literature of the social and national political movements. He also had the advantage of being a skilled leather maker of the uppers of boots; he thus earned his living in the shoe factories and gave thanks that he was "not a shoemaker poet but a poet who makes shoes."

With the chutzpah of the insufficiently educated, I set out to demonstrate what I took to be the undervaluing of the poet's artistic achievement. In fact, I argued, this apparent versifier for children used *pashtes*, from the Hebrew term for plainness, as his touchstone for beauty, truth, and moral clarity. Adhering to the strict sonnet form, like a Jew restricted to the confines of Jewish law, he had fashioned a secular liturgy in celebration of life, in the process transposing the Jewish virtue of modesty into a modern aesthetic of restraint. He had done this in his illness, in the shadow of death.

In the audience for my lecture, besides my parents and relatives, were members of the local Yiddish intelligentsia. Their applause and appreciative questions assured me that I had passed what was probably the most rigorous test to which I would ever be subjected. But at the point of leaving, one of my former teachers drew me aside and whispered, "*Men zogt*[one says]*'sarfen,'*" correcting my mispronunciation of the word "to burn" in a Mani Leib sonnet I had quoted. Never having heard the word spoken, I'd said *sreyfen*, inferring the pronunciation from the noun *sreyfeh*, conflagration, a Hebrew root word that had been adopted by Yiddish and also turned into a verb, here meaning to set afire.

Though I was sure that all the teachers and writers in the room had taken note of this gaffe, none had exposed my ignorance by correcting me during the question period. This community of Yiddish speakers embodied the refinement in which I had been raised and the delicacy that Mani Leib extols in his verse. Need I draw the invidious comparison between these cultured Jews and the provincial bigot who headed the graduate school's literature program at Columbia?

CR

AT THAT POINT I WAS still very much my parents' daughter and even as Len and I were on our own, living downtown at the heart of the city, we stayed in close touch with the Yiddish sector. When our son Billy was born at the end of December 1962, we showed our gratitude for the gift of this wondrous child by celebrating a *pidyon ha-ben,* the ancient ceremony in which the father of a firstborn son "redeems" him for five pieces of silver from a member of the priesthood—the *kohanim.*

We were not then affiliated with any synagogue, and it was not necessary to involve a rabbi; we needed only a *kohen,* one who traced his lineage to the priesthood. During my studies in New York, I had befriended the Yiddish book publisher Israel London who happened to be a kohen, so I phoned him and ask whether he might do us the honor of coming to Montreal to serve in that role.

"Why me?" London asked. "Bashevis Singer is speaking in Montreal that day. Ask him."

Bashevis promptly accepted my invitation, saying that although he had never before performed as a kohen, "it could no longer do him any harm" (*s'ken mir shoyn nit shadn*). Although he was gaining a reputation through his English translations, he was by no means yet the celebrity he would later become. On the appointed afternoon, he graciously showed up at our home and kissed my hand like a Polish count. During the brief ceremony (photographed by Ben) he was visibly more nervous than Len in reading his part, and when handed the required coins—new silver dollars Len had gotten from the bank—he timidly asked what to do with them, uncertain whether to accept our assurance that he could spend the money as he liked.

A shy and awkward man, Bashevis resembled the protagonist of much of his fiction, and there seemed to be no way of making him feel at home in this room of Yiddish speakers who delighted in his presence. But he managed to form a high opinion of our community. In his regular column for the daily Yiddish *Forverts* under the pseudonym Yitzhak Varshavski, he reported "one of my loveliest experiences serving for the first time as the kohen for a *pidyon haben*," and praised our home for being "filled with Yiddishism in the good sense of the word"—meaning, untinged by the socialism that was one of his pet aversions. He also cited his rabbinic grandfather's teaching that the most fortunate rabbi was one whose parishioners were better scholars than he:

> Each time I speak [to a Yiddish audience] I am newly persuaded how many intelligent people come out to hear Yiddish lectures. The Yiddish writer and the Yiddish press must reckon with this. We must be careful with every word because we are paid close attention. The expression *oylem-goylem* [the stupid masses] was always false and cynical, today more than ever. Our audience grows ever more refined, asking questions it is not easy to answer, with no patience for mistakes or empty rhetoric.

I had just discovered as much in my talk on Mani Leib. Billy was redeemed from the priesthood, and I was grateful that Bashevis had not treated the occasion cynically as he sometimes did Jewish rituals in his fiction.

The talk on Mani Leib led to others in English about Yiddish literature. Encouraged by local interest in the subject, I proposed to the director of the YM-YWHA that I set up an institute of Jewish studies for adults. I would pull together a group of local scholars to offer evening courses in Jewish philosophy, literature, history, and art, with their salaries covered by registration fees. The director managed to override objections from several members of his board who considered my proposal "too Jewish," that is, too divergent from the YMCA model of sports facilities and recreational activities that they had adopted as their template.

But a younger generation with greater cultural self-confidence, buttressed by survivors who had come after the war, was about to turn the Y around, to the point where even its cafeteria was made kosher. Once I got my go-ahead, I launched the Harvey Golden Institute for Jewish Studies, named for the director who had approved the project.

Benjamin Roskies took this photo of Len with Isaac Bashevis Singer at the *pidyon haben* (redemption of the firstborn son) of William Reuben Wisse, Montreal, January 1963. In accepting our invitation to serve as the Kohen for the ceremony, Bashevis wrote that though he had never yet served in that capacity, doing so "could no longer do him any harm."

CR

I ALREADY KNEW THAT THE Institute's biggest draw would be Rabbi David Hartman, who had arrived in Montreal in 1960 to head the city's largest Orthodox congregation. Born and raised in Brooklyn, educated in the finest yeshivas, and granted rabbinic ordination by Rabbi Joseph B. Soloveitchik, Hartman had also done graduate studies in philosophy at Fordham University and his thinking reflected the excitement at bringing these two intellectual traditions together. The leading rabbinic figures in America, his teacher Rabbi Soloveitchik and the Lubavitch (Chabad) Rabbi Menachem Mendel Schneerson, had likewise studied philosophy—in Germany. But whereas their starting and end point was the rabbinic tradition, his seemed to be independent inquiry, with the emphasis on *independent.*

Acculturation—a term we preferred over assimilation, implying selective adaptation rather than conversion to the dominant culture—had made the synagogue both more and less important in American Jewish life. Distinguishing features like language and dress that once separated Jews from the rest of the population now identified only those labeled *ultra*-Orthodox, and much like churchgoing Christians, the rest of us expressed our affiliation mainly through the synagogues we joined, as many of us did once we started having children. Yet rabbis had lost much of their authority. They were rarely consulted other than in scheduling bar mitzvahs or arranging funerals. Montreal's wealthiest and largest synagogue, the Shaar Hashomayim, then affiliated with the Conservative Movement, had successfully spun off a number of loosely affiliated study groups which ran on their own, without rabbinic supervision.

Hartman was like no other local rabbi: he took intellectual charge. Lithuanian Jews like my parents valued skeptical intelligence in their standard-bearers over the magnetism for which Hasidic rabbis were famed, but Hartman combined a hard intellect with emotional flair. The first time I heard him lecture I confided to my journal that I was like one "awakened from sleep." Both the sentiment and its expression now embarrass me, but I welcomed the intensity he brought to the study of Jewish sources. And when others carped that he was an actor using his hands and voice for calculated effect, I asked why we never accused those of acting who concealed all trace of emotion?

Hartman interpreted Jewish texts through whatever happened to excite him. In those days it was Norman O. Brown's manifesto *Life Against Death,* much discussed at the time, but which I left unread, relying on what he made of it. In this I suspect I was like most of his listeners, well versed in our own professional and intellectual spheres, but not about to check out all his references, though some did challenge his interpretations. Hartman used Brown as an argument against Freud's idea of civilization that is based on repression and offered Judaism's affirmative energy as a corrective. He was not seriously engaging Freud—as Brown does—but using both as springboard for his own ideas. While I was learning to be ever more attentive to the integrity of "the text," Hartman saw himself differently, drawing from Jewish and general sources for whatever he needed in working out his own ideas.

His congregation soon became a destination. An Orthodox synagogue that did not yet include women on its board, it was lax in admitting people who lived beyond the prescribed Sabbath walking limits. This allowed Len and me to become members and park on neighboring streets to complete our journey by foot. If asked what kind of Jew that made us, I said nonpracticing Orthodox, inventing the term that I later found already in use.

In general, rather than emphasizing *halakhic* observance, Hartman urged us to "get on the bus" of Judaism and travel as far as we were prepared to go. Rabbi Schneerson, whose Chabad movement was also gaining strength in Montreal, advocated something similar but in the opposite sequence, urging observance of a single mitzvah as a pathway to a fuller Jewish life. Yeshiva boys came to Len's office to persuade him to perform the mitzvah of *tefillin*, the ritual of phylacteries, in the hope that he would make it a daily habit. Chabad and Rabbi Hartman—Duvy to his friends—were drawing those of us from nonobservant homes closer to Jewish practice.

I somewhat distrusted how Hartman's changing enthusiasms influenced his definitions of Jewishness, like adapting Judaism to Norman O. Brown, but I could not resist the liveliness of his mind. He would begin a lecture by commending the ancient Greeks for their intellectual mastery, go on to demonstrate their striving for absolute perfection through the ideal form of the circle, and then, just as he seemed on the point of reaching for an ultimate tribute to their genius, his semantic register would change, his body language shift, and he would show us how the Talmud, in total contravention of the Greek ideal, surpassed it by discussing the ritual purification of the high priest in the ancient Temple *alongside* directives on the positioning of toilets in the Temple edifice. How sterile the rarefied air of the Athenian agora suddenly felt compared with the intricate, messy, complexly human struggle of the Jewish way of life.

But he did more than lecture. Anticipating the approach of the famous Hartman Institute that he would later establish in Jerusalem, he drew together the most dynamic rabbis on the continent for "inclusive" annual retreats in the Laurentian Mountains. It was a way of claiming the intellectual center of Jewry that was otherwise denominationally divided. Those all-male gatherings generated less tension—a word he adored—among Orthodox, Conservative, and Reform participants than between religious conservatives and liberals in each group.

Among the regular participants, the one probably closest to him in background was a fellow student of Rabbi Joseph Soloveitchik's, Irving "Yitz" Greenberg, who was then trying to establish an Orthodox branch within the college Hillel Association. Yitz, like Hartman, was actively engaged in revitalizing Jewish life; most of the others were dedicated scholars and teachers with a pronounced intellectual bent. Among those, I formed strong impressions of the theologian Michael Wyschogrod, who seemed at odds with his Orthodoxy, and Jakob Petuchowski, who tacked to the right of his Reform movement.

In one memorable lecture, biblical scholar Moshe Greenberg of the Jewish Theological Seminary took issue with the thesis of the "two Adams" favored by those who were on the lookout for discrepancies in the first two chapters of Genesis. Greenberg stressed Adam's singularity instead, and illustrated his point with a lesson he had learned from his father: at the top of the blackboard he drew a stick figure—Adam—and beneath it, an inverted pyramid to show that only thus, from Adam's single "rib," could one prove the common origin of *all* humankind. I filed this away as a lovely demonstration of the universalism from which the covenantal people emerged and differentiated themselves.

Another speaker reinforced something I had already thought about in my studies of Yiddish literature. Shmuel Leiter, who taught Hebrew literature, deplored the dearth of Jewish biographies. He attributed this lacuna to the Jewish emphasis on modesty and the otherwise salutary inhibition against hero worship, but pleaded for more works in this vein. I had already experienced this frustration in studying Yiddish writers and I would eventually write my second book on Mani Leib and his fellow American Yiddish poet Moishe Leib Halpern to provide a little of the biographical and cultural bibliographical background that I found missing.

No women were invited to participate in the conference. Allowed to audit, I happily ran errands on my way back and forth to the city, like picking up Elie Wiesel at the airport and driving him to the retreat. Best known as the survivor-witness of Auschwitz and author of the novel *Night*, Elie was at no disadvantage among the rabbis and scholars. He had a solid Talmudic education and thought deeply about Jewish matters. I liked him tremendously. He was so similar to the narrator of his books that I felt I knew him well though this was our first meeting. Speaking Yiddish together certainly had something to do with it. We otherwise used it mostly with members of the family, so it made us feel like family.

By then I had read the first three of Elie's books, which made me a little uneasy because I would not have wanted to lie to him and I could not fully admire them, not even *Night*, the first, which I had by then read also entitled *When the World Kept Silent* in its original Yiddish. The book recounted how Germany's deportation of Hungarian Jews, relatively late in the killing process, had turned this fifteen-year-old yeshiva boy into a cipher in Auschwitz. It described his experience of the torture intended to destroy him that had indeed destroyed millions, including his father, but had left him determined to flourish, morally intact. One does not read such accounts for their literary merit, but this writer gained power by constructing his book around the father's fate as well as his own, and its literary qualities drew attention to its artistry as well as its content. I and others would later compare the Yiddish and subsequent versions of what became an iconic "Holocaust book" to show how he had shaped each of them to its intended audience. Their very titles conveyed the contrast between the unfiltered emotion of the Yiddish and the existential distancing of the French *La Nuit*, of which the English was a translation. Mendele, too, had rewritten his works to suit the different Yiddish and Hebrew readers, but he mostly adjusted the prose to the educational sophistication of the readers, whereas the gap here was much wider between a Jewish readership suffering national agony and Gentiles with no necessary connection to the events. Neither book was any less truthful on that account, yet I preferred the angrier, less literary book.

I needn't have worried. Elie was more curious than concentrated on himself and we talked mostly about other writers, not about his work. But he seemed uneasy at the start of the drive, and I could not account for his nervousness until he asked for my assurance that he would not have to share a room with anyone at the retreat. His insistence on rooming alone was the only oblique allusion to his wartime experience. Once I told him that everyone had a private room and bathroom, he relaxed and the hour's drive seemed too short. We met infrequently in the years that followed. The works of his I liked best were the nonfiction accounts of Soviet Jewry and his memoir of his postwar life in Paris.

Returning to that conference, I must admit that I did not mind being relegated to the sidelines, having come to consider Jewish women so much better off than their menfolk that I never begrudged males their confederacies. I condescendingly thought of Talmudic competition as the Jewish male sport, and feared that without this intellectual equivalent of boxing, Jewish men would cease to be as manly as I needed them to be. I knew with certainty that the inclusion of women in this retreat would have adversely affected the "yeshiva atmosphere" that I preferred to witness rather than disrupt. The precepts of maleness were soon to weaken, in any event, in ways that almost everyone (myself excluded) assumed made for a healthier society.

Meanwhile, Hartman included me when it mattered. Just as I had organized the Harvey Golden Institute for adults, he had the idea of organizing a summer evening series of Jewish studies courses primarily for college students, held in his synagogue and timed to begin after the end of the spring semester.

In this enterprise, and at his invitation, I taught an early, abbreviated version of courses on Yiddish and Jewish literature that I would later offer at McGill. Since literature had always interested me as a carrier of ideas, I chose works that lent themselves to such discussion. Yiddish literature had developed in tandem with Jewish modernity and interpreted that process. The other classes, including Hartman's, taught traditional Jewish sources. Mine extended "Jewish sources" to include modern Jewish fiction and poetry.

One of the students, Richie Cohen, who had told me that he intended to go on to study the Holocaust, and is now a retired professor of Jewish history of the Hebrew University in Jerusalem, recently thanked me for the "lectures at Hartman's shul ... at a turning point in [his] life." I myself experienced memorable instruction in the class of Yochanan Muffs, professor of Bible, who traveled in from New York. Using ancient texts like the Code of Hammurabi that bore obvious similarities to parts of the Bible, Muffs demonstrated what it meant that "God speaks in the language of men." He offered as proof the very correspondences that others considered *disproof* of Divine Provenance. A student troubled by this elegance blurted out, "Sir, the trouble is you don't know the meaning of absurd." Muffs choked up. "Absurd?! Bach died! What could be more absurd than that?!"

Circumstance determines opportunities. In the 1920s, Europe's hostility to Jews inspired the rise of independent Jewish institutions of learning because neither Jewish teachers nor Jewish subjects were welcome in their universities. The YIVO in Vilna was one such innovation; another was the Lehrhaus of Frankfurt, where Franz Rosenzweig offered acculturated German Jews the chance to explore their own sources. We in Montreal were creating embryonic versions of such centers, but our liberal North America encouraged Jews to move out into the mainstream.

The success of our informal courses made me eager to procure academic credit for them. Why pour effort into high-level studies in separate institutions if they could be offered in places where students earned degrees?

CR

AT COLUMBIA, I HAD STUDIED with several professors like Fred Dupee who taught without PhDs, but I knew that McGill would make no such exception for me, especially if I intended to introduce a brand-new subject into its curriculum. So I enrolled as one of the first students in the university's newly inaugurated doctoral program in English literature. The only consideration I asked and was given was that in the fullness of time I be permitted to write my dissertation on a topic in comparative rather than strictly English literature.

Along with McGill, I, too, had expanded. By the time I returned in 1965, I was eight months pregnant with our second child. Raising a family focused me on coursework to the exclusion of whatever else was happening on campus. On class days, I would return home early enough for a long stroll with three-year-old Billy, who seemed almost capable of raising himself.

It was sometimes maddening to realize that I was studying Edmund Spenser, Jonathan Swift, and Percy Bysshe Shelley in order to get to teach Suzkever, Sholem Aleichem, and I. B. Singer. Most of the professors I had already encountered as a McGill undergraduate. The school atmosphere was chilly: our son Jacob was born so conveniently in mid-October that I did not have to miss a single session of my weekly seminars. No one in that class commented on the transformation or asked about the outcome.

Determined to stick it out, I completed the coursework and written comprehensives on everything in English literature between *Beowulf* and Virginia Woolf in a little over two years. Like the biblical Jacob who labored seven years for Leah so that he could work another seven for the hand of Rachel, I looked forward to writing my dissertation on a subject of my choice.

When that happy hour arrived, adapting the topic of Yiddish humor that I had chosen with Uriel to the requirements of an English department, I proposed to write on the *schlemiel* as hero in Yiddish and American Jewish fiction, tracking this comic figure from his European sources to Anglo-American language and culture. I sought out Louis Dudek as my adviser and confided to him my intention of introducing Yiddish literature into the curriculum.

"Why would you do that?" he asked, pointing to the bookcase behind him. "All you have to do is master the books on this shelf and you could become a professor of Canadian literature!" He himself was that very professor. Was he belittling his own academic pursuit, or mine? I could not tell.

With Saul Bellow in his home, Boston, December 2001. (Photo by Janis Bellow)

The only book Dudek had read of my proposed bibliography was Saul Bellow's *Herzog*, a novel so good and so central to my thesis that from its opening sentence it alone was almost enough to make the case:

"If I am out of my mind, it's all right with me, thought Moses Herzog."

Until now, the cuckolded man, or schlemiel, had been strictly a figure of fun, seen from the outside in gentle or ribald comedy, but Bellow enters the mind of the traditional foil of such humor and presents him from the inside, with humor at his own expense—and at the expense of his betrayers. Herzog is a Jewish intellectual, likewise a perpetual target of derision, since if he is so smart, how come he is always losing the woman and his status? Dudek's question—why not rather specialize in Canadian literature when it is already profitable—seemed an extension of that challenge, and *Herzog* responds by turning the tables on estimable Western thinkers.

Dear Doktor Professor Heidegger, I should like to know what you mean by the expression, "the fall into the quotidian." When did this fall occur? Where were we standing when it happened?

The Marx Brothers specialized in this puncturing wit and Woody Allen would soon make it his calling card, but *Herzog* aimed much higher. Saul Bellow had composed a Jewish equivalent of James Joyce's *Ulysses*, starring a real Jew who was infinitely more interesting and entertaining than Leopold

Bloom. Bellow admired Joyce, but when it came to writing *his* masterwork, he trusted his own tradition, experience, and talent to do it (for my taste) even better.

Dudek's respect for Bellow was one of the reasons he accepted our unusual arrangement, and his requests for clarification as the thesis progressed often elicited my best explanations and most ambitious interpretations. I was helped by the scarcity of secondary material, which gave me free rein to develop my own ideas about my chosen figure: the Jewish innocent who outmaneuvers his superiors.

The schlemiel was the comic hero of perhaps the most tragic story ever told of a people determined to remain morally innocent in a determinedly hostile world. I had begun tracking this character in the works of Mendele Mocher Sforim, Sholem Aleichem, and Peretz, the three reputed classics of Yiddish literature. But he was also everywhere in folk humor—for example, as the Jewish soldier in the Austrian army who, when commanded to unsheathe his bayonet for hand-to-hand combat, says, "Please, sir, show me my man. Maybe we can come to some agreement." He thus functions in a high-stakes struggle for sanity and survival within a politically dependent and threatened community, and only at great cost does his foolishness command the moral high ground. My literary sources credited the character's resilient strength, but given the fate of Jews in World War II, I myself remained ambivalent about whether to admire or condemn this celebration of the loser-as-winner.

The Hasidic master Rabbi Nahman of Bratslav, who enters the annals of Yiddish literature as an inspired teller of stories, sets up in one of them a radical dichotomy between the wise man and the fool. The former is a brilliant Renaissance man, modeled on the Jews of the then-emerging Jewish Enlightenment, and the latter is a *tam*, the third of the four sons in the Passover Haggadah, the simple, intellectually limited member of a cerebral people. Nahman's story tries to uncomplicate the contrast: the skeptic who trusts his intelligence becomes the prey of dissatisfaction and evil while the apparent simpleton accepts his tradition on faith and thereby succeeds in everything that matters.

Later Jewish works such as Peretz's "Bontshe the Silent" and Isaac Bashevis Singer's "Gimpel the Fool" probed the theological and real-life implications of this naiveté. Some deemed gullible what others found blameless. That Bellow had translated the story "Gimpel the Fool" substantiated the transition I was tracing from Yiddish to Anglo-American literature. I looked for writing where the balance between innocence and defeat could not be resolved except through incongruity or humor. Around that ambivalence, I built my thesis, later to be published as a book. Within the same decade, Bellow and I. B. Singer had received the Nobel Prize for Literature.

CR

ONCE THE DOCTORATE WAS IN reach, it was time to persuade the university to let me teach Yiddish literature. I started with my department, where I was already teaching a freshman section of the English literature survey. Along with a sample outline of the course, I circulated Irving Howe and Eliezer Greenberg's *Treasury of Yiddish Stories,* the impressive anthology that I intended to use as its anchor.

Anticipating the objection that Yiddish did not "belong" in the English department, I said that, in the absence of a comparative literature program, there was no other more appropriate home for such a course. Surely the linguistic relation between Yiddish and German did not suggest that it belonged in the German department! Besides, I explained, the high proportion of Jews and Yiddish speakers in the student body would generate a constituency for courses in the original language as well as in English translation.

The vote in my favor was almost unanimous. As if to confirm my earlier experience at Columbia, the sole vote against the proposal was cast by the department's only other Jew, a recent hire who had come from America to Canada to evade the draft for the Vietnam War. This first encounter with a draft resister reinforced what I already knew of the Left-wing enmity that Jews had faced and always would face from Internationalists in their own ranks. But for the moment there was only one of him, and the senior professors paid him no attention. Departmental endorsement in hand, I now had only to secure administrative approval and, crucially, community funding, since the English department could not support my position if I was not teaching its curriculum. Both the dean's office and my former employer Saul Hayes at the Canadian Jewish Congress gave me what I called the "cotton candy treatment," not refusing the proposal but never scheduling the meeting I requested.

In the biblical book of Esther, the ever-vigilant Mordecai warns the young queen that if she fails to intercede with the king on behalf of her people, "relief and deliverance will come to the Jews *from another source.*" Just as I was growing impatient, I learned that someone else at the university was making a pitch like mine, only not on his own behalf. David Hartman had independently decided to complete at McGill the PhD in philosophy he had left unfinished at Fordham in New York. Now his McGill adviser, Professor Harry Bracken, wanted to hire his protégé to teach in the philosophy department.

When Harry and I learned of one another, we teamed up for a two-pronged operation. His credentials as a tenured professor, and a Gentile, carried the day with the Montreal Jewish Federation, which promised three years' seed money if we could get the university's approval. Once we paired up, we found ourselves pushing open doors. The university was eager to enlarge its scope, and the Jewish community was ready to invest in that expansion.

Thus, by the time I got my PhD in 1969, I was teaching Yiddish literature at a university where David Hartman was teaching Maimonides. Within a few years a full-fledged program in Jewish studies, later to become a full-fledged department, had its own premises and secretary and several full-time faculty members. Harry served as provisional chair; I took over three years later.

To avoid being marginalized, we made most of our appointments jointly with the departments of history, literature, and philosophy, and with the divinity school that then housed courses on religion. McGill's may have been the only Jewish studies department in North America established by a university not through special endowments but modestly gifted with seed money and supported wholly by the university itself.

In 1970 Harry and I drove down to Brandeis University for the second annual conference of the Association for Jewish Studies, founded the same year as our program. The approximately fifty members who came together at Brandeis constituted most of the tenured or tenure-track college professors of Jewish studies on the continent. Several were on the Brandeis faculty; many were rabbis educated and ordained by the Jewish Theological Seminary. Without encouragement from their institutions or colleagues, they had founded AJS as part of the "normalization" of Jewish studies in American higher education.

In fact, their predecessors, European born and trained men with rabbinic ordination who taught in the various denominational seminaries, had established the American Academy for Jewish Research in 1920 on an elitist model that accepted only those whose work adhered to the highest "proven" standards of scholarship. By contrast, the founders of the AJS, mostly American born and trained, only briefly considered making membership conditional on a working knowledge of Hebrew and dismissed even that qualification as impractical, instead opening registration to anyone in the field.

The Civil Rights Act of 1964 had outlawed discrimination based on race or religion and it followed that universities aspiring to teach world civilization should include study of other races and religions. Bestsellers and films about the wrongs of prejudice against blacks and Jews prepared the ground for Jewish and African American Studies. But there were those who did not share Martin Luther King's slow and steady approach to social justice. Our university appointments in Jewish studies were springing up in tandem with the Woodstock Festival, the antiwar movement, and everything entailed in what Lionel Trilling referred to as the period's "adversarial culture."

We Jewish studies academics intended to strengthen the universities, not trash them. We were for the enhancement of academic rigor, for shoring up hard-won gains of rational enlightenment. We were determined to enrich our institutions with our contribution. Not for a moment did it occur to me that our drive for the inclusion of Jewish studies could form part of a movement to undermine the university's role in reinforcing Western civilization. Had I known then what became clear to me by the time I left the academy forty-five years later, I could not have proceeded with the confidence that I was doing only good.

Seven months pregnant with our third child at the convocation that granted me my PhD, I was aware of my parents in the stands as I could not remember them at any earlier ceremony. I would have denied that I chose my profession on their account, yet my place in Mother's Yiddish chain of transmission was too obvious to ignore. Grateful for having been granted the chance to reach my goal, I ought to have pronounced the *Shehekhiyonu* prayer that thanks God, Lord of the Universe, for granting us life, sustaining us, and enabling us to reach this occasion. Odd as it may seem, the harder I persevered, the more thankful I felt for my *unearned* blessings.

8

ASCENT

*W*ith me embarked on my professorial career, Len collaborative at work and competitive at squash, and our children in a new Jewish day school founded by Hartman, we had a wonderful life.

The choice of school had been a surprise. Rabbi Hartman had a daughter the same age as Billy for whom he determined to create a better school than any of those available in Montreal. On the way to the interview that he had requested, anticipating that he would pitch us his project, Len and I rehearsed why we were sending Billy to the Folkshule, the Jewish elementary school we had both attended. On our drive back, we discussed how to explain our change of mind to my father who had been a member of the Folkshule board for twenty-five years. I had tried to persuade Duvy that we could improve one of the existing schools, but he persuaded me it would be better in every respect to open a new one. Akiva School became part of our lives; Len served a term as its second president.

In those years, departing from the irregular practice of my parents, we also began observing Sabbath eve at home, I lighting candles, Len reciting kiddush. I was no good at public worship, but we needed a context to give thanks for all that went well and the eve of Sabbath became that ceremonial acknowledgement.

At first, I fretted about the inauthenticity of praying without belief in a God of whom I had no knowledge. In the Jewish tug of war between Hasidic spirituality and rational intellect, I was a thoroughgoing Litvak—the hard-headed Lithuanian branch that was accused of being halfway to apostasy. Until one day it occurred to me that if I did not yet feel connected to God (as I thought of Him in English), I could pray to the *reboynesheloylem* (*Rebono Shel Olam*, Lord of the Universe) of my grandparents. Since prayer was for me not petition but gratitude, and I awaited no supernatural intervention, I could address that homey Presence with heart and soul.

During the Vietnam War, Canada's political irrelevance served us well. But this is not to say we were wholly unaffected by the shouts from across the border. "What do we want? *Freedom!* When do we want it? *Now!*" Pent-up demands that brought about the 1964 Civil Rights Act were now fueling the Black Panthers, Timothy Leary's promotion of mind-altering substances, and the O'Neills' (Nena and George) endorsement of "open marriage." While thinkers like Herbert Marcuse and Saul Alinsky fired up radical faculty and Left-wing community organizers, Leary and the O'Neills advocated the liberation of mind and body and inspired large sectors of the middle class to practice sexual hedonism and "inhale." Meanwhile student revolutionaries were trashing the offices of their professors in the name of "free speech."

The poet Allen Ginsberg famously howled, "I saw the best minds of my generation destroyed by madness." I had seen the best minds of my generation go into physics and accounting, and I hoped the psychedelic action would remain in the States. The times they were a-changin', but whereas some of my fellow Jews probably agreed with Bob Dylan that "the loser now will be later to win," I was not sure that reversal would include us Jews, who were so recently the butt of discrimination. I half-suspected that the revolutionaries trashing Columbia University and those at Berkeley burning their draft notices would eventually turn against us bourgeois citizens. In short, I took none of our good fortune for granted and thought it was time to consolidate our blessings.

CR

WHEN MONTREAL RECEIVED THE GO-AHEAD to host the 1967 World's Fair, our once-provincial backwater became a prime destination. The city's bilingualism and biculturalism were burnished to cosmopolitan sheen for what was until then the largest ever international exposition. On a mild evening in late April, Len and I previewed the displays with artist friends who had worked on the exhibitions. We toured America's geodesic dome, lingered at the Israeli display, and enjoyed the beguiling Czech pavilion that included along with its exhibition of Bohemian glassware an interactive Kinoautomat at which the audience determines the direction of the film at key turning points in the plot, and a technically dazzling multimedia Laterna Magika where live characters emerge enchantingly from the screen. Our official greeters at the Fair said they expected more than six million visitors over the summer.

Already, threats to Israel troubled that lovely evening. Arab opposition to the Jews of Palestine had begun long before 1948 and the Jewish State remained surrounded by hostile neighbors—Egypt to the west, Syria to the north, Jordan to the east, and many other Arab and Muslim belligerents beyond them. That spring Egyptian president Gamal Abdel Nasser had opened hostilities to full throttle. By May, he had massed troops on Israel's southern border, expelled the protective United Nations Emergency Force from the Sinai Peninsula, and closed the Straits of Tiran to Israeli shipping.

The Soviets were clearly behind the escalation, providing military, logistical, and diplomatic support. One had learned to take enemies at their word, so that when Nasser said, "We aim at the destruction of Israel," and that Egypt's national goal was "the eradication of Israel," there was obvious cause for alarm.

Len and I had been to the Sea of Galilee and seen for ourselves the way Syrians on the Golan Heights had the kibbutzim along its shores directly in their sights. More threatening than the boastful enmity of Arab leaders was the lack of international response. In the weeks that followed, the free world's abandonment of Israel to its fate made such a mockery of the spirit of the World's Fair that I never wanted to visit it again. Letters from Montreal friends who were working in England and South Africa carried the almost identical message: "I know what's on your mind. I'm feeling the same."

Israel's military triumph in the Six-Day War of June 5–10 was the more extraordinary because of the anxiety preceding it. The recapture of the Old City of Jerusalem that opened access to the Western Wall was especially dramatic, given Jordan's decision to join the attacking Arab armies when Israel's leaders had urged the king not to. But there was none of the delirium that one sees in newsreels of 1945 with sailors kissing girls in the streets. We felt more relief than exhilaration. Not only were there the many casualties, whom we mourned, but soon enough the brief military reprieve was cut short by the Arab War of Attrition along the Suez Canal. The genocidal threat was in in no way diminished.

Meanwhile, my older brother Ben had discovered a second front in our Jewish fight. After the war he and his wife Louise traveled to the Soviet Union to visit her father's family in Baku, Azerbaijan. One of her cousins, a young man in his teens, gave them a Russian poem he had written about the Jewish struggle for national rights, and announced that he intended somehow or other to leave for Israel. Ben and Louise, who had not expected to meet a passionate Zionist among these formerly unknown relatives, had her cousin's poem translated into English. The next year we incorporated it into our Passover seder along with our tribute to the 1943 Passover uprising in the Warsaw Ghetto.

The Soviet Jewry movement had galvanized through the early 1960s, but Israel's victory greatly spurred its growth. The Soviet Union had militarily backed the Arabs, and now anti-Jewish discrimination was practiced more openly on the excuse that Jewish-Zionists were a fifth column acting against Russian interests. The spike in anti-Jewish policy combined with newfound pride in the Jewish state inspired Soviet Jews to demand the right to emigrate to Israel. The incongruous Jewish victory over incalculably larger and Soviet-backed Arab forces produced a new line of humor: An instructor at the Russian War College, to demonstrate how the Soviet Union might defeat the greater manpower of China, shows that Israel's two or three million Jews won the Six-Day War against the Arabs' hundred million. "Yes," a student objects, "But where can we find three million Jews?"

Israel had fostered contacts with Soviet Jews who were prohibited from studying or practicing their religion, and American Jews created a parallel movement to free Soviet Jewry. Montreal soon had its own active chapter of the Group of Thirty-Five, a consortium of women's organizations that mobilized political resources on behalf of Russian "prisoners of Zion." Ben and Louise were part of the movement that matched Russian Jews determined to leave for Israel with Jews on the outside determined to get them there.

The family encounter in Baku may also have finally determined the aliyah to Israel that Ben had been contemplating since his teens. He and Louise arrived there, with their children, years ahead of the Russian cousins, spending several months in an absorption center learning Hebrew and then settling in Jerusalem. From the moment they landed, Louise applied herself to the domestic side of the challenge of adjustment that confronts every new immigrant and demonstrated that aliyah may be easiest for those with little ideological investment in the move. With fewer expectations and less idealism, she may have found it easier to face the indignities and hardships that accompany every such adaptation.

When Louise had confessed to the Israeli consul who was helping with the transition that she did not know what she could contribute to the country, he said, "Well, what if you find yourself in a line at the supermarket that you feel is moving too slowly?" Louise replied, "That's just it. I would go to complain to the manager." "You see," the consul told her, "*that's* what you would contribute to the country." Thus, the conditions did not take her by surprise.

Ben's own adjustment was harder. He did not want his family to suffer economically and intended to support them as he had done in Canada. Since he could neither start a new textile business nor find one in Israel to work for, he became the sales representative of an American firm, which required months of travel abroad. The move that was to have brought him home to Israel ended up keeping him away from it. Happily for us, his travels sometimes allowed for stopovers in Montreal where he stocked up with comestibles still in short supply in Jerusalem, and within a year he had moved the family into an ideal apartment in easy walking distance of the city center in one direction, the Israel Museum in another. The confidence that Ben inspired in me and everyone who knew him made it easy to ignore his personal undertow of depression.

In the summer of 1968, before their move, Len and I took a trip to Israel, the highlight of which was a week in the Sinai Desert. Our cousins Itzhak and Rina Zamir recommended the trip organized by Haganat Hateva—Society for the Protection of Nature—and lent us the camping equipment we would need. We set out from Jerusalem, about thirty passengers in two large open jeeps, with three guides who lectured alternately in Hebrew, English, and French. During that brief interval when the country was still enjoying the geographical fruits of its military victory, we were able to revisit the landscape of the ancient exodus from Egypt, and swim in the pristine pools our guides pretended to discover for us along the way. The guides were wild about spending time in wilderness, and we tamer explorers fell in with their choreographed adventure, each with our own supply of knowledge and sentiment.

As its name implied, Haganat Hateva was more about terrain than Torah, but the guides' focus on environment and archeology—sun and stone—left us free to experience the mystery. The eponymous mountain we climbed before sunrise was among the smaller in the area. We were a rabble, stumbling upward even where some makeshift steps had been carved. Yet the moment of creation that most mattered to the Jews had happened here. This was where the Law was conceived and delivered, and where Jews forged the covenant to which we still adhered. Hard as it was to imagine God's rendezvous with Moses, it was even harder to imagine the Commandments *without* the presence of YHVH.

That trip was the immediate catalyst for our decision to move to Israel. Though it may have seemed sudden, it felt at the time like the logical next step for our family in the overall trajectory of the Jewish people. It did not need the *push* of Soviet Jewry escaping political suppression to feel the *pull*, the attraction of Israel at this momentous time. My parents were about my age when they left a comfortable home in Czernowitz with two small children to relocate across the globe and now, in blessedly changed circumstances, we could do the same. They escaped the danger, while we were confirming that the danger was past. I had often followed my brother's example and once again, his move showed that it could be done.

Not everyone approved of our plans. A friend said that Len and I were experiencing a midlife crisis and that any decisions taken in such a state of mind would come to grief. My father begged us not to sell our home. The market was at an all-time low and we had no reason to cut ourselves loose. We could always return to complete the move. But I knew in my bones that immigration meant there could be no going back. I quit my job at McGill and insisted the department hire someone to replace me. Akiva School tendered us a bittersweet farewell. If I felt any qualms, it was only about Billy, who was least happy about the move and may have felt anxieties that Len and I suppressed.

At no other time in our marriage were Len and I so united in action or so separate in our thoughts. The many practical details we had to cope with in closing up and planning the transition meant that we never talked about our expectations or how we imagined this adventure. In preparation for the move, Len undertook an additional year of legal studies so that he could have a degree aligned with the kind that Israel recognized. This was one reason I never suspected he was unsure we would succeed. In fact, he informed his law partners that he would let them know at the end of a year whether he was returning. Len was a third-generation Canadian with grandparents and parents in Canadian cemeteries and a deep attachment to his native land. Though I appreciated Canada no less than he did, I did not realize how much more rooted he was in all that we were leaving behind. I was looking only ahead.

Len may well have realized, but never let on, that we were foolhardy to give up the professional positions we had fought hard to acquire, remove our children from their schools, leave parents, family, friends, and a community in which we felt perfectly at home in order to move to a foreign country where we would never completely master the language. Our move defied the normal pattern of voluntary immigration for material advantage.

Yet while many impoverished European Jews once fled to America for that material advantage, some of the well-off and well-educated among them had gone to "drain the swamps and make the desert bloom in the Land of our Fathers." They had pioneered—and there was still more to be done.

In contrast to Canada, where history came ready-made, in Israel a new script was being written on weathered parchment, inviting us to what had anyway become the center of our concerns.

CઠR

MY EUPHORIA ON ARRIVING IN Israel in June 1971 extended for several months, thanks to the Jerusalem absorption center that housed us until we could get our bearings. Len began an intensive Hebrew instruction program and within six months passed the Hebrew exam to qualify for the Israeli bar and then the law exams that he was permitted to write in English. Billy and Jacob, nine and six, spent that first summer in preparatory Hebrew classes to ready them for the regular school they would start in September. From her first day in nursery school, Abby—just short of her second birthday—came home potty-trained.

Jacob and Billy celebrating Abby's second birthday during our year in Israel, August 1971.

As for me, knowing it would take Len time to requalify as a lawyer and find employment, I had secured both a tenured position at Tel Aviv University and a part-time teaching appointment at the Hebrew University in Jerusalem. I had been hired for the Tel Aviv position by Benjamin Harshav, the founding chairman of the university's Department of Comparative Literature, at a Hungarian cafe in downtown Montreal during a break in a conference he was attending at McGill. At the time, we were both writing about Sholem Aleichem, and during a terrific conversation he told me that his department was about to add a Yiddish position. When I said we were coming to Israel, he offered me the job on the spot and I gratefully accepted. In the meantime, Khone Shmeruk at the Hebrew University had hired me to teach one course on Yiddish literature, with prospects for more if he could secure a line in the budget. By the time the Tel Aviv contract came through, I thought I had better take both jobs for the extra money.

If my luck seems too good to be true, it was. The two departments were so different that I was unable to adopt the same approach or the same curriculum for both. Moreover, Len, retooling for work in a different language, legal system, and society, was even more harried than I, making us all the more grateful for the help we received from Israeli relatives and from Ben and Louise, who had a head start in the process.

By September, with the help of cousins, I had found an apartment to rent, but did not realize how tightly wound up I was until Jacob and Abby took sick one day. How could I have failed to anticipate that we would need a pediatrician? A doctor recommended by our cousin kindly came to the apartment and left me a prescription—but then informed me that Jerusalem pharmacies did not deliver. Asking a neighbor to look in on the children, I drove to the nearest pharmacy where the proprietor was serving another customer, with several others already waiting in line. Warned by the pediatrician that the medicine might not be available everywhere, I bypassed the line to ask the pharmacist just to tell me whether or not he had it in stock. He instructed me to wait my turn. When, after the proverbial eternity, I finally handed him the prescription, he said he couldn't fill it and directed me to a pharmacy in midtown. Exploding, I heard myself shouting, "Are you crazy?! Couldn't you see that I have sick children at home? Why couldn't you tell me instead of keeping me waiting?"

Where did I imagine I was? Yanking up the sleeve of his white coat to show me—and the customers behind me—the blue numbers tattooed on the inside of his arm, he yelled, "Are *you* crazy?! Do you think you can come into my business and tell me how to run it?!" In a flash everyone seemed to be shouting—at him, at me, and at the absent pursuers who were still hunting some of us down. Among the pursued, I had gotten off easiest.

I returned to the car and, working hard to calm myself, drove to the midtown pharmacy, filled my prescription, and returned home to be reassured by the neighbor that the children were no worse off. But I had learned my lesson.

My resolve was often tested. Once after picking up the children at school I took them for supper at Wimpy's (pronounced Vimpy's), Israel's precursor of McDonald's. As they enjoyed their burgers, seeing my chance for a couple of easy meals for the rest of the month, I asked for a half-dozen frozen Wimpys to take home—at the full regular price. The manager refused and shouted at me, "Here in Israel, mothers *cook* for their children. They do not rely on frozen food." Rude to a mother in front of her children, stupid to turn down an easy profit, he was outspoken in a style I tried to appreciate—when it did not bring me to tears.

The care of Israel's Jews for one another often took the form of interference. Riding the bus one day, the woman in front of me caught sight of a young boy smoking at the bus stop. "*Yeled!*" she shouted through the open window: "Boy! Stop smoking!" The boy looked up with no visible resentment, smiled a little, and put out the cigarette.

Not all problems were of the same magnitude. One of my hardest assignments came from Jacob's teacher when his grade was about to receive their first real *book*, having been taught to read from mimeographed pages. To mark the festive occasion, mothers were given cloth covers and asked to bring them back embroidered with the child's name. I had never sewed more than a button. In a needle craft shop I found transfers that one could iron on to the cloth, but the four Hebrew letters of *Yakov* I had to stitch. Jacob could not boast of the result and that memento I did not keep.

Reading with Jacob and Billy, Montreal 1968. (Photo by Shelly Schreter)

One evening, I was invited to attend the wedding in Tel Aviv of a student whose family had recently come from the Soviet sphere. The event in a rented hall reflected disparate aspects of a society that had not yet fused. The bride's family and guests were Yiddish intellectuals. The groom was a native Israeli on leave from the army; some of his friends were there in uniform. Neither family was religiously observant, so the Orthodox ritual directed by the rabbi under the *huppah* was jarring rather than familiar. The band played rock with a Middle Eastern touch, with little deference to the occasion or the musical culture of the guests. I found myself hoping that bride and groom were better matched than the components of their wedding.

Unable to stay over in Tel Aviv, I had arranged for a ride back to Jerusalem, and was joined by the Yiddish writer Leib Rochman. On our drive, I said how glad I was for his company and his decision not to stay the night. "Oh," he explained, "since arriving in Israel in 1950 I have never spent a night away from Jerusalem. I am her jealous husband. No matter how late, I make sure to return to her before dawn." It took me a moment to realize that he was speaking not of his wife but of the city.

Among the Yiddish writers I met in Israel, Rochman was the most exceptionally faithful to the khurbn he had survived and the most devoted to his newfound home. He had opposed with all his strength the government's decision to accept reparations from Germany and made a point of refusing to purchase anything associated with that country. At the same time, there was no one as eager to welcome newcomers or more receptive to new ideas. If in my Montreal Jewish community I had observed that some of the most inflexible people espoused the most progressive ideals, here the gentlest people I met held the toughest political views: so-called hard-liners like Rochman were exceptionally tender. His attachment to Jerusalem made me realize how deficient I was in spirituality.

Yet, on one Sabbath in Jerusalem, I *knew* how desperately, during the many centuries His people were in exile, God had longed to return to His city. Len and I had gone out for a stroll, and suddenly I experienced the Sabbath quiet of the streets not from my point of view, but from God's. It was He who needed the Jews back in the city so that Jerusalem could once again know the Sabbath peace. With no talent for faith, I will not make any claims for this knowledge, nor do I expect anyone who has not felt it to believe me. Since then, on subsequent trips to Israel, I sometimes recovered this same impression, but only as an idea, not a sensation. That certainty came to me only the one time, possibly after I traveled with Rochman back to his beloved.

☙

ONE OF THE THINGS I had hoped to find in Israel, in addition to the ease many Jews feel when landing in the Jewish state, was a place to argue. If you've been consigned to playing tennis on asphalt pavement in a municipal facility where you have to sign up in advance for a half-hour of court time, you know how to appreciate a sports club with reactive surfaces and limitless membership privileges. Montreal had been a fair training ground for spirited argument, but Israel was the Wimbledon of Jewish disputation. And not just disputation. I looked forward to being where Jewish culture was the culture of the land.

My friend Gita in Montreal had put me in touch with her friend Marcia, wife of the writer Hillel Halkin, one of the two men in Israel I most wanted to meet. Hillel had been raised in the Hebraist culture of the Conservative Movement's Jewish Theological Seminary where his father Abraham taught medieval Hebrew philosophy and poetry. Gita, too, had been raised in the Conservative Movement. Her father, Rabbi Bernard Segal, a chaplain during the war, was its executive director. She had filled me in on Hillel's *yikhes*—the high lineage that included his uncle the Hebrew poet and Hebrew University professor Simon Halkin and on his mother's side, her father, Rabbi Meir Bar-Ilan, who inspired the founding of the university that carries his name. We were all alike in having been raised in a Jewish language, but Hillel's Hebrew was obviously a greater asset in adjusting to Israel than my Yiddish. Even before moving there—shortly before we did—he had been translating works by modern Hebrew writers.

I had read Hillel's article, "Hebrew as She is Spoke," about the complications of adapting the sacred language to common speech. With the stirrings of Zionism in the nineteenth century had come the realization that if Jews were to reclaim their national sovereignty, this would have to include the resurrection of their national tongue. Hebrew was used throughout the Diaspora in the liturgy, in study, and selective communication, but wherever Jews founded enduring communities they developed accompanying Jewish vernaculars, like Yiddish or Ladino, for daily use. Hillel's article described how Jewish nationalists at the turn of the twentieth century, most vociferously the lexicographer Eliezer Ben-Yehuda, championed the revival of Hebrew so that the "sleeping beauty ... once awakened would again become a princess among tongues."

Following the princess from her sequestered palace into the streets, Hillel moved gracefully in this essay from dense philological analysis of classical sources to anecdotes about slang usages he'd discovered after his own move from America to Israel. I came upon this article in *Commentary*, my favorite magazine, and liked everything about it.

Commentary was the only publication that our father, my older brother Ben, and I regularly read in common; I will soon say more about this magazine that was to become my intellectual home. I loved good critical thinking, especially about literature and politics, and there I found it in every issue.

Editor Norman Podhoretz and his writers fearlessly attacked their subjects, wrestling them to the ground like street fighters, I thought, without ever having seen a fist fight except in the movies. My only complaint about the magazine had been the scarcity of knowledgeable essays about Jewish culture and here was this terrific essay about Hebrew by someone who had made aliyah.

Accordingly, I was delighted when Marcia invited us over for an evening. They were renting a Jerusalem apartment from Yehuda Amichai, Israel's favorite contemporary poet, who was abroad for the year. I am not name-dropping, just conveying the effortless interconnectedness of our new life with Israel's literary community. In Montreal the linguistic separation between English and French created a regrettable barrier between the two literary communities, while here the common language brought academics, critics, writers, and poets into perhaps too close proximity. I had the feeling that everyone knew everyone else and that every major writer in Israel was after Hillel to translate his or her work. There were not yet fixed political battle lines that I was aware of, only personality differences and the inevitable competitiveness among academics and creative artists.

It was already dark as Len and I stumbled through Yemin Moshe, today one of the most desirable neighborhoods in Jerusalem but then a designated artist-and-writer's colony undergoing construction. Getting to the house required descending a poorly lit stone stairwell and crossing a single-file wooden plank linking sidewalk and doorstep over what looked like a dark sea of mud. The adventuresome approach stoked my excitement.

When Marcia opened the door, she said she had also invited another couple and introduced us to Judy and Ezra Mendelsohn—the second person I had most wanted to meet! Like the Halkins, they, too, had just made aliyah, and Ezra was teaching at the Hebrew University. I had discovered his book, *Class Struggle in the Pale: The Formative Years of the Jewish Worker's Movement in Tsarist Russia*, when I was looking for information about the Jewish Labor movement.

His book, like mine on the schlemiel, was also a reworked version of his doctoral dissertation, but I found it more helpful than the work of senior scholars. Ezra moved easily between politics and culture in just the way I aspired to do in my teaching and writing. He read the fiction of Y. L. Peretz to understand the Jewish Labor movement just as I read about the Jewish Labor movement to appreciate the writings of Peretz.

Hillel and Ezra constituted the intelligentsia I'd dreamed of joining, and here they both were. I had been drawn to the two as *intellectuals*, except that by their Zionist or socialist standards, each would have considered the term an insult.

That evening we talked about neither Hebrew nor the class struggle—at least not directly. Someone's comment about a cleaning woman spun into reflections on employer-employee relations, which led to the question of whether interaction with Jewish domestic help in Israel was in any way different from our experience with Gentile help in North America. Hillel floated the idea that instead of relying on others, we should be required to clean up after ourselves. As the ones handling most of the housework, we women parried, "Easy for you to say." Hillel, unfazed, rejoined that who did what did not affect the principle of the thing. I suggested he was mistaken on moral grounds, citing my father's teaching about the importance of decent pay for those in one's employ. Had Hillel considered the women who depended on work for their livelihood?

Our discussions were Talmudic rather than Socratic, which is to say they were unresolved, and in my case, they continued long after my head hit the pillow, arousing fears lest good arguments fracture new friendships.

Ezra was tall, dark-skinned, a natural athlete—and compulsively ironic about the things he loved. Hillel was slighter, blond, a sailor rather than a basketball and tennis player, not as biting at his own expense. Though I assumed they were close friends, they had actually been brought together by their wives, both of whom were talented dance therapists. I liked both women very much, but common interests made me friendlier with the men, which no one seemed to mind.

Both Hillel and Ezra said they moved to Israel to be Jews on their own terms. Too skeptical to assume religious obligations and too independent to join any community of belief, they had come to a place where membership in the Jewish people was just a normal attribute of citizenship. Given that they intended to spend their professional lives immersed in Jewish sources, languages, and ideas, Israel *logically* best suited their needs.

Their reasoning left out that they would have to serve in the military, including the reserves, until their mid-forties, live with bank overdrafts, and endure the constrictions of a tiny country surrounded by enemies. In my eyes, they were fervent Zionists who had actually come to Israel out of love, fulfilling an ancestral dream. I felt certain of this because I had come out of the same wish to be at the vibrant center of Jewish experience and the same obligation to shore up the beleaguered Jewish state.

Hillel's parents had moved to Israel before him. Ezra likewise knew Hebrew from home. His father Isaac had left his Orthodox home in pre-Soviet Russia to turn first socialist, then Zionist-leftist immigrant to Palestine in the 1920s. A decade later, judging the Yishuv to be not communist enough, he lit out for the U.S., becoming a professor of Semitic languages at Columbia University, where Hillel had studied with him (without knowing Ezra). Ezra's father took him to baseball games and used the time to work on "Cuneiform Documents from the Sumerian, Old-Babylonian, Kassite, and Neo-Babylonian Periods." His scholarship was literally grounded in the history of ancient Israel.

Had my father followed his original plan to study agriculture, he would have settled in Palestine and I would have grown up there. Rerouted instead to chemical engineering, he'd found work in the rubber industry, which then led to deployment in Romania. Like my brother Ben, I undoubtedly absorbed our father's Zionist aspirations just as Hillel and Ezra did theirs. This common attraction of Jews to the Land of Israel, stretching back to God's call to Abram in the twelfth chapter of Genesis, had brought us together. But our friendship was bound to be strained.

Len and I returned to Canada after the end of our first year. There is no elegant or painless way to handle that sentence. The hardest part about leaving was informing our Israeli cousins and friends, fully aware that, had they been the ones leaving, we would have felt betrayed.

All the while he was struggling to retool as a lawyer, Len had seemed happier than I'd ever seen him. Only when he started working at an entry-level job did he feel he had lost his professional competence. If he did not return now, he would forfeit his future in Canada, leaving him without sound prospects in either country. Ben had likewise concluded that he could not support his family in Jerusalem and yielded to our parents' entreaties to return to work in the family textile factory that needed his presence.

Returning to Canada had never entered my mind. Everyone we knew in Israel seemed to live so precariously that I had not yet even begun to compute how we could support ourselves, taking it for granted that we could make do on two sources of income. Had I been more mature and better prepared, I might have provided steadying reassurance to Len, but the tremor of both pillars, my husband and my brother, made me fearful too.

I was afraid that our family might collapse, and I did not consider breaking up the family in order to stay. We left with as little fanfare as possible. A decade later, during a high-school class trip to Israel, our son Jacob refused to believe the relative who said that we had once come on aliyah with the intention of permanency. We were no less taken aback when he asked why we had deceived him. Len and I had never concealed the truth from the children. We had never spoken about it at all.

I was humbled by our return to the Diaspora. My Israeli employers had taken a risk in hiring me, and at Tel Aviv University some students had registered for a sequence of Yiddish courses entailing my ongoing presence. And I had considered living in Israel a moral imperative. All Jews were not required to live in the Jewish homeland, but as long as the burden of defense was as great as it was, I felt we should be sharing it.

CR

WE REMAINED FRIENDS WITH THE Halkins and Mendelsohns, but what had formerly clinched our friendship now challenged it. Within a year of our departure, in one of his "periodic bouts of optimism," Hillel wrote it was harder and harder for him to grasp:

how anyone who is conscious of living a Jewish destiny could deliberately choose to live it anywhere else than here. (Which is one reason I suspect you will be back some day, and perhaps sooner rather than later.) It seems so—self-denying, somehow; and self-evading, ultimately, too. . . .And though I know you will disagree, I really don't believe in a Jewish future anywhere else than here: the Jewish novel, yes, maybe, at least for another generation or two, but Jewish history—no. Jewish history already exists only here, and among those Jews who will someday be here.

Far from resenting this proposition, I was glad to be held to its standard, and flattered when Hillel said that in planning *Letters to an American Jewish Friend*, the book-length polemic he published in 1977, he had considered inviting me to serve as his real interlocutor instead of the fictional one he created. He was right in assuming that I could not give up on the Diaspora because there I was—and no matter how blissful life in Israel might be, some Jews and Israelis were bound to continue living outside it. But on the imperative of ascent, I agreed that one did not shift the goal posts just because one could not score a touchdown.

I could have responded to Hillel's challenge saying that I intended to pursue the same goals abroad, teaching and encouraging others to become teachers of Yiddish literature, knowing that students in one place might become teachers in another. I could try to inspire our own children and those around us with love and knowledge of Israel and use the wider reach of English to fight for the country's rights and security.

Len and I could and did undertake a higher level of Jewish observance and affiliation in Montreal than we would have in Israel, where just living might have felt Jewish enough. The story of Jewish leadership, be it Moses or Herzl, starts outside the country in order to get there and secure it, and one of the ways Judaism differed from imperial religions was its intrinsic acceptance of coexistence, living among the nations. One of my functions in America could be to oppose the Yiddishists and communists who tried to turn Jewish political dependency into a value. Our task was to help secure the Jewish homeland as much from abroad as from within the country, as much among our fellow Jews as our fellow citizens.

On American Jewry, Hillel and I were in basic accord. He scorned those who redefined Jews as a *spiritual* people: "Ethical idealism and the philosophical mind as Jewish traditions indeed," he wrote, "as if these were the distinguishing marks of historical Jewish existence rather than the very symptoms of its disintegration in modern times!" He had little use for those who wanted to turn Judaism into a new religion of social justice, pointing out that on every contemporary issue that arose—environment, transgenderism and sex change, health care, abortion rights, labor unions, U.S. foreign policy—the *tikkun olam* crowd claims that Judaism's position "just happened" to coincide with that of the American liberal Left. "Judaism has value to such Jews to the extent that it is useful, and it is useful to the extent that it can be made to conform to whatever beliefs and opinions they have even if Judaism had never existed." I often wondered whether there was any point writing if he did it so much better.

Hillel expressed my ideas about Zionism so well that I would have given him my proxy on every subject except on what to do about most of the territory Israel had captured in the Six-Day War. He could have put me at a disadvantage by pointing out that he, not I, faced enemy attack. But though I never challenged his right to determine what constituted his security, this did not necessarily make his judgment on political matters sounder than mine. He started out advocating the establishment of a Palestinian state along Israel's pre-June 1967 borders "subject to certain conditions," on the grounds that a more homogeneous Jewish society on less land was better than more land with a restive Arab population. As if the choice were his to make! I predicted that his "restive Arab population" would see an even easier target in a smaller, more vulnerable Jewish entity than the one it had originally attacked.

Several years later, badly chastened by the escalation of Palestinian terrorism, he called me from Israel to ask how I, who lived outside the country, could have grasped the situation better than he did. I answered that I had learned political realism from Yiddish literature.

What I meant by this was that circumstance had forced Yiddish writers to confront the hostility directed against them. They were that same small and vulnerable entity surrounded by hostile neighbors, and Mendele Mocher Sforim was not alone in figuring out some of the dos and don'ts of their predicament. Self-proclaimed idealists in the late-nineteenth and early-twentieth centuries had attributed pogroms and hatred to Jewish deficiencies that were presumably correctable by Jewish reforms. Russian Jewish revolutionaries had likewise tried to reduce anti-Jewish hostility by renouncing "capitalist" occupations in favor of communist or socialist commitment. Now their modern Israeli counterparts advocated renunciation of land won in a defensive war to pacify those who intended to displace them. All were dissembling in the same fatal pursuit.

With Hillel, the apparent divide between dove and hawk dissolved, but not so with Ezra who became one of the earliest members of Peace Now, the movement claiming that surrender of the West Bank of the Jordan was the necessary prerequisite for peace with the Palestinian Arabs. As its name suggested, it held that peace could be achieved through Israeli concessions and ran a public relations campaign to force Israel to "return" the disputed territories on the assumption that this would alleviate Arab hostility.

The movement opened a branch in the United States whose function it was to urge the American government to oppose rather than support Israel's presence in most of the territories it had just regained or won. I thought it wicked to give the enemy unwarranted benefit of doubt while caricaturing one's sober fellow citizens as enemies of peace for resisting the real and present danger.

About all this I later wrote: "Since Israel's acquisition of the disputed territories was the *result* of the Arab war against Israel, it could not retroactively have become its *cause*." The unilateral war would stop, and peace might come only when Arab leaders agreed to coexistence. Until then, and beyond, Israel would need to prove stronger than those seeking to destroy it.

It was much harder arguing with Ezra who resented my interference in Israeli politics than with Hillel who welcomed my involvement. I told Ezra he was conveniently turning me into his enemy so that he should not have to face the intransigence of his real enemies. Jews are by no means alone in blaming the messenger of unwelcome news, but as subjects of more aggression, they specialize in trying to befriend their aggressors and vilifying those who warn against them.

Growing up in a communist family had made Ezra a more complicated Zionist than I was. When the Jewish "atom spies" Julius and Ethel Rosenberg were executed for treason, Ezra's parents anticipated a pogrom. It must have been a tense household, and the parents' vacillation between competing allegiances to communism and Zionism was never resolved.

And there was more: He had followed his father into the profession of scholarship, but his mother was a Soyer, sister of the twin brother artists Raphael and Moses, and in Ezra the creative genius struggled with the academic. He had to suppress some of his love for art, music, and literature to become the dedicated scholar of political history who wrote a two-volume *History of Zionism in Poland Between the World Wars*. He did not suppress his dark side. Our son Billy who adored him remembers Ezra musing aloud on the phrase "being as" and smiling when he came up with the perfect example to demonstrate its use: "Being as I feel lousy, I'm going to kill myself."

That dark wit broke through every letter in our extended correspondence. It would not have occurred to him to shirk his annual army service, which he found even more tortuous once he was transferred from artillery to the education department "to give ludicrous lectures to miserable soldiers in various holes." After the Yom Kippur War, probably the grimmest time in the life of the nation, he wrote me, "The worst thing we can do is to give in to depression, but it's hard to resist." Sounding like Sholem Aleichem, "Our *shikun* was lucky—only one dead—most of the men are not in battle units, and there are lots of *olim* who will have to wait for the next war to die for the *moledet.*" Use of Hebrew terms for *apartment complex, new immigrants,* and *homeland* was the ironic cloak of his Zionism, his *tsiyonut.*

I try not to psychologize people's politics, but I couldn't help thinking that his conflicts originated elsewhere than in his battles against the Israeli Right. When I had anticipated the pleasures of argument with Israeli intellectuals, I had in mind discussions of Peretz and Jewish politics of Poland, not aggravating a dear friend who wanted to believe that Jewish withdrawal could reduce the Arab threat. On my visits to Israel or his sabbaticals abroad I would vow not to broach this subject, but one of our arguments turned so ugly that Len took me by the arm and pulled me out the door.

Yet Zionism finally did bring Ezra some peace, as I would happily witness at a conference in 2004 marking his formal retirement from the Hebrew University. The festive closing dinner included a table for the consuls of the several Central and East European countries whose histories Ezra had plumbed. In rising to respond to the accolades of his students and colleagues, he asked the indulgence of the dignitaries who would not be able to follow the rest of his remarks and, switching from English to the native Hebrew of his children, he said he had undertaken the study of history to understand his father. Failing at that, he did, however, discover that during his sojourn in 1920s Palestine, Isaac Mendelsohn had registered as member number thirty-seven of the newly founded National Library at the Hebrew University. Ezra imagined that while studying ancient Semitic languages his father Isaac had dreamed of becoming a professor at that same university, and he was happy to have fulfilled his father's dream.

It was Ezra I most had in mind when I once wrote that Israelis are hypocrites in reverse: if the traditional hypocrite professes the virtues he declines to practice, the Israeli practices the virtue he declines to profess. A student or friend who knew my feelings would occasionally ask whether I did not think it hypocritical to uphold the value of living in Israel without living there myself—to which I responded with the defense of hypocrisy that I would repeat and refine in the years ahead. Better to fall short of your standard than to abandon it. Ezra could not assert the greatness of Israel, even as he bequeathed it to his children.

I'd had the idea of publishing with Hillel and Ezra a trio of essays about our three fathers, representing, roughly, modern Orthodoxy (Halkin), Jewish leftism (Mendelsohn), and Jewish national culture (Roskies). Hillel and I wrote essays along those lines, and Ezra's talk at the conference might have become the kernel of the third; but I ought to have tackled the project with greater urgency.

At the end of May 2015, I happened to be in Israel, sitting with Hillel in a café, when we learned that Ezra had died the previous day. Neither of us knew that he had been diagnosed with cancer and given only months to live. I managed to make it to the *shiva*, where Judy was surrounded by colleagues and neighbors, children and grandchildren.

9

INTELLECT

*I*n the fall of 1972, upon returning to Montreal, I resumed my academic duties teaching Yiddish literature at McGill. That my university rehired me was not to be taken for granted and impelled me to work even harder. I was still so frustrated by the college professors who had lectured out of their ancient notes that I tore up mine at the end of every school year lest I fall into the same habit. Though I enjoyed research, I vowed not to write books at the expense of teaching, and never to give the same lecture twice. Fortunately, after a few years I realized that one could *replenish* used material instead of starting each time from scratch.

Of course, on any given workday I still had to choose between reading primary works in Yiddish or secondary sources on literature when writing academic articles and preparing classes. But this was mostly a matter of prioritizing, and it still left time for musing on when and whether I would dare to try becoming an intellectual and write for *Commentary*.

Maybe because "intelligent" was the most prized adjective in my childhood—in Yiddish, *inteligént* with a hard "g"—I valued the work of "intellectuals" before knowing what they actually did. The term took shape for me as a form of thinking that flows from reading yet differs from erudition. My original model was the talk around our dining table that began in my teens, where that magazine was often our primary text. Among the many features that appealed to us in its far-ranging analysis of domestic and foreign culture and politics was that it included Jewish subjects in its coverage, albeit not with the intimacy or consistency of the Yiddish press. But the keenness of these pieces in *Commentary* often made up for their infrequency.

That it was also important to others in Montreal I learned one day in the late 1960s when I happened to meet my elementary school principal Shloime Wiseman at a public lecture and he asked me, out of the blue, "What do you make of Cynthia Ozick's attack on Yiddish!?" Wiseman was assuming that I had read that month's *Commentary*, where the lead item was a full-length novella by Cynthia Ozick.

"Envy; or, Yiddish in America" is a brilliant fictional study of Yiddish writers in New York, one of whom breaks through to international renown while most of the others languish in embittered obscurity. The central character burns with jealousy of the figure who is clearly based on Isaac Bashevis Singer and feels that he is being squelched by the indifference of the young Jews who run after celebrity, and secondarily, by the antagonism to Jews out there in America. Wiseman, who could identify some of the writers on whose jealous competitiveness the story was based, thought the story itself bordered on anti-Semitism. I tried to persuade him it was not against Yiddish but an affectionate portrait of what Yiddish in America was *up against*, and sympathetic to the part of European Jewish culture that appears to have no chance of surviving here.

Though I did not yet know the author, I had reason to admire her prescience. As it happened, my first commission in Yiddish literature—from the National Foundation for Jewish Culture—had been to translate the Yiddish novella *The Well* by Chaim Grade, and when I was done, the author asked me to undertake another. We had been carrying on a friendly correspondence, and while never complimenting me in his own name, Grade relayed favorable comments by others, including that I had captured 75 percent of the original—"the best one could hope for." Translating, however, was not work I truly enjoyed, and since I was already teaching full time and raising two children, I very respectfully declined the proposal. But I made a fatal error that Cynthia's story would have warned me against, had she already written it. I suggested that Grade choose from among Isaac Bashevis Singer's several good translators, never realizing that the enmity between them was perhaps even fiercer than the one described in the story. That was the end of our correspondence and of any relations between us; the insult Grade thought I had done him he repaid me in kind in his final letter to me. The situation and the atmosphere that Ozick describes were not identical with my experience, but spectacularly true to life. My appreciation for Grade grew with every new work that he published, wholly independent of his temperament and this incident.

Ben had begun subscribing to *Commentary* in the early 1950s, so that by the time I was in college I was familiar with the names Milton Himmelfarb, Will Herberg, Lucy Dawidowicz, Irving Kristol, Nathan Glazer, Dan Jacobson, and what seemed like an army of serious thinkers. I was eager to join their ranks. In my senior year, mild praise for one of my assignments in Hugh MacLennan's creative writing class prompted me to send it to the magazine—minus the obligatory return envelope, as if to signal my serene confidence that it would be accepted.

The story, big surprise, was about a Jewish college senior who accompanies her parents to an evening commemorating the April 1943 Warsaw Ghetto uprising and then goes home to complete the paper she is writing on the German poet and playwright Heinrich von Kleist. Far too subtle to attempt an actual plot, I believed the girl's implied re-creation of the impossible tension between the allure of German high culture and the fact of Germany's murder of the Jews would emerge by itself. The rejection letter stung; in later years, I winced at how sophomoric my submission must have seemed to the editors.

As an example of what Ben and I found exciting in *Commentary*, consider this 1964 item by the psychiatrist Leslie Farber—not to be confused with the cultural critic Leslie Fiedler who also wrote for the magazine. "I'm Sorry, Dear" opens on a dialogue between two unidentified individuals. The male speaks first.

Did you?
Did **you**? You **did**, didn't you?

Yes, I'm afraid I—Oh, I'm sorry! I **am** sorry. I know how it makes you feel.

Oh, don't worry about it. I'm sure I'll quiet down after a while.
I'm **so** sorry, dearest. Let me help you.

I'd rather you didn't.
But, I...
What good is it when you're just—when you
don't really want to? You know perfectly well, if
you don't **really** want to, it doesn't work.

But I **do really** want to! I **want** to! Believe me. It **will** work, you'll
see. Only let me!

Please, couldn't we just forget it? For now the thing is done, finished.
Besides, it's not really that important. My tension always wears off
eventually. And anyhow—maybe next time it'll be different.

Oh, it **will**, I know it **will**. Next time I won't be so tired or so eager.
I'll make sure of that. Next time it's going to be **fine**! .... But about
tonight—I'm sorry, dear.

Disquieting as it was in that era to see sex discussed so frankly in what
we treated as a family magazine, we were intrigued by the article's reflections on the (William) Masters and (Virginia) Johnson experiments in sexology. Actually, Farber was less interested in the dubious reliability of the
science than in how the setting of explicit standards for sexual satisfaction
had inhibited romantic ideals of intimacy and love. Technical mastery, he
wrote, tempts humans with visions of omnipotence while exposing their
fundamental and irreversible mortality.

Moving from the physical to the metaphysical, the essay throbbed with
larger anxieties:

[The] manner in which lovers now pursue their careers as copu-
lating mammals—adopting whatever new refinements sexology
devises, covering their faces yet exposing their genitals—may
remind us of older heresies which, through chastity or libertinism,
have pressed toward similar goals; one heretical cult went so far as

187

to worship the serpent in the Garden of Eden. But the difference between these older heresies and modern science—and there is a large one—must be attributed to the nature of science itself, which. . . by means of its claims to objectivity can invade religion and ultimately all of life to a degree denied the older heresies. So, with the abstraction, objectification, and idealization of the female orgasm we have come to the last and perhaps most important clause of the contract which binds our lovers to their laboratory home, there to will the perfection on earth which cannot be willed, there to suffer the pathos which follows all such strivings toward heaven on earth.

Even when I did not fully understand the argument of an essay like this—the fault presumably mine—I saw the way it marvelously peeled open a subject or wrestled it to the ground or otherwise probed or amplified it in pursuit of a finding that could rarely be inferred at the start but seemed inevitable and proved by the end. A lovers' dialogue that could have been played for laughs by Mike Nichols and Elaine May expands into a meditation on the dangerous hubris of the rational intellect and points to the deeper mysteries beyond.

The essay that disturbed us most was Norman Podhoretz's "My Negro Problem—And Ours," published in 1963 at the height of the American civil rights movement. We were hardly unique in our reaction, since the essay brought the magazine several hundred letters (including one from Ben). The essay seemed to share our basic view of anti-Semitism—that we owed no apology for enmity that we had not earned.

Podhoretz, who in 1960 at the age of thirty had succeeded founding editor Elliot Cohen as the chief editor of *Commentary*, notably moved its focus to the Left during this decade of social upheaval and political radicalism. But his ultimate relocation on the Right was clearly presaged in "My Negro Problem." On the basis of hard-won experience as a Jewish kid in Brooklyn stalked and bullied by bigger black boys, he challenged prevailing stereotypes of rich Jews versus persecuted Negroes, unearthing in himself emotions like envy and hate that, he was certain, characterized the "twisted and sick" feelings most American whites harbored against blacks—who heartily returned the compliment.

Rather than defending himself against presumptive charges of racial prejudice, Podhoretz admitted these feelings for the sake of a larger argument: that, contrary to the facile belief of many liberals, relations between blacks and whites were so tortured as to negate the dream of amicable coexistence. Fiercely following his logic to the end, he concluded that the only way of resolving the underlying problem, and then only incrementally, was racial intermarriage. And since ideas, to be persuasive, had to undergo the test of personal honesty, he asked himself in print whether he would like one of his own daughters to "marry one." No, he answered, he would not *like* it at all, but he would accept it as the man he had "a duty to be."

This masterpiece of political incorrectness has lost none of its bite, as I would learn on the several occasions when I later included it in a college course. What troubled our family back then in Montreal, however, was not the essay's contentious treatment of race, which hardly resonated on our side of the Canadian border, but Podhoretz's apparent indifference to whether his daughter's hypothetical suitor was *Jewish*. So the boy was black, we said; big deal. But how could the editor of a Jewish magazine treat so casually his daughter's marriage to a Gentile?

True, the Jews made an appearance in the essay. Imagining himself in the position of blacks despairing of a society in which color would cease to matter and driven to wonder whether their survival as a group was worth the struggle, Podhoretz added:

> In thinking about the Jews, I have often wondered whether their survival as a distinct group was worth one hair on the head of a single infant.... Did the Jews have to survive so that six-million innocent people should one day be burned in the ovens of Auschwitz? It is a terrible question and no one, not God Himself, could ever answer it to my satisfaction.

I found this question terribly wrong. Did it not undermine his argument? The genocide of the Jews was the consequence of Nazism's perverted definition of the "fittest." Should the Jews, having been forcibly made aware of the extravagant price of their survival, now surrender—for example, through miscegenation with Gentiles—because they wanted to solve the problem of anti-Semitism? If God did not flinch after the book of Lamentations, why would He flinch after the ovens of Auschwitz?

By the time I came to know the authors of these and other articles on matters of Jewish concern, they themselves had come to regret some of the things that had bothered me. Nathan Glazer later wondered why *Partisan Review*, a magazine created in large measure by Jewish editors and writers, "had so little to say about Jews, Jewishness, or Judaism." In truth, I had never subscribed to *PR*, but whenever topics spilled over from *Commentary*, as they often did, I looked up the articles and thus got to know the magazine fairly well. I had noticed that it seemed to shy away from Jewishness even when, as in reviewing certain books and authors, the subject ought to have figured in the discussion. Sidney Hook's 1987 autobiography would cite the underestimation of Zionism as one of the two great miscalculations of his generation (the other was underestimating capitalism). This corrective was particularly important since Hook, a former Marxist, remained an expert on Marxism and a person of searing honesty who believed in keeping every iota of the historical record straight. Once Norman Podhoretz took up the cause of Israel, moreover, no one ever defended it more effectively.

Indeed, by the 1970s, *Commentary* had thrown its intellectual resources behind the neoconservative reorientation that Irving Kristol would immortalize as that of "a liberal who has been mugged by reality." My veneration of these thinkers was tempered only by disappointment at how long it took them to get there. Perhaps it was my father's earlier experience in Vilna, our flight from the Soviets in 1940, or my own college encounters with people raised in communism that put me ahead of the New York intellectuals in this respect. I seem to have always appreciated the conservative strain in Jewishness and could not understand how such intelligent people could have subordinated that to anything less substantial and less *interesting*. At the same time, I sometimes envied their evolution from youthful Marxism that gave many of them a wonderful subject.

Writing as a child of his times, Robert Warshow, a pioneer of serious popular culture and film criticism, described the legacy of the 1930s as the period when "virtually all intellectual activity was derived in one way or another from the Communist Party. If you were not somewhere within the party's wide orbit, then you were likely to be in the opposition, which meant that much of your thought and energy had to be devoted to maintaining yourself in the opposition." This was precisely how I perceived the atmosphere in the communist circles of Montreal, and the same intolerance persisted among liberals who absorbed their rigidity, sometimes unknowingly.

Warshow died in 1955 before the term *neoconservative* was applied to reformed liberals like himself, but he identified the essential untruth of communism that turned him resolutely against it. Irving Kristol and other mild leftists like Leslie Fiedler and Lionel Abel appear to have spent most of their college years in the famed alcoves of the lunchroom at City College of New York, debating the followers of Joseph Stalin. They could not have been surprised to find their former classmate of the Stalinist alcove, atomic spy Julius Rosenberg, in the service of an ideology that denounced America as the capitalist enemy, yet his actual treason seemed to bother them less than the culture of deception it demanded—the double-think defined so brilliantly by George Orwell. For intellectuals who believed in the power of ideas, betrayal of truth was more culpable even than betrayal of country.

One of best expositions of liberalism's failure to confront communism early and strongly enough was Lionel Trilling's 1947 novel, *Middle of the Journey,* which I later (when I taught it in the 1990s) called "the first neoconservative novel," though Trilling never applied the term to himself. The Left-leaning liberal protagonist, John Laskell, loosely modeled on the author, experiences successive challenges to his progressive faith beginning with a near-fatal illness akin to one that Trilling himself had experienced. This slightly unsettles his rational materialism and readies him for the second challenge when he is visited by Gifford Maxim, recognizably modelled on Whittaker Chambers, whom Trilling had known at Columbia College. Maxim-Chambers had worked underground as a spy for the Soviet Union.

Now repentant and about to resurface as a citizen, he is fearful of the fate he knows awaits him at the hands of would-be Soviet executioners and needs Laskell's help in visibly establishing himself so that it will be harder to make him disappear. Laskell gradually admits the realities of Stalinism. Moreover, recuperating in the company of friends in his leftist circle, he recognizes that the handyman whom they prize as an authentic "man of the people" is actually a brutal and selfish character. As Laskell is weaned of Marxist pieties, he thinks more clearly about good and evil, but is not yet ready to acknowledge with Maxim the deeper sources of morality in religion and God. We leave him still in the *middle* of his journey.

Strange to say, Trilling, who as a Jew could not be denied a teaching position at Columbia University once the university president had read his doctoral dissertation on Matthew Arnold, and whose essays and books became my signposts at what he unforgettably called "the dark and bloody crossroads where literature and politics meet," was so uncomfortable with his Jewishness that he let it undercut his own literary potential. The novel describes the mental struggle of his mostly Jewish intellectual circle without making any of them Jewish. This excision prompted Robert Warshow's observation that its characters exist "in a kind of academic void of moral abstractions, without a history," whereas the Stalinism it treats was a particular response to particular historical pressures: "Mr. Trilling might have come closer to the 'essence' of the experience he describes...if he had been more willing to face his own relation to it." The Jewish author could present in Gifford Maxim a man of Christian faith, but he could not animate a believing or any other kind of Jew. I agreed with Warshow's assessment of the novel, yet the flat and deracinated quality of Trilling's characters brought its ideas into sharper relief. It fit neatly into the category of "political novel" that Irving Howe was in the process of defining.

I did not so much get my ideas from these writers as admire how well they were expressed. Growing up beside Ben, who by the time of his bar mitzvah understood that the British had betrayed the Jews in Palestine, I could never swoon over British culture, as Trilling did, to the exclusion of our own. As a student of literature, I knew that Jews had no Shakespeare or

Dostoevsky, yet while I did not let the bias of such great writers diminish my appreciation for their work, I also knew that great drama and the modern novel were not the sum of a civilization. Talmudic thinking came to me largely through my mother's hundreds of sayings and the way she applied them to the challenges of everyday life. In particular, her teaching that *a rakhman af gazlonim iz a gazlen af rakhmonim*—"pity for the cruel is cruelty to the truly pitiable"—became the basis of my frustration with liberalism and helped me understand why it so often betrays itself by sliding into the illiberal left. I had the chutzpah to think I understood this better than my intellectual betters.

ɒʀ

THE FIRST MEMBER of THE *COMMENTARY* CIRCLE I met and befriended was Neal Kozodoy, less than a year after he had joined its editorial staff. During McGill's winter break in 1966–67, I attended a student Zionist conference at a kosher lakeside hotel in the Laurentian Mountains north of Montreal. Neal was brought in from New York as a speaker. He was not much older than the student participants and was still also pursuing his own graduate work at Columbia, but his lecture about the image of the Jew in modern literature displayed the verve I associated with the best of thinkers.

The informality of the conference gave us time to talk about the magazine. Very gingerly, I complained about what I saw as its failures of omission on matters Jewish and Zionist. Perhaps I mentioned the need for items on subjects like Jewish education and must have somehow gotten the impression that Neal shared some of my misgivings. But if so, he did not let on, and we moved to other topics.

While majoring in English literature at Harvard, Neal had also attended the Hebrew College of Boston, spent a year studying in Jerusalem, and at Columbia written a master's thesis on the Hebrew poets of medieval Spain. Around the time I met him, he had already become a "go-to" freelance editor in Jewish publishing for books like Elie Wiesel's *The Jews of Silence* and Abba Eban's *My People: The Story of the Jews*. As I was then writing my doctoral dissertation under an adviser whose expertise in modern fiction did not extend to Jewish languages, it was delightful to speak with this polymath who demanded clarification of my inchoate ideas and suggested readings and approaches I hadn't thought of. The ensuing improvements to my dissertation made up for the damage to my ego.

Neal and Maud Kozodoy enjoying comedian Modi at the *Commentary* roast of Joe Lieberman, December 2018. Neal had hosted many *Commentary* dinners as editor of the magazine 1995–2009. His successor John Podhoretz instituted the annual roast. (Sarah Merians Photography)

Unlike Norman Podhoretz, *Commentary's* prolific editor-in-chief, Neal rarely wrote under his own name, evidently preferring to express himself through the writers and works he edited both at the magazine and outside it. One of those outside projects became a series of books published by Behrman House and intended for use in the then-forming field of Jewish studies. (Among the early titles were Isadore Twersky's *A Maimonides Reader*, Michael A. Meyer's *Ideas of Jewish History*, Lucy Dawidowicz's *A Holocaust Reader*, and Robert Alter's *Modern Hebrew Literature*.) He invited me to edit a volume geared to courses like those I was teaching on Yiddish literature in English translation.

Lucy Dawidowicz, with her book, *A Holocaust Reader* (1978) on the shelf behind her. She created the "Fund for the Translation of Jewish Literature," and in other ways encouraged the author with advice and friendship.

Mine would emerge as an anthology of short fiction, *A Shtetl and Other Yiddish Novellas,* bringing together various literary representations of the East European Jewish market towns that were the major setting of the Jewish fiction I was teaching. By bringing together five different treatments of this subject I felt I could demonstrate stylistic, thematic, and political varieties of fiction and challenge the homogenization of the European Jewish past that was occurring in the wake of its destruction. The case would be made—without need for comment—by the contrast between the sleepy impressionism of David Bergelson's *At the Depot* and the missionary zeal of the ex-yeshiva students in S. Ansky's *Behind a Mask,* between Mendele Mocher Sforim's memoir of a traditional childhood and Joseph Opatoshu's *Romance of a Horse Thief.* When offered the choice of a 10 percent royalty on prospective sales or a flat fee of $5,000, I declined Neal's advice and chose the former, indulging every novice's fantasy that legions of professors of politics, let alone literature, would adopt my reader for their classrooms.

Perhaps someone (maybe Costa-Gavras?) would buy the film rights for Itche Meir Weissenberg's *A Shtetl*, about the strike by Polish Jewish workers over the right to important Passover matzos from a neighboring town that escalates into internecine violence. The anthology worked fairly well as a sourcebook, and though three subsequent editions still haven't brought me close to that lump sum, I'd probably make the same choice again, in the firm belief that what interests me will eventually garner the attention it merits.

It was likewise thanks to Neal that, before I'd worked up the courage to try to write for the magazine, I first visited the *Commentary* offices on a trip to New York. Readying myself for the visit, I was reminded of the accounts by Yiddish writers of their first trip to Warsaw to the home of the great Y. L. Peretz, there to offer homage and show their work. One acolyte pocketed Peretz's discarded cigar as a keepsake and was mortified when it started burning a hole in his vest. Another, who had borrowed a cape to cover his torn trousers, was at the point of leaving when his perceptive host slipped him some money to buy a new pair. A third was advised to forget his choice of writing in Hebrew and switch to Yiddish instead (though Peretz himself wrote in both languages). These nervous memories conveyed my own provincial excitement at getting to meet *Commentary*'s editors on the seventh floor of the American Jewish Committee's building on East 56th Street. Although I had secured a university appointment, a goal that some of the magazine's earlier editors had aspired to, I considered theirs much the higher accomplishment.

Marion Magid was *Commentary*'s wise-cracking associate editor, her sassy voice and sinewy figure reminiscent of Rosalind Russell in *His Girl Friday* and Katharine Hepburn in *Woman of the Year*. You haven't appreciated the art of the book review until you read hers of *Jewish Wit* by the then well-known Freudian psychoanalyst Theodor Reik (1962):

> The book has apparently not been edited at all, leaving Dr. Reik's incredible prose Style intact. There is a fresh surprise on every page. No sooner has the reader built up an immunity to the continuous

present, the Germanic inversion ("Late resounds in us what early sounded"), and the mangled citation ("Be Kent unmannerly when Lear is crazy") than he is faced with new challenges: "While he still lived in Germany, he identified with his Jewish friends and emigrated to America." In the end it becomes a game and there are rich incidental rewards: women who are "chase and virtuous"; a man who "spoilt his changes in life"; "the saving grave of the Jewish people." (Has no one read the gallows?)

On a later visit I would receive my own (jovial) slashing when I turned up in the doorway of Marion's office wearing my favorite buttoned up navy blue shift. Among my idiosyncrasies was the conviction, not shared by my husband, that vestal clothing was more alluring by virtue of the mystery it concealed. Marion took one look at me and declared, "Oy, it's *Hashomer Hatsa'ir.*" It broke me up to be consigned to the sartorial brigades of a Marxist Zionist youth movement that eschewed bourgeois accoutrements like lipstick and marriage. Being the target of Marion's wit made me feel almost like an insider.

Podhoretz's office was protected by a secretary, but he was wonderfully cordial when I gained admittance. Over time he taught me to accept hostility as an inevitable reward for exposing unwelcome truths. This is the man who would write, "If I wish to name-drop, I have only to list my ex-friends," and for whom it was a point of honor to speak out against rotten ideas even at the cost of social disadvantage. His instruction was the more admirable since, when I met him, he was already losing the kind of celebrity the pursuit of which he had called "the dirty little secret" of the New York intellectuals—that is, his own community.

His book *Making It*, published in 1967, struck like a bolt of lightning. I already admired Norman for his boldness as an essayist and editor, but this masterful memoir caught me up in its opening and never released me till its final breath.

Let me introduce myself. I am a man who at the precocious age of thirty-five experienced an astonishing revelation: it is better to be a success than a failure. Having been penetrated by this great truth concerning the nature of things, my mind was now open for the first time to a series of corollary perceptions, each one as dizzying in its impact as the Original Revelation itself. Money, I now saw (no one, of course, had ever seen it before), was important: it was better to be rich than to be poor. Power, I now saw (moving on to higher subtleties), was desirable: it was better to give orders than to take them. Fame, I now saw (how courageous of me not to flinch), was unqualifiedly delicious: it was better to be recognized than to be anonymous.

This ironic self-advertisement led into the account of how the boy from Brooklyn won scholarships to Columbia College and Cambridge University, then rose through stages of writing and editorial advancement to the point of producing this book. Victorians had suppressed the admission of sex; he aspired to do for the dirty secret of ambition in his circles what D. H. Lawrence and Henry Miller did for sexuality. He had considered exposing this in a book about Norman Mailer, who wrote *Advertisements for Myself*, but then realized it could only be done in the first person, demonstrating the process through the product. In the short run, it added to his roster of ex-friends; in the long run it became an American classic.

I was nearing thirty-five when I read this, still riddled with middle class guilt, uncomfortable with power, and uncertain about the pursuit of fame. My mother's voice curdled when she said of someone, *Er iz ambitsyez!*— warning against precisely the pursuit of fame and fortune Norman was ready to admit. The inhibition against self-promotion was actually deeply ingrained in Jewish culture, manifest in the custom of referring to rabbinic masters by the title of their works rather than their names. Keeping a low profile among the gentiles made modesty a communal requirement. Jewish communities were not allowed to build their synagogues to the height of churches, and although customs varied according to local circumstance, it was often considered unwise to flaunt one's wealth. On the other hand, there was not the same discomfort among Jews about money as there was in polite Gentile society. I delighted in telling people that the Montreal Jewish Federation in the 1950s published an annual booklet listing all contributors of more than twenty-five dollars alongside their current and last year's donations. The horror of my listeners resembled the reaction of Lionel and Diana Trilling to Norman's allegedly vulgar display in writing this book.

Making It inspired me, but also reminded me why I was not like its author. I was ambitious, yes, but while I tried learning from Norman not to *fear* dislike or to avoid confrontation, his scrappier childhood left him with fewer outstanding debts than my protected upbringing. I had learned from my father the responsibilities of ownership. Director and part owner of a factory, he knew that providing decent work for decent pay and producing useful goods benefited many others as well as himself, and that he could do this more efficiently and fairly than government, but that he therefore dared not fail. His primary obligations to consumers, to the workers and their families, spun off into myriad commitments to Jewish and philanthropic causes. Mother resented those who took advantage of her husband's generous nature, yet her oft-repeated saying, "A good name is like a precious jewel," was meant to remind us—or herself—that helping people was more important than banking checks. Money, power, and fame were certainly better than poverty, dependency, and obscurity, but each imposed so much responsibility that I never wanted more of them than I could comfortably shoulder.

CR

IN 1976, WHEN I BEGAN teaching courses on American Jewish literature, Neal invited me to write a review essay for *Commentary* on new works of American Jewish fiction, primarily *The Pagan Rabbi* and *Bloodshed: Three Novellas* by Cynthia Ozick who had recently foretold the emergence of an authentic Jewish culture in the English language. At a conference in Jerusalem that was meant to bring Jewish writers from abroad into contact with their Israeli counterparts, Ozick had described this idea for a "new Yiddish" through the image of the *shofar*, the curved ram's horn that is sounded during the Jewish Days of Awe: "If we blow into the narrow end of the *shofar*," she wrote, "we will be heard far. But if we choose to be Mankind rather than Jewish and blow into the wider part, we will not be heard at all." Blowing through the wider part was what Trilling had done by deracinating the characters of his novel, but her immediate target was Philip Roth who had said at the preceding conference that he was an American, not a Jewish writer. Ozick saw through the unseriousness of this declaration, its lack of dignity. She herself was a practicing and quite learned Jew, the niece of American Hebrew poet Abraham Regelson, and her fiction could be read as demonstration of her thesis that Jewish particularity could only enrich, never impoverish fiction.

Despite my admiration for her brilliant metaphor, I was not yet persuaded that the new cultural amalgam was actually emerging. My review would put her augury to the test. Pitched as a piece of literary history, "American Jewish Writing, Act II" contrasted the so-called triumvirate of Saul Bellow, Bernard Malamud, and Philip Roth, each of whom bridled at being labeled "Jewish," with newer writers whose fiction tackled a distinctly Jewish issue. Among these were Arthur A. Cohen's *In the Days of Simon Stern*, a contemporary treatment of the messianic coming; a first novel, *My Own Ground*, by Hugh Nissenson, recalling immigrant New York circa 1915; and Ozick's own two story collections, which deserved to be called "midrashic" literature for the way they recast traditional Jewish themes. Thus, the title story of the first collection (set among Orthodox Jews in London) cites as its epigram the Talmudic saying, "He who is walking along and studying, but then breaks off to remark, 'How lovely is that tree!' or 'How beautiful is that fallow field!'—Scripture regards such a one as having hurt his own being." That admonition is brought to life when a brilliant Talmudist falls in love with a tree and hangs himself from it to bring about their pantheistic union. The author invests in the rabbi some of her own aesthetic struggle with Judaism and in the rabbi's pious widow her equally profound rejection of the man's "abomination." Ozick's prose was as bold and original as her imagination, and I became a lifelong fan.

However, much as I wanted to cheer both the intention and the books, I did not yet find the artistic results of this body of writing as successful as I'd hoped. In part, I thought, the reason lay in the still relatively impoverished cultural ground of mainstream Judaism in America—a circumstance that forced the writers who were intent on engaging meaningfully with Judaism to situate their plots elsewhere: in Israel, in the Jewish past, or in an ultra-Orthodox community. American Jewish life did not yet supply the rich soil they needed, and their books reflected the strain of having to invent the absent context that Yiddish had in overabundance.

Nissenson and Ozick, joined by Norma Rosen, whom I had included in my first version of this review, took offense at my essay and attacked my credibility. I had not previously known that they were friends. In a letter to the editor, Cynthia charged me with reading literature as "sociological reality," and said that I had demonstrated "an essential disbelief in fiction *as* fiction." Her letter possessed all the verve I appreciated when her displeasure was directed at others:

> The light-years distance between a cultural critic and an imaginative writer is made most explicit in Ruth R. Wisse's argument that "for those who take Judaism seriously as a cultural alternative, the wish to weave new, brilliant cloth from its ancient threads, the sociological reality of the present-day American Jewish community would seem to represent an almost insurmountable obstacle."

As I had no intention of becoming an "imaginative writer" of fiction, I held to my view that for the time being, American Jewish reality lent itself more easily to satire, nostalgia, or fantasy than to the serious probing of Jewishness. The point she called sociological was not meant to limit the capacities of a novelist, but to note that a *new Yiddish*—her coinage and dream—could arise only among modern practicing Jews who were still somewhat outside the mainstream. While Yiddish writers were coping with the erosion of their culture, those writing in English worked with shoots of a Jewish culture that had not yet ripened.

It was painful to find myself at odds with a writer I so much admired and would have wanted to befriend; fortunately, Cynthia seemed to bear me no grudge. We eventually became long-distance friends and comrades-in-arms against the enemies of Israel. She herself was no slouch as a "cultural critic," but it was easier for me to take unpopular positions since I was more than satisfied writing for *Commentary* whereas as a committed writer, she was well advised to stay at least nominally in the good graces of the PEN association and the editors of left-leaning magazines.

ℭℜ

BY THE TIME I DEBUTED in *Commentary* I was twice as old as when I had sent in my first unsolicited story, and though I was now reviewing books and writing about literature, I still looked to others to say what was most on my mind.

One day, I found myself urging a colleague in Jewish studies to write an article about an issue then heating up in the Jewish community. "You might want to say," I began, and outlined the points he could make as he listened with interest.

Suddenly, as I was talking, I realized that this admirable scholar would never write the article I had in mind, and certainly never write it as I thought it should be written. I felt silly for whatever it was that was holding me back.

If I were now to attempt the kind of self-scrutiny I normally distrust, I would be compelled to note that I did not begin to write for *Commentary* until after my brother Ben died at forty-three, leaving sheaves of poems and a diary he had started keeping in his late teens. But though this is intended as an intellectual memoir, and though no one had been more important than my brother in that development, I can't fully deal with his dying. After he married and I married soon after, we saw each other less often and almost never face to face, so I did not really know what was on his mind and I did not really try to know. He had always seemed perfect to me, and so I continued to regard him in his marriage, work, friendships, his mind and character, his love of music…and when he began to slide, I was not alone in wanting to ignore it.

Sometime in his late twenties he started drinking. Len and I had a close friend who drank more at a sitting than Ben did in a week, but the two men did not have the same chemistry or temperament. It pulled Ben down. My father loved being an industrialist, and despite his preference for rubber production over textiles, I think he enjoyed directing the family mill. Ben took it up as an obligation. When he could no longer ignore his depression, he sought the help of a psychiatrist, but to no avail. Whatever transpired in those sessions remained between them; the doctor's response to my one tentative request for some posthumous understanding was enough to dissuade me from asking again. Ben had developed pancreatitis but continued to drink. He died on November 25, 1974, two days after returning from a textile fair in Frankfurt.

He was survived by three children, a loving wife, stricken friends, and parents, one of whom would soon die of grief. They mourned him, but I was incensed. He had been my guide and shield since earliest childhood, my model of integrity and grit. He was also the buffer between me and our immigrant parents, absorbing their bewilderments, reorienting them in their uncertainties, and reassuring them that all would be well. For as long as I could remember, I had been expecting him to write whatever had to be written.

On the day of his funeral I was in a rage. At the time I believed that he had it in his power to live. Simply, I blamed him for dying, held him responsible for his death. Part of me wept for his poor children and worried for my sister-in-law, but the anger was selfish. "Stupid man, how could you squander a life our parents had gone to such lengths to save? How could you abandon *me* who needs you so badly?" At the burial, as the gravediggers made ready to fill the grave after the family had dropped their symbolic shovelfuls of earth on the coffin, Ben's friends waved the men off and insisted on filling the grave themselves according to Jewish tradition. He was the first of their cohort to die.

So there we stood in the cold, shoveling the hard ground, who with love and who with sorrow, who with regret and who with wrath. I knew

I was being cruel but didn't care. I hated death and took it personally. It was unbearable to lose Ben and it took me years to calm down.

The colleague I urged to write that article on a similarly bleak November day may have reminded me a little of Ben, but it is wrong to keep picking at this sore. Families are gnarled, death does not come to everyone in his time, and writing isn't easy. Maybe I waited to write what I thought until I was middle aged simply because it took that long to gain the understanding I needed.

CR

HAD MONTREAL PRODUCED AN INTELLECTUAL circle like the one that sprang up in New York around *Partisan Review* and *Commentary* in the 1930s and '40s, I might have fashioned myself an intellectual and published in little magazines. (Ben might have preceded me.) I was too far removed, geographically and otherwise, to become part of that circle, but I warmed myself by its fire and approached close enough to know that, for all my appreciation, I would not have exchanged my experience for theirs.

According to Elliot Cohen, founding editor of *Commentary*, the only difference between those two magazines was that "we admit to being a Jewish magazine and they don't," but to the extent that this was true it only pointed to the huge stable of such writers available to both publications, whose contributors also overlapped. Other differences stemmed from *Partisan Review*'s beginnings as a vehicle of the Communist Party and *Commentary*'s as an organ of the American Jewish Committee. The former engaged with Marxism and Modernism, apparent opposites both opposed to the bourgeois status quo. The latter, more liberal, tacked leftward in the early 1960s but stayed relatively centrist on economic and political issues.

Irving Howe's defining essay on "The New York Intellectuals" appeared in 1968, during an interval when its members were less divided on political issues than ever before or after. Those whom he included in his roster were by then (like John Laskell of Trilling's novel) anti-Stalinists, persuaded of the guilt of Julius Rosenberg in having spied for the Soviet Union, and solidly on America's side in the Cold War against communism. They all condemned the viciousness of Senator Joseph McCarthy's hunt for domestic communists through the House Un-American Activities Committee, but they did not use his excess to excuse the communists who kept perjuring themselves in service to their Soviet controllers. On the Eichmann trial, almost all criticized Hannah Arendt's theory of the banality of evil. After decades of indifference to the rise of Israel, the scare of the Six-Day War had turned the Jews in the group into warm supporters. There was enough agreement in this sprawling cohort to keep them within the same orbit of argument. Howe neatly summed up their interrelationships: "Attention was paid."

Given the absence of anything like this in Canada, I had chosen the same path as several of my college friends to become a professor—in a field as open as California in the gold rush—and I wrote my first post-dissertation book about an earlier cohort of Yiddish New York writers, poets, and intellectuals whom I had begun to investigate when I had prepared my talk on the poet Mani Leib. These literary stars were reaching their prime in the 1920s while the mass of immigrant Jews around them were abandoning their language. It was the pathos of such writers and their situation that Cynthia Ozick addressed in her story "Envy: or, Yiddish in America;" I was out to capture the pulsating heart of the movement when its writers and especially its poets were at the height of their powers. Perhaps I could begin to give them their due.

I constructed *A Little Love in Big Manhattan* around the contrast between two wonderful poets: Mani Leib, from the rural Ukraine, who tried to cope with the immigrant cacophony by withdrawing into the lyricism of his native region, and Moishe Leib Halpern, who injected into American Yiddish verse the harsh contrarieties of Vienna where he had spent part of his adolescence. Mani Leib's beloved word *aleyn*, alone, led him into *aleyen*, Yiddish for "avenues" that in its musicality and image evoked the French "allées" more than the bustling streets of the Bronx. If Moishe Leib Halpern was his opposite, that was not entirely accidental: he knowingly cast himself as the antitype of Mani Leib's school of quietude—as the "street drummer" whose boom-boom-booming drowns out the urban noise. On good nights, these two poets came to me in dreams so that when I sat down to write I had only to bring them to life as I had "seen and heard" them talk in the coffee shops of New York's Lower East Side.

Each of the two seemed to have simply emerged fully formed from his formative environment before coming to America in their teens. Yet Mani Leib, the exemplar of harmony, began publishing verse and defining himself as a poet while earning his living in the local shoe factories, making the leather uppers of boots. His private life was equally riven when he fell in love with fellow poet Rachel Veprinski and left his wife and children to live with her. Halpern, for his part, married the love of his life and addressed some of his finest lyrics to her and to their son, their only child. That "little love in big Manhattan" was a line I took from one of his poems, and it was far less ironic than he sometimes made it sound. More than with each other, they wrote out of the tension in themselves.

Keeping their poetry in the foreground I also wanted to probe their American experience. Though Jews valued literary culture, this immigrant society was too harried and poor to properly sustain it. The blessings of freedom in *di goldene medine*, the golden land, came with no accompanying support for literature. Cut off from their families by the First World War, they learned day after day about the brutal destruction of home communities they may once have hoped to revisit. What we would later call the poetry of Holocaust, khurbn in Yiddish, they already composed after the earlier "Great War" and civil war in Russia.

No less traumatic in its impact was the Bolshevik Revolution, which brought American Jews the mixed blessing of the Yiddish daily *Freiheit* that the Soviets founded in New York to spearhead and promote the Communist International. For a time, it gave Moishe Leib Halpern a platform, a small but precious weekly stipend, and a taste of fame. But the paper's affectation of granting its writers *freedom* concealed strict Soviet control that kept contributors on for only as long as they toed the party line: Halpern was cruelly dumped when he deviated. Writers in the sphere of Yiddish were under the direct pressure of world events and could not escape them if they tried.

If my college education had once raised doubts that Yiddish belonged in its curriculum, I now felt that the Jewish historical predicament had produced writing of exceptionally profound importance to Western civilization. Except for Keats, I had little interest in the Romantics whom I had once adored, and no patience for the idea of poets as guides to action. King David managed to win battles and write psalms, Disraeli to govern and write fiction, and Churchill to save Western civilization and dazzle with his writing and painting—but it was not as artists that they attempted to legislate. Alas, there was no obvious correlation between wisdom and the individual talent. Nonetheless, Yiddish writing, composed under exceptional pressure, had a unique perspective on its time and circumstance, and the more I read of it the more consequential I found it to be.

Quite by chance, I had come to know the Yiddish writer who provoked such questions, the object of "envy" in Cynthia Ozick's novella about Yiddish in America. In the years since he had come to our home to perform the symbolic ceremony of redeeming our son Billy from the priesthood, Isaac Bashevis Singer had achieved the kind of celebrity no other Yiddish writer had ever been accorded, not even Sholem Asch, whose novels, including a trilogy about Jesus, had made him famous in the 1930s. Bashevis continued to publish in the Yiddish press as Varshavski, maintaining personal contact with his newspaper readers and juggling literary identities the way his male protagonists juggled two, three, or more women simultaneously.

When appearing on American talk shows he peddled jokes rather than Talmudic homilies, and in supervising translations of his fiction he flouted any notion of literary "authenticity" by giving one of his finest novels, *The Family Moskat*, two separate conclusions, the road to Zion for his Yiddish readers and, for Americans, the figure of Death as the promised messiah. The latter ending was closer to his instincts. If William Blake said of the author of *Paradise Lost* that "Milton was of the devil's party without knowing it," Bashevis went Milton one better by writing some of his best works in the voice of the Devil.

His cynicism, including about the future of Yiddish, I experienced at first hand. In the early 1970s, on my own initiative and as follow-up to my earlier collection of novellas about the Jewish shtetl, I began to translate David Bergelson's novel, *When All is Said and Done* (Later translated by Joseph Sherman under the title *The End of Everything*). I wanted to teach courses on the Yiddish novel in translation as well as in the original, and though I did not warm to this novel, it demanded inclusion in the canon. Around the figure of an unfulfilled young woman, Mirele Hurvits, Bergelson describes the sector of Russian Jewish youth that *did not* leave for America or Palestine. A female heroine was rare enough, and Mirele's indeterminacy captured the Chekhovian strain of Russian Jewish life. I learned from this book the Hebrew-Yiddish word *alakhsen*, literally "diagonal" but here implying life experienced "indirectly" as though secondhand. I appreciated Bergelson's style, often called impressionist, which uses indirect speech and description to convey the dejection and philosophic pessimism of the period after the failed 1905 revolution. Translating the novel was the only way to get it into the classroom.

When I was about a third of the way through, I got bogged down and realized that I could only persevere if I had the prospect of publication in hand. I phoned Bashevis to ask if he could suggest a likely publisher. His response: "No one is going to read Bergelson." He is not responsible for my dropping the project, though this certainly lent me no encouragement. That failure, however, did lead me to plan a Library of Yiddish Classics and to arrange for others to translate a series of books that would bring some of the best of this literature to English readers. After I had launched it with the indispensable help of Lucy Dawidowicz and Neal Kozodoy—more about them to come—I went back to Bashevis to ask for his support in publicizing the first volume, Sholem Aleichem's *Tevye the Dairyman.* This time, he dismissed that most popular and beloved of all Yiddish writers for being too "sentimental." I bit my tongue to refrain from saying that he sentimentalized evil more than Sholem Aleichem did goodness. "What is there then?" asks the title character Gimpel the Fool in the most famous of his stories, to which the Devil answers, "A thick mire, *a tifeh bloteh*."

My disappointment in the man never led me to dismiss the writer (or take his literary judgments seriously). Besides, his fame was drawing attention to Yiddish literature as a field of study and I could understand some of his distrust. This son of a rabbi and a rabbi's daughter was the most extreme example of the whiplash transition from tradition to modernity. Isaac grew up in the teeming heart of Jewish Warsaw but spent part of the First World War in the town of Bilgoray in his maternal grandfather's rabbinic household that functioned as the family had for generations. When he then returned to postwar Warsaw, his older brother Israel Joshua, who had gone AWOL from the Russian army, was already a well-known writer, part of a bohemian artistic circle. Isaac followed his brother in abandoning Jewish practice, but without ever trusting any alternative. In a moral no man's land, he doubted communism, socialism, and all ideological substitutes for Judaism without being able to return to their parents' Orthodoxy.

In Israel Joshua's shadow, he was given a job as proofreader at the literary weekly, *Literarishe Bleter*, where he began publishing under their mother's name (Batsheva's=Bashevis) to distinguish himself from his older sibling. His first published novel, *Satan in Goray*, appeared in 1936, on the eve of his move to New York, where his brother had immigrated before him and arranged for his visa and a job on the Yiddish daily *Forverts*. This maiden novel about the mid-seventeenth-century hysteria around the false messiah Shabtai Zvi I read as a brilliant fable about the frenzies propelling Nazism and communism, but the unfortunate timing of its publication and its conservative bent in a time of zealotry left it mostly ignored. Bashevis called his memoir of those years *Lost in America*, chronicling his personal insecurity in his early years of immigration.

Most urgently, Bashevis Singer had to find a way to cope with the annihilation of their parents and younger brother and their entire formative world. Of some of his wartime writing the South African Jewish novelist Dan Jacobson, who otherwise admired him, noted (where else but in a review in *Commentary*) how unfairly Bashevis "imported" radical evil into depictions of traditional Jewish society where they were explicitly abjured.

Y. L. Peretz had written similar neo-folktales about the devilish temptations of otherwise pious rabbis and good Jewish housewives, but whereas Peretz ultimately champions the good, Bashevis demonstrates the energy of evil. Inhabiting a young Devil, he seduces a young wife from inside a mirror. He shows a butcher launched into debauchery on the corpses of his slaughtered animals. Why, asked Jacobson, would he have attributed such invented acts of fornication and corruption to the Jews of Poland and Lithuania when he knew only the *murderers* of Jews had actually done such things—and worse?

I had a stake in this troubling question because Bashevis Singer was now the face of Yiddish literature for Americans who knew nothing else about it. The great writer, I had come to recognize, is one who works within the constraints of his language. So, for example, before creating his masterful character Tevye the Dairyman in 1894, young Sholem Rabinovitch had wanted to write great novels like Balzac and Zola about young men trying to find their place in societies that were becoming fluid enough to let talented individuals rise above the stations of their birth. After trying his hand at it, he had the artistic good sense to realize that such a project could not succeed under the given socio-political conditions of Yiddish speakers. Yiddish society and its language lent themselves to homier conflicts and more intimate expression. Recasting himself as the humorist Sholem Aleichem, he drew from the riches of the oral language for monologues and stories whose characters spoke for themselves. His writing unleashed the inherent genius of Yiddish that makes much of little, tasty gefilte fish from leftovers. He became both beloved and a "classic" by exploiting the *limitations* of his language.

The same was true for Bashevis, a gifted storyteller who had one of the richest Yiddish vocabularies of his generation. In fact, I had approached him for help in publicizing Sholem Aleichem because I thought he would recognize his affinity with the only other Yiddish storyteller in his league. Dan Jacobson's question answered itself. This Polish-Jewish boy had absorbed more of traditional and modern Jewish life than almost any of his contemporaries, yet without access to Hitler's Germany or Stalin's Russia he had none of the tools he needed to describe the evils they had unleashed. He could not avoid that subject, but neither could he hope to describe *them*. He put the demon to work in the idiom he had available. He had no surer way to portray the power of wickedness than through the language of its victims, and this he did in story after remarkable story. He delivered its ingenuity, energy and skillfulness, trickery and recklessness, mastery and power; no one reading Bashevis Singer would ever prattle about the "banality of evil."

To be sure, this wasn't all he wrote. In awarding him its Prize in Literature in 1978, the Nobel committee singled out *In My Father's Court*, in which the author appears as a child observing the goings on in his father's neighborhood rabbinic court. Bashevis honored this parental heritage in accepting the award.

> My father's home on Krochmalna Street in Warsaw was a study house, a court of justice, a house of prayer, of storytelling, as well as a place for weddings and Chassidic banquets. As a child I had heard from my older brother and master, I. J. Singer...all the arguments that the rationalists from Spinoza to Max Nordau brought out against religion. I have heard from my father and mother all the answers that faith in God could offer to those who doubt and search for the truth. In our home and in many other homes the eternal questions were more actual than the latest news in the Yiddish newspaper. In spite of all the disenchantments and all my skepticism I believe that the nations can learn much from those Jews, their way of thinking, their way of bringing up children, their finding happiness where others see nothing but misery and humiliation.

No matter how much he indulged the skeptic or heretic, Bashevis held up the faith of his parents as the gold standard of civilization, even as he insisted that gold was nowhere to be found. To apply a metaphor that he might have enjoyed, he worked both sides of the street. And for the Yiddish reader, unlike those who read him in translation, the bad comes swaddled in the language of the good.

ੲ

THE CULTURAL CRITIC IN ME would not bow altogether to literary genius, by which I mean that I could not judge a work solely by its literary merit without taking its ideas into account. I ran into this problem early on when I came upon anti-Jewish passages in world literature and realized that unless I simply read on, I would be deprived of much entertainment and enlightenment. (I once thought of writing on the Jew in the British murder mystery, where he was a frequent suspect and unpleasant besides, but never the killer.) Jews apart, could a work be truly insightful if it condoned or ignored racial prejudice or promoted what I considered evil? On the other hand, the moralizers who banned certain books were a warning against censorial judgments. What a letdown to read *Lady Chatterley's Lover* expecting to find some salacious material and how funny to realize it had warranted censorship!

I found just the writer I was looking for in Saul Bellow when I first read him in that pocketbook issue of *Discovery* that Ben brought home one day and was never disappointed reading him thereafter. His novel *Herzog* was the anchor of my dissertation and book on the schlemiel as modern hero. His every new story and novel and essay, capped by the memoir *To Jerusalem and Back,* filled me with gratitude, as though a battalion of reinforcements had just come over the hill to help me fend off the enemy. The military image comes to mind because we both knew the importance of confronting enemies, though we occasionally disagreed on who they were. We were also alike in not wanting to let go of the dead. *Humboldt's Gift,* his 1975 homage to the poet Delmore Schwartz, was close enough to my feelings for my brother who had died the previous year to make me ache with loss when I read it.

The New York Intellectuals were thinkers who valued literature higher than philosophy, and since the novel was their favored literary genre, Bellow was *primus inter pares* even before being awarded the Nobel Prize in Literature in 1976. His protagonists are all bookish, sensitive beings who can say things like, "At times I feel like a socket that remembers its tooth," or, about historically unwarranted optimism, "I had a Jewish life to lead in the American language, and that's not a language that's helpful with dark thoughts."

In the boldest of his novels, the eponymous spokesman is Mr. Sammler, an elderly Jew who had dug his way out of a Nazi mass grave, and during the fortnight of the novel in the late 1960s resides on New York's Upper West Side. Intelligent, learned, experienced, but blind in one eye and frail, he is frightened less by the pickpocket who stalks him or the students who shout him down or even by the penury he might have to endure in feeble old age than by the decline in civilized behavior all around him and the absence of authority to monitor that bad behavior. Because what frightened Sammler was precisely what was frightening me, reading his diagnosis offered hope of a cure. From a shrewd adult's perspective, he exposed the madness of the sexual revolution, the anti-intellectual distrust of anyone over thirty, the circus of irresponsibility. "[This] liberation into individuality has not been a great success."

Mr. Sammler is provoked into sharing his wisdom by the various characters who either seek or resist his advice, and though he is never stentorian, his defining point of view comes across with greater authority than in any other of Bellow's novels.

> [I]t is sometimes necessary to repeat what all know. All mapmakers should place the Mississippi in the same location, and avoid originality. It may be boring, but one has to know where he is. We cannot have the Mississippi flowing toward the Rockies for a change.

This was one of my favorite passages. Bellow endowed this character with the acquired experience of a European and someone fifteen years older than he was at the time he wrote this. I aspired to be that reliable mapmaker. A teacher's duty, an intellectual's duty, was to restore the reputation of plain Truth, if not the thing itself.

10
POLITICS

*W*hen I began writing on political subjects in the 1970s, I
prepared by imagining myself in the kosher bakery that was
a seven-minute drive from my Montreal home. My women friends, who
thought my affection for the place perverse, baked their own hallahs or sent
their husbands to do the shopping. But for over two decades I'd gone there
for encouragement in times of stress.

The bakery's staff had long since given up trying to keep order by
means of numbered tickets. The largely immigrant customers paid such
things no heed, shouting, "I was here first!" or elbowing others aside as if the
next loaf sold from under them might mean they would never feed their
families again. The cacophony on a Friday, not to speak of a holiday eve,
peaked when the trucks bearing gefilte fish arrived and the women grabbed
the packages before the deliverymen could reach the refrigerated shelves.

This fevered behavior sometimes proved too much even for me, but
this was where I felt I belonged, and when I began writing about politics, I
thought of it as my audience. My beloved author Mendele Mokher Sforim
had said he switched from Hebrew to Yiddish, the lower-status vernacular,
after asking himself for whom he wrote, and in the same vein, that bakery
is where I would have mounted my soapbox, if only to urge my readers/
listeners to turn down their anxieties a notch. "You are now in Montreal,
not in Munkacs. The Nazis have been defeated. The Canadian government

is formally committed to our protection. Israel is up and running. And there is enough food here to feed us all."

CR

IN THE 1960S, WHAT HAD been the Province of Quebec's "Quiet Revolution"— its measured evolution out of nativism and the grip of the Catholic Church—was transformed into a separatist movement promoting the French-speaking province's break from the rest of Canada. Its beginnings were violent. Members of the Front de libération du Québec (FLQ; Quebec Liberation Front) announced their presence through a series of bombings and the kidnapping in 1970 of the British trade commissioner and Quebec's labor minister Pierre Laporte. Laporte's murder justified then prime minister Pierre Trudeau's passage of the War Measures Act that brought in the army, curtailed civil liberties, and effectively ended the insurrection.

Regardless, the drive for political sovereignty became much more potent through the formation that same year of the Parti Québécois (PQ) whose leader René Lévesque fought for the sovereignty of Quebec through the democratic process. By 1976 he was elected premier of Quebec and called for the first referendum on the question of independence. The prospect of separation from the rest of Canada set off an exodus among English Canadians, including many Jews whose fate under nationalist movements elsewhere had hardly disposed them to welcome this latest incarnation.

Until this time, Montreal had been an ideal Jewish Diaspora, with two strong ethno-religious communities—English Protestant and French Catholic—encouraging our smaller one to flourish between them. Additionally, the influx of thousands of French-speaking Jews from Morocco beginning in the late 1950s had served to make the otherwise largely English-speaking Jewish community more at home with the province's French majority.

But now the "stay or leave" question became the default topic of every local Jewish gathering. Len and I did not seriously contemplate leaving. For one thing, having tried moving to Israel, we were disinclined to move again.

For another, Len's law school education at a French university and our ensuing friendships with his classmates had already made us almost as comfortable among French Canadians as among the English.

Hence our surprise when, at the end of an otherwise pleasant evening at
a French movie, a former law school classmate of Len's began scolding us for
having always conducted our conversations with him in English. Switching
instantly, we said, "*Mais si tu préférais....* But if you preferred French, why
didn't you say so?"

It soon became apparent that this was not the real point at issue.
Mutual friends told us that our friend had joined the PQ—from which we
were implicitly excluded. I might have sympathized with his predicament.
Obviously, he did not wish to be perceived by us either as an old-style
Roman Catholic xenophobe or as a new-style Quebec anti-Semite. But he
had preempted the possibility of my good will by effectively blaming us
for the estrangement *he* was initiating. This was such a familiar ploy that I
wondered how much more of that politics of blame would play itself out if
Quebec nationalism were to succeed in removing the province from the rest
of the country.

It would be several decades before Len and his old friend attempted
another serious conversation. Meanwhile, the debates swirled around us.
Some adherents to or fellow travelers of separatism even tried to solicit our
support for French sovereignty by reference to the state of Israel: "How can
you favor an independent Jewish state if you deny one to the Québécois?"
This analogy ignored the fact that French Canadians already enjoyed the
benefits of both an ethnic community and an unthreatened larger polity
that was equally *theirs.* Had I been in their place, I would have thought my
Québécois ambitions for maintaining the French language and culture could
best be achieved within the Canadian framework. That had worked so far to
preserve French identity and could be relied on to continue doing so.

Did French Canadians have legitimate grievances? Certainly not by the
standards of Jews, who had always lived as an ethnic-religious-linguistic
minority among others. What more could a group want than the freedoms
it already shared with all its fellow Canadians? Naturally, they saw it dif-

ferently: if they were a majority in the province, why not claim national sovereignty? Canadian business was conducted in English, putting French Canadians who were not bilingual at a disadvantage. Were they to create a sovereign state they could make French its *only* national language!

As I saw it, the rapid collapse of religious authority in Quebec with the death of Premier Duplessis had left a vacuum that nationalism came to replace. Some of the authoritarian features French Canadians objected to in the Church were passing into their politics. Tracking the history of the Jews under various kinds of governments and the behavior of different countries occupied by the Nazis, I had come to realize the importance of political culture in the life of a people and I trusted the British tradition more than the French, Edmund Burke more than Rousseau and Voltaire, and the Canadian mosaic more than ethnocultural hegemony. We were not about to leave Montreal, and hoped the separatist fervor would eventually peter out. But Len's French-Canadian former buddy was not alone in making us uncomfortable.

℞

I WAS EAGER TO WRITE ABOUT the implications of Québécois separatism for the Jewish community, urging engagement on the side of federalism that had served us—and not only us—so well. But I also felt inhibited, lacking proper certification.

Looking for a coauthor to supply the missing sanction, I found him in Irwin Cotler, who was already prominent in Jewish and political affairs and would later serve as member of Parliament for the Liberal Party, Canadian minister of justice, and attorney general. We had attended the same high school and summer camp a few years apart and became colleagues after he completed his legal studies and started teaching law at McGill. His interest in international law and human rights went hand in hand with his commitment to the security of Israel and the Jews, each strengthening his ability to advance the other. He and his American counterpart Alan Dershowitz of the Harvard Law School represented Soviet Jews wanting to emigrate to Israel and other victims of repressive regimes.

The McGill Law School was conveniently located right across from the Jewish studies office. It took us only one meeting to sketch out an article called "Quebec's Jews: Caught in the Middle." The piece appeared in *Commentary* in September 1977, not quite a year after the PQ, for the first time, won a majority in provincial elections and was now wielding power: "With a sense of eerie familiarity," we wrote, "Quebec's community of 115,000 Jews finds itself beset by a *crise de conscience*." On the one hand, we understood and even sympathized with aspirations for autonomy; but at the same time we worried about the inevitable fallout of these nationalist impulses. We also wondered at what point Jewish particularism, so acceptable in what was an atmosphere of ethnic pluralism, would "stick in the craw of a nationalist bid for domination."

Irwin and I resembled our French-Canadian counterparts as members of a community with a tremendous stake in its local institutions and way of life. Should Montreal Jewry make a special effort to adapt to the changing conditions? Or was this just further proof that the Diaspora can never provide a wholly comfortable home for Jews? We were posing a question that depended less on our proven ability to coexist with others than on the not-yet-certain ability of others to continue coexisting with us.

In describing the conflicting national aspirations of Jews and French Canadians, our article made one bad mistake that would return to haunt us:

> There are things in Jewish history too terrible to be believed but not too terrible to have happened. When the jubilant mass of *Parti Québécois* supporters at the victory rally on November 15 [1976] sang a French version of "Tomorrow Belongs to Me," the Nazi party song from *Cabaret* that has unfortunately been adopted as a French-Canadian nationalist hymn, it triggered in countless Jewish minds fresh images of stormtroopers and jackboots in the night.

Irwin and I had relayed this morsel about the song from local media without checking it out. In a damning response to the editor of *Commentary*, the Montreal composer Stéphane Venne protested that *"Demain nous appartient"* ("Tomorrow Belongs to Us") was *not* the French version of the song from *Cabaret* but his own original composition. This was deeply embarrassing, even though we certainly hadn't likened French Quebecers to Nazis but were rather reporting an instinctive Jewish reaction to the delirium of the PQ victory. We knew we were never in danger for our lives. At most we could be interpreted as saying that, whatever their intentions, those who unleashed nationalist passions could not necessarily keep them in check.

But one mistake was enough to challenge our credibility. Because our article appeared in a respected American publication, PQ leaders took it seriously and peppered us with protests. Irwin was already active in politics—on his way to a distinguished career—and his alarm over the damage to his reputation prompted me to write to Premier Lévesque taking exclusive responsibility for the essay. The internet can retroactively do what print cannot, which is why, in the web version, unlike in archived print copies, Irwin's name no longer appears as coauthor. For the record, though, I do insist on stating that the marvelous line "There are things in Jewish history too terrible to be believed but not too terrible to have happened" was his.

In the end, I resolved that I would henceforth (a) double check all of my facts and (b) never again partner with anyone. Irwin was certainly feisty and brave, and he and Alan Dershowitz, his friend and fellow law professor, put themselves at risk when they took up the defense of political dissidents. Alan was, like Irwin, a brilliant debater as well as legal prodigy, likewise a prominent political and legal commentator. Both were also passionate advocates for Israel and the Jews.

Yet this miscarried partnership forced me to see how I differed from these two champions of human rights. They needed always to be seen as the good guys, as *liberal* defenders. This meant not only staying formally within the Liberal and Democratic parties but continuing to insist that they were politically, philosophically, on the Left. Meanwhile, the PQ had flipped the political equation by turning our legitimate liberal concerns into a putative Right-wing, Anglo-American assault on *them*. The PQ stood for defensive ethnic nationalism and a centralized government that selectively *restricted* civil liberties. The separatists were now incipiently anti-liberal in the cause of an aggrieved minority. Like our erstwhile French-Canadian friend, they blamed us for the antagonism their party had initiated.

People who knew me at college have sometimes asked, "When did you turn *conservative?*" The short answer—when liberalism turned illiberal—fails to show the deviltry that lay in the details. Opposing Quebec's separation from Canada was a quintessentially liberal position: the position, in fact, of Canada's Liberal party. Irwin and I were fully justified in claiming that a Canadian federation offered its minorities better guarantees of toleration than would a small nationalist state. Using the Nazi analogy is rarely a good idea, and it was admittedly too freighted for the purpose. We would have done better to add that the British political tradition stood for pluralism, liberal democracy, and decentralized authority and to ask the PQ for better assurances that in seeking its rights, it would continue to respect ours. Minority rights were being threatened not by Canada but by the minority that wished to curtail those rights by claiming that theirs were being abridged.

Some of our fears proved justified: no sooner did the PQ assume power in the province than it passed a French-only language law, complete with policing force to monitor infractions. In seeking to impose linguistic hegemony on a pluralistic society, it denounced as regressive those who intended to protect Canada's guaranteed freedoms. Quebec's democracy had earlier been controlled by the autocratic union between the premier and the Catholic Church to which he and most of the population were faithful and which "protected" the faith as it saw fit. The control had now flipped to the side of a minority intent on righting what it considered historical injustice. Liberals, having emerged as a political force to fight autocracies, were on guard against such forms of repression, but could they recognize and repel leaders with ideologies intent on curtailing their freedoms from populist forces below?

Thankfully, most Quebecers would eventually choose as we did and rejected the separatist option, but on the rest of the continent coalitions of victimhood had begun mau-mauing the elites in the universities, media, and boardroom, all the way up to the highest political offices—mau-mauing being the offensive urban idiom for intimidating the white man into accepting his guilt. I coined the term "gliberals" for the gutted and gutless liberals who failed to stand up for classical liberal tenets when they were confronted by grievance and blame. I saw their collapse early on, but could not have imagined its speed.

C3

For all the anxiety it caused us, our situation in Quebec bothered me less than political challenges elsewhere on the North American continent. Culture and politics of the United States mattered so much more not just because they played out on a larger scale, but because America was the mainstay of liberal democracy. What happened there would determine its feasibility everywhere else. Drawing heavily on biblical and British sources, the founders of the United States had produced the world's largest, and so far most effective, democratic polity and now some of its clearest thinkers were warning that its future was imperiled.

Sharp warnings came from Norman Podhoretz, whom I had come to rely on as a "first responder" to current events. Norman was fearless about making enemies, which may be the greatest asset in political writing. Taking a political position is bound to be unpopular with at least one sector, sometimes the one to which one already belongs or aspires to join. Whether his clarity made him fearless or his fearlessness demanded clarity, he exemplified the connection between good English and morality that George Orwell draws in his essay, "Politics and the English Language." In Norman's case, speaking clearly meant breaking with the liberal consensus.

In *Breaking Ranks*, published in 1979 as a letter to his teenage son John, Norman explains his political evolution from a "young fogey" in the 1950s, to a radical in the 1960s, to a neoconservative in the 1970s. The intellectuals around *Partisan Review* and *Commentary* when he was starting out, including his teacher Lionel Trilling, had already repudiated communism and tried to free liberalism from any false nostalgia for the Marxist "idealism" of their youth. As part of their circle, he was old before his time, never having experienced their revolutionary phase.

He married young, assumed responsibility for his wife's children by a previous marriage and then two of his own, and ran a major magazine funded by a Jewish organization. That alone stamped him with the despised bourgeois label. But in the spirit of "better late than never," he rebelled in the early 1960s, when as *Commentary's* editor he published parts of Paul Goodman's anarchic *Growing Up Absurd* and Norman Mailer's insurrectionist *The Armies of the Night*—vivid antibourgeois writing that tested and proved his editorial independence.

That was the easy part. Anyone, Jew or Gentile, can stand up with impunity to a "Jewish establishment" that has very little political power because it is reluctant to exercise the power it has. By contrast, standing up to the Left required true grit. Podhoretz saw developing on his watch a "spiritual plague" that he understood all the better for having helped it spread: *Young whites* contemptuously repudiated everything American and middle class, and in the guise of idealism refused the responsibilities of becoming adult; *young blacks* had real external oppression to contend with but they, too, refused to accept responsibility for ills they alone could cure.

Norman was not alone in his concerns. In 1965 Irving Kristol and Daniel Bell founded *The Public Interest*, a periodical they said expressed "a trend in social thought that has been called the 'pragmatic left' or the 'new right.'" They knew its direction without precise definition. When critics dismissed them as "neoconservative," Kristol seized the advantage: it had not been a political movement until it acquired a name, and though it did not exactly fit my trajectory, I placed myself in their company. Meanwhile, from inside the academy, political scientist Jeane Kirkpatrick, who would soon make her appearance in *Commentary*, called it the movement of "blame America first," and formally switched her political allegiance from the increasingly Left-leaning Democrats to the Reagan Republicans.

President Reagan led the Republican party to electoral victories, and the United States went on to win the Cold War, but in the academy and the media it was still the Left that "determined what you were to think about and in what terms." Robert Warshow's description of communist influence in the 1930s was amazingly apt: the Left once again seized the moral high ground under the banner of progress and deployed the negative terms of racism and oppression to malign those who stood for old-style constitutional democracy. Montreal absorbed some of this process a little more slowly and mildly than Washington and New York, but by the late 1970s, many old-style liberals had lapsed into moral submission.

There was also a shift in social behavior to contend with. Montreal friends invited us to join them in smoking pot. "Would you like to try this joint?" "How about inhaling from this teapot?" Someone gave me a tab of what he assured me was a safe dose of LSD, which Len flushed down the toilet. In a single week I heard about two couples divorcing, a happenstance once seemingly as remote as malaria.

Not all the changes were equally unwelcome. I thought decriminalization of homosexuality and abortion long overdue. What hadn't occurred to me was that, in the rush to nonjudgment, tolerance would turn to advocacy, and advocacy into reverse orthodoxy. In our little Canadian corner of the world, young men and women who a generation earlier would have entered into heterosexual marriages now declared themselves gay and began living their lives accordingly. Having held standard views about the primacy and nature of family, I was stunned at how quickly those assumptions fell away.

Once, driving to the court for a tennis game, I mentioned to my friend that I was thinking of writing on this subject. "Oh, Ruth, don't!" she said. "Six of your friends will think that you are writing about their children." Even had I wanted to ask her to fill in that sentence she would not have done so—she observed the prohibition against such gossip more strictly than I did—but flipping through my mental rolodex for the rest of the ride I realized that I could have named those children, that I knew what I had not known that I knew. Though I would have wanted to continue to distinguish between *marriage* (as between man and woman) and *civil union* or some lovelier term for members of the same sex, my friend was right: I would not have wanted to hurt my friends or their children. No other social issue made it harder to defend "traditional values" against individual inclinations.

Abortion proved more complicated. There I had started out with no scruples at all, in fealty to my mother's experience in Romania when her obstetrician insisted on aborting a life in embryo, thereby enabling the escape and survival of our family. I assumed all obstetricians including mine would be of a similarly "realistic" cast of mind. When a friend and fellow patient of his complained to me that our doctor had refused to terminate an unwanted pregnancy, I confronted him expecting some witty comeback. Instead, he muttered, "I didn't go into medicine to become a human sewer."

Who knew that an obstetrician would nurture a passion for initiating life, and balk at ending it? After Quebec law was liberalized, a hospital administrator whom I knew took advantage of a retrenchment in medical facilities to shut down his hospital's obstetrics ward because abortions were outnumbering births. He, too, voiced his revulsion.

If I recoiled from the idea of terminating the life of a child-to-be through a form of retroactive birth control, I felt obliged to help those confronting the practical consequences of unwanted pregnancy. An opportunity arose when a social worker friend asked whether we could accommodate for several months a young pregnant woman who was going to give up her baby for adoption.

Quebec law at the time insisted that adoptions happen only within the same religious group; the result was plenty of unclaimed Catholic infants and a shortage of Jewish ones. In response, the local Jewish federation had come up with the idea of temporarily housing Jewish girls with unwanted pregnancies until they gave birth, thus enabling a local Jewish family to receive the child. Comfortably sequestered outside Jewish districts, these girls could pretend to be out of town and, after giving birth, resume their adolescent lives.

Our experience had a happy ending. The young mother who lived with us for five months gave up her child as arranged, went on to marry and raise a fine family of her own, and was later sought out by her grown daughter who wanted to know her birth mother as well. The longer I lived, the more I was persuaded that decriminalizing abortion was one thing, equating it with appendicitis quite another. Before long, however, any reservation about abortion as a given *right* was being silenced as reactionary heresy, along with any other limitations on "freedom of choice."

With Norman Podhoretz and Midge Decter. (Photo by Jill Krementz)

❦

DESPITE HAVING JOINED AN ORTHODOX synagogue, I felt a kinship with the Conservative Movement, and particularly with the Jewish Theological Seminary in New York, the denomination's rabbinic and intellectual center. It was there that most of the founding members of the Association for Jewish Studies had been educated, combining rabbinic ordination with advanced degrees in secular disciplines. At various times the husband-and-wife teams of Norman Podhoretz and Midge Decter and Irving Kristol and Gertrude Himmelfarb had studied at JTS, which also offered joint programs with Columbia University for undergraduates. My good friends Hillel Halkin and Gita Rotenberg had grown up in its afternoon school and Hebrew-speaking Ramah summer camps. The decision in 1972 by historian Gerson Cohen to leave his tenured professorship at Columbia University to assume the chancellorship of JTS seemed the harbinger of a newly energized American Jewish community.

JTS had been founded by European born and trained rabbis and scholars, all of whom I believe were still "Orthodox" in their practice. We tend to think that becoming modern meant moving from orthodoxy to reform, but the pattern of Jewish immigration to America had reversed that process. The early influx of German Jews established the reform version of Jewish religion in America, and only at the end of the nineteenth century did East European Jews form the Conservative Movement. As its intellectual center, JTS restored the traditional basis of Jewish learning and observance while taking for granted the benefits of acculturation and responsibilities of citizenship. Gerson Cohen was an American-trained Jewish historian who had succeeded Professor Salo Baron at Columbia and was now returning to one of the schools that had trained him. When he said he would "cease to write history in order to make history," I saw it as he did.

Cohen's move also alleviated some of my anxiety—and not mine alone—about one troubling aspect of the burgeoning field of academic Jewish studies. If the finest Jewish minds were to choose the university over the rabbinate, what would happen to the golden chain of the Jewish tradition in America? Cohen's decision to head JTS meant that centers of modern Judaism could coexist with secular universities. His intelligence and devotion to Israel convinced me that under his stewardship JTS would become one of the two foremost institutions of higher Jewish learning outside Israel, Yeshiva University being the other. Cohen solidified my faith in his leadership when he appointed my brother David to teach Yiddish literature and culture as part of JTS's academic and rabbinic curriculum.

David's account of his own career attributes to me his college choice of Brandeis over McGill. I was concerned about the hothouse quality of his life as Mother's muzinik, her youngest child, and since by that time Montreal students were attending American universities in greater numbers, I urged our parents to let him move out on his own. He flourished at Brandeis and went on there for a PhD in Jewish studies that included study at the Hebrew University in Jerusalem.

But the most decisive part of his education happened at the Boston Havurat Shalom, founded while he was a student. In 1968, Arthur Green, ordained rabbi at JTS with a PhD from Brandeis, created a countercultural urban commune modeled on the Hasidic movement that he was studying. Defying the exclusive attention to Talmudic learning that prevailed among

the Jewish communities of Eastern Europe, the Hasidic movement emphasized direct experience of the sublime—attachment to God and to the charis-
matic leaders who galvanized communities of worship.

The Havurah brought this Hasidic paradigm up to date, combining
study with passionate observance. The Havurah's house in Somerville was
just close enough to the surrounding universities to attract some of their finest students. David became an enthusiastic member and chronicler. He called
it a "combination ashram/ monastery/ *shtibl*/ *Lehrhaus*/ urban kibbutz"
embodying varieties of religious experience, though its lasting importance
to him was learning Jewish prayer and ritual. He brought to the group the
sophisticated Yiddish culture of our home and his native Montreal community, though we had never really learned to worship. Through the Havurah
he became a practicing Jew, and the religious instruction he acquired there
enriched his teaching of Yiddish and Hebrew literature.

The Havurah's official designation as a Seminary meant that its members were not subject to the military draft, a feature that did not apply to
David as a Canadian, but may have attracted others. It was almost exclusively male, and at first women who joined the group individually or as
spouses were not included among the ten males required to form a *minyan*. This changed after a few years, the very years David calls the group's
golden age. He does not make the connection between the abandonment of
Orthodox practice—the most consequential feature of which was the admission of women in prayer quorums—and the decline of the Havurah, which
quickly evolved into a center for feminism and gay rights. Much as I had
distrusted the Havurah's emphasis on spirituality, its male camaraderie and
intellectual competitiveness was something I considered a healthy part of
Judaism. But neither the Havurah nor the Conservative Movement from
which it spun off seriously considered how to expand the role of women
while resisting the feminist crusade.

One of the main impressions I had formed from my study and personal
experience of Jewish life was the unique vulnerability of maleness. The main
task ordinarily assigned to the male of the human species was protection of
the female. Warrior and lover defined the hero from Arthurian legends to

American Westerns, and in the Bible too if one thinks of Joshua and David. Militant feminists were arguing that these cultural traditions were no more than patriarchal constructions to rationalize male dominance at the expense of female autonomy, but Jewish political dependency in the Diaspora had upended that standard of heroism in any event because Jewish men were not allowed to soldier in defense of their families. Whether biological or political, Jews could not match the militant idea of maleness and so they elevated intellect and learning instead. They praised rabbis who "swim like Leviathan through the sea of the Talmud" and Jews who soldiered in the army of the Lord. Sexuality was domesticated. "Who is a hero?" asks the Talmud and answers, "He who conquers his urge." Jews had ingeniously adapted to the Diaspora by creating models of masculinity that suited their circumstance, and the reckless removal of those independent standards could be the undoing of Jewish men altogether. Israel had too many real enemies to give up on male protectors but not so American liberalism or the Jews in its orbit.

CR

I DIDN'T LOOK FOR CONTROVERSY, but it came to me unasked. A mere seven years after Gerson Cohen became chancellor of JTS, the Conservative Movement issued a twenty-seven-page ruling approving the ordination of women as rabbis. Even someone as deficient in Talmudic expertise as I could see that the movement's avowedly cautious and "conservative" approach to innovation had been unceremoniously sacrificed to modern feminist pressure. Had JTS's rabbinic authorities really framed their arguments for this decision in conformity with the movement's own guidelines? Had a cohort of female Talmudists risen to rival or surpass their teachers in mastery of sources? Had growing synagogue membership and intensified devotion on the part of conservative women required such a tradition-defying innovation?

Had any of those been the case, the decision might have marked a religious breakthrough. Instead, Judaism was being asked to align itself with the tenets of the new women's movement without subjecting those tenets themselves to the slightest scrutiny. The relaxation of norms, I felt certain, would simply hasten the *decline* in religious observance that had prompted the movement to inaugurate such a change, and JTS to bless it in the first place. Judaism's hard internal logic was necessarily in tension with the pressure for progress at any cost, and giving in to change without anticipating the unanticipated consequences was a recipe for even greater assimilation.

Commentary's invitation to review this ruling and its supporting documents gave me a chance to register my dismay and the basis for my concerns.

> When the women's movement began to show some muscle in the late 60s and early 70s, I decided it was a passing fad, like the Hula-Hoop. It did not seem possible to me that ideas in such obvious contradiction of the facts should be able to inspire and propel a serious mass movement. Convinced that women were the practical gender, I was sure they would never be deceived by false ideology, and I expected the movement to evaporate as quickly as it had materialized. It was the worst cultural prediction of my life.

By the time I wrote that passage in the late 1980s, it was clear that a secondhand Marxism, in the form of second-wave feminism, had already prevailed. A friend had given me Betty Friedan's book, *The Feminine Mystique*, saying it had made her an ardent advocate. I dutifully read: "The feminine mystique says that the highest value and the only commitment for women is the fulfillment of their own femininity."

Friedan accused male-dominated American society, operating through women's magazines and Madison Avenue advertising agencies, of guilt-tripping housewives who aspired to anything beyond their daily drudgery. Psychotherapy had allegedly assisted the process. Freud, in whose Vienna women had been denied all opportunities to realize their full potential, developed theories rationalizing their culturally induced anxiety and making it seem essential to female nature. Although feminists and suffragettes had won the fight for civic equality, they had been defeated by the *mystique* that prevented women from exercising their acquired rights. And whereas American women had earlier served in the workplace, especially when needed in wartime, that interval of empowerment was brief, quickly yielding to re-infantilization in peacetime. Friedan urged these stunted creatures to emerge from the "immaturity that has been called femininity to full human identity."

Reading this, I could not have been more surprised had my friend offered to sell me the Brooklyn Bridge. Women infantilized by men? Nothing was more condescending to women than Friedan's image of us as so many dependent childlike puppets. My female contemporaries and I had married young, and fortunate were we whose husbands cherished and supported us. When our son Billy was born at the start of Christmas week I sang along with the radio, "For unto us a child is born. Unto us a son is given!" The births of Jacob and Abby were the subsequent high points of our life. Our children are the best contribution we women would make to society and the universe. Men, subordinate players in this ultimate human act of creation, would assert their power in other ways.

About the inner motivations of Southern women like the civil rights heroine Rosa Parks or the brilliant literary artist Flannery O'Connor I knew very little. But I saw precisely how a Jewish woman like Friedan had crudely applied Marxist economic assumptions to relations between the sexes, substituting gender warfare for class conflict. About Jews I knew she was wrong. In traditional European communities, which placed a premium on study as a religious imperative, the equivalents of Friedan's "middle-class" women had been expected to support their studious husbands. When Jews turned modern, they attacked those socioeconomic arrangements and mocked Jewish men as irresponsible *luftmentshn* who lived off their wives or abandoned them to run off to America.

At the turn of the twentieth century, Jewish polemics, rising to the level of slander, portrayed husbands, fathers, and brothers feebly witnessing the rape of their womenfolk by rampaging pogromists. In a caricature that would be cheerfully exploited by Nazi Aryan propagandists, Otto Weininger's *Sex and Character*(1903) assessed Jewish men as genetically feminized. Yiddish and Hebrew literature condemned Jewish men's reliance on working women as against the "positive" Western European standard of male breadwinners. In fact, Jewish immigrant women in America who worked in the sweatshops dreamed of the day when their fathers or husbands would earn enough to let them raise their families at home. Friedan denigrated all that her predecessors had aspired to.

Of course, greater leisure had created a vacuum as well as an opportunity. But suburban women had been relieved of some of their heaviest burdens—and fears. On Rosh Hashanah, the Jewish New Year, when synagogue attendance was highest, the biblical readings featured the experience of two barren women, Sarah and Hannah—childlessness having been from time immemorial the greatest misfortune of women and humankind, with the death of a child a close second.

All of my female forebears had lost children, my mother one, her mother several, my paternal grandmother five of the ten she bore. Ours was the first generation that could expect to raise all of our children to maturity. Scientists—men, until recently—had worked this miracle. Birth control and fertility treatments, epidurals and cesarean sections, vaccines and antibiotics, vitamin supplements and mammograms prolonged and improved our lives. The incredible lightness of being a modern woman in a Western democracy ought to have elicited hosannas beyond the thanks we owed God for the gift of life itself. Whatever anxieties accompanied the fact of greater opportunity, how could women confuse their relief from the historical dangers of childbirth and child rearing with some kind of patriarchal oppression?

In fact, in both my friend's family and mine, responsibility fell unfairly on firstborn sons. My older brother Ben loved music and literature, composing and writing, and would have wanted to pursue the bookish professions of his younger siblings. But men were expected to support families, giving their wives the option of working outside the home or not.

I myself had taken full advantage of being female to work part time when it suited me, and I thought so little about wages that from the time McGill first hired me I initiated no discussion of salary or rank. After a committee meeting to consider a colleague's promotion, the dean of arts asked me why I was still at the associate level. When I said I didn't know, he replied that, very well, he would put the process in motion, and the next thing I knew I was a full professor. My casual approach to salaried employment changed only in the 1990s when we moved to Cambridge so that I could assume a position at Harvard, and Len gave up most of his Montreal legal practice. Only then did I appreciate what insouciance I had enjoyed at his expense.

None of this prevented me from pressing for women's legal and political rights, properly understood. Some unfairness was a reality as I knew from experience. I lobbied the Quebec government for the right to deduct expenses for a proportion of childcare—otherwise, I could not earn my salary—and fought our hospital when told only fathers could authorize operations on their children. These and other holdovers from Quebec's Catholic patriarchy were in any case being phased out. Once women in greater numbers joined the McGill faculty, the university opened its formerly restricted faculty club to us for membership.

I never thought such welcome evolutionary developments warranted an ideological power struggle between the men and women whose loving partnership was the bedrock of any sane society, and I feared that the politicization of gender would damage America at least as much—if not more—than communism did Russia. The resemblance of politicized feminism to Bolshevism was never far from my mind.

CR

SWITCHING PARTY AFFILIATION IS GENERALLY the last phase of political evolution. Though hers had no direct influence on mine, I associate my own realignment with Jeane Kirkpatrick and her November 1979 essay in *Commentary*, "Dictatorships and Double Standards." Her analysis of American foreign policy became a key text in the emergence of neoconservatism and won its author President Ronald Reagan's appointment as U.S. Ambassador to the United Nations. In that article she set out—as I later tried to do with different evidence—how "liberalism" slips from its moorings into the adversarial illiberal and potentially totalitarian camp.

Kirkpatrick, a professor of political science, was writing this when the Cold War between America and the Soviet Union was still at its height. The

United States had already suffered its defeat in Vietnam when President Jimmy Carter took office in January 1977, and while the Soviet Union used the period of his tenure to dramatically expand its weaponry and influence in Africa, Asia, and Central America, the United States experienced a cascade of economic miseries and setbacks in foreign influence. Kirkpatrick focuses on failures on two fronts: the takeovers by Marxists in El Salvador and Nicaragua and by the theocratic Ayatollah Khomeini in Iran. About Central America she writes:

> The pattern is familiar enough: an established autocracy with a record of friendship with the U.S. is attacked by insurgents, some of whose leaders have long ties to the communist movement, and most of whose arms are of Soviet, Chinese, or Czechoslovak origin. The "Marxist" presence is ignored and/or minimized by American officials and by the elite media on the ground that U.S. support for the dictator gives the rebels little choice but to seek aid "elsewhere." Violence spreads and American officials wonder aloud about the viability of a regime that "lacks the support of its own people." The absence of an opposition party is deplored and civil-rights violations are reviewed. Liberal columnists question the morality of continuing aid to a "rightist dictatorship" and provide assurances concerning the essential moderation of some insurgent leaders who "hope" for some sign that the U.S. will remember its own revolutionary origins. Requests for help from the beleaguered autocrat go unheeded, and the argument is increasingly voiced that ties should be established with rebel leaders "before it is too late." The President, delaying U.S. aid, appoints a special emissary who confirms the deterioration of the government position and its diminished capacity to control the situation and recommends various measures for "strengthening" and "liberalizing" the regime, all of which involve diluting its power.

Through that series of reproving quotes, Kirkpatrick reconstructs the way America's policies encourage the worst consequences over the merely bad. She traces the same pattern in the fall of the shah in Iran, and this article, appearing as it did—just after Iranian students had attacked the U.S. Embassy in Tehran to seize and hold more than fifty American hostages—explained with eviscerating precision how liberal policies had all but ensured this humiliation.

> The failure to distinguish between authoritarian and totalitarian regimes actually collaborated in the replacement of moderate autocrats friendly to American interests with less friendly autocrats of extremist persuasion. In Jimmy Carter–egalitarian, optimist, liberal, Christian–the tendency to be repelled by frankly non-democratic rulers and hierarchical societies is almost as strong as the tendency to be attracted to the idea of popular revolution, liberation, and progress. Carter is, par excellence, the kind of liberal most likely to confound revolution with idealism, change with progress, optimism with virtue.

I was struck by how closely her analysis matched my understanding of the moral fiasco of various misguided Israeli "peace" initiatives and realized that I could neatly have substituted "Jewish" for "Christian" in what was really the failure of liberal thinking.

Like other Montreal Jews, I had always voted Liberal in the reflexive way that most American Jews vote Democratic. When my cousin Hela's new American husband revealed he had voted in 1964 for Barry Goldwater, my instinct was that she needed to be rescued from this ill-fated match. By the time Reagan became president in 1980, I was ready to welcome his leadership in the Cold War—my conversion, like Kirkpatrick's, having been largely determined by considerations of foreign policy.

In the way that she worried for Central America, I worried for Poland—a once-independent country that had fallen under Soviet domination. Her distinction between authoritarian and totalitarian governments applied to the efforts of Poland's anticommunists to free their land from what Reagan was not afraid to call "the evil empire." Indeed, among my overseas concerns, Poland, the land of my immediate ancestors, was second only to Israel. I had long wanted to visit, and in the spring of 1978 had seized on the chance to join W. on a trip to Warsaw.

The two of us had met as McGill graduate students when W.—the only person in that painfully polite crowd to comment on the advanced stage of my pregnancy—had offered to take notes for me when I would be absent. Now a freelance writer, she had a grant from the Canada Council to travel to Poland to interview Fred Rose, a one-time member of Canada's parliament later convicted of spying for the Soviet Union. It was rumored that W.'s communist parents had once hidden this man from the Royal Canadian Mounted Police, yet she was now being subsidized to visit a person the government had condemned to permanent exile.

Though political opposites, W. and I were ideally matched as travel companions, since we could pursue our separate daytime quests and come together for respite in the evenings. Sharing a hotel room would be efficient and pleasant.

A strange mood came over me that week in Poland. I had never been timid, but from the minute we landed I became fearless to the point of bellicosity. I pretended to speak Polish, of which I knew but a dozen phrases, and felt utterly at ease in this place where almost three million Jews had been murdered. On a cold late afternoon, I kept my taxi driver waiting while I trekked around the former Treblinka extermination camp, recalling everything I had read about what transpired there. In the nearby town of Tykocin, where I had been told the local synagogue was being restored, the caretaker insisted she did not have the key. I sat down on the ground and commanded: "I am from Canada. I stay here until I am allowed in." Reinforcing my sense of invincibility, she managed to retrieve the key. Once she opened the door, the beauty of the synagogue so overwhelmed me that I collapsed on the floor and couldn't stop sobbing.

Though we had no intention of meshing our interests, W. felt obliged to bring me along when Fred and Fanny Rose asked to meet me. After a few minutes, I realized that this elderly couple may have had more in common with me at that point than with W., who had shed the Jewish part of her leftist inheritance. They knew they had made the wrong choice and were eager for news of Israel. As the editor of an English language Polish state publication, Fred already had access to information about Israel's domestic and foreign affairs. But I was able to supply fresh impressions of the country and even a little news about some of their acquaintances who had moved there after an uptick in Polish anti-Semitism in the late 1960s. I kept to myself that I found contemporary Warsaw circa 1978 shockingly worse off than Tel Aviv in 1957, when rationing was still in force.

Saying our goodbyes, Fred asked what further sites lay ahead of us. When I said I planned to spend a day at Auschwitz, he insisted that W. accompany me, either because he thought I needed someone to stand by me or, more likely, for her edification. It was snowing when she and I entered the camp in early May, and we encountered very few other visitors as we walked through the empty barracks, some of them still equipped with special torture facilities.

After going through a couple of buildings, each devoted to a different ethnic subset, I asked to see the recently announced "Jewish pavilion," and refused to take no for an answer when informed it was not yet open to the public. Staging a sit-down as I had done at Tykocin, I declared that *jestem za Kanadu*—as a Canadian I intended to stay until we were shown the building. A guard summoned an administrator who escorted us by flashlight through the unfinished exhibition.

On one wall of this pavilion, a full-length blown-up photograph showed an armed Nazi soldier herding naked women, some trying to cover their breasts, to their death. As we left the building, W. said, "Did you get a load of those tits?"—an indelicate but piercing commentary on the way this presumed commemoration catered to and exploited pornography. These women had not signed releases for the use of their images.

Unlike W., I had come to Poland that first time with no one to contact except a woman originally from Vilna who had acted as go-between for Mother in sending parcels to her former schoolfriend Ida Erik in the Soviet Union. Her schoolmate's late husband, Max Erik, had been one of the rising Jewish intellectuals of Vilna in the 1930s, a Yiddish literary historian who had slipped across the closed border in 1929, lured by the communist regime's support for Yiddish scholarship. It is hard to know how forcibly or willingly he had adjusted his literary criticism to state directives that kept tightening over the next few years. However hard he tried, it was not judged to be enough: he was arrested, sent to a labor camp, and executed in 1937, which was one of the reasons Mother feared to place his widow under further suspicion by trying to reach her directly and used the Polish liaison instead.

Mother's intermediary undertook to give me a guided walking tour through once-Jewish Warsaw, ending at the memorial to the Warsaw Ghetto Uprising of 1943, which stood in the small, cleared area still so shabby I could almost envision the ghetto conditions I had been reading about for years. But my companion wanted to talk about something other than the war. She had been a student and political conscript of Erik's, and several years after his departure, she followed him to the Soviet Union. Arrested there and sent into the Gulag, she was shocked to meet him in a labor camp, after (so she heard) he had already attempted suicide. He did not want to talk except to tell her, "It was better under the Tsars." This was the message she wanted to impart to me.

Everything I saw and experienced on that trip turned me all the more strongly against communism (and possibly turned W. more strongly away from her Jewishness), but closer to Poland. A few years later, Len and I traveled there with our children. In subsequent years, I joined scholars from the Hebrew University on several study tours to Poland and Lithuania. On one of my private visits, I met with distinguished Catholic intellectuals and their younger counterparts who had started a dissident Polish version of *Commentary*. I felt more at home sitting with these intense anticommunists in a dark Polish coffeehouse than with my politically indifferent friends in Montreal. The small rural churches overflowing on Sundays convinced me that the Polish people would someday win back its sovereignty from the Soviets just as it had from the Tsars and the Germans.

CR

As MENTIONED ABOVE, I HAD always voted Liberal. And so, in the heady days when Pierre Elliot Trudeau served as Canada's prime minister—1968–1984, with a brief intermission—Len and I were close to his political circles. The two men had graduated in law from the Université de Montréal, Trudeau as the consummate insider and Len (several years earlier) as one of eight "Anglos," six of them Jews, in a class of 125. Len had prepared Trudeau's marriage contract to Margaret Sinclair in 1971, and he would eventually take our children and a nephew to Ottawa to visit our Liberal prime minister in his office. Only in 1981 did the camaraderie and the politics collide when Trudeau supported the Soviet-backed Polish government's crackdown on dissidents.

The main foreign policy function of Western liberal democracies, as I saw it, was to oppose the Soviets and the Soviet-Arab alignment against Israel. Solidarity—in Polish, Solidarność, led by Lech Wałęsa—was the first independent trade union in a country ruled by communism, and thus the most hopeful presage of democracy since the failed Hungarian uprising of 1956. Wałęsa joined Poland's Catholic intelligentsia in what then became a two-pronged challenge to Soviet might.

How could Trudeau justify the communist suppression of Poland's striking trade unionists? Some said that, having himself called in Canadian troops against threats of violence by Quebec nationalists, he had to support the Polish government's analogous jailing of Polish strikers. I thought, to the contrary, that our prime minister's determination to keep Quebec free in a united Canada should have made him all the more supportive of a free and politically independent Poland, and I'd expected him to lend his political support to the Polish workers.

It took me a while to realize that, as an ideological leftist, Trudeau was reluctant to appear in the guise of a cold war anticommunist. Even as, in Washington, President Reagan was creating the Strategic Defense Initiative to stave off the Soviet nuclear threat and readying himself for the day he would demand that Mikhail Gorbachev "tear down" the Berlin Wall, our prime minister was failing the cause of Polish independence.

From my own gnarled relation to Poland I recognized clearly enough that politics requires triangulation—that one set of values can contradict another. I knew of Jews killed by Poles for money or spite, and in wartime by Polish collaborators with the Nazis. I knew that Jews returning to their towns after the war were often chased off, and sometimes killed by locals. There was plenty of blood on those hands. Yet Poland had housed Jews for seven centuries, and its innate democratic traditions made it the most promising potential ally of America and Israel in the years ahead. Without deprecating the need for historical reckoning, I put the cause of political freedom higher. Here was yet another example of Jeane Kirkpatrick's differentiation of bad from worse and of the cautionary teaching of my guide in Warsaw. If Trudeau wavered on supporting solidarity, in what meaningful way could his government pretend to be "liberal?"

We do not owe the same allegiance to political parties as we do to God, our families, our people, and our countries of citizenship. When parties change what they stand for, so must we. After Trudeau, I never again reflexively voted a Liberal-party ticket or any other, and in time I began writing a column to argue these dissident views of politics and culture.

11

CONTENTION

A student would occasionally ask me whether political adversaries could also be friends. I would try to explain that circumstances govern the answer. Otherwise compatible Gentile and Jewish laboratory partners in 1930s Berlin would have discontinued their scientific collaboration had the former decided to join the Nazi party; by contrast, tennis partners in the United States were unlikely to split up after the 1984 election if one had voted for Ronald Reagan and the other for Walter Mondale.

But why not offer a complicated case of my own?

Irving Howe was important to me as a writer and editor before I came to know him as a friend. In an earlier chapter I've described how *A Treasury of Yiddish Stories*, the 1954 anthology he coedited with the American Yiddish poet Eliezer Greenberg, helped me persuade McGill's English department to let me teach Yiddish literature under its auspices. Howe's introduction to this brilliant collection did much to establish the cultural, as opposed to the narrowly ethnic, value of Yiddish literature.

The child of Yiddish-speaking immigrants, Irving had come of age during the Depression and this experience of hardship continued to define him more than anyone else I knew. His family had suffered a reversal, which is harder than growing up in poverty and may have given him a personal stake in the socialism he began to preach on soap boxes in his teens and continued to expound as editor of *Dissent*, the quarterly magazine he cofounded with Lewis Coser in 1954. On Irving's political map, socialism was not on the far left, as it figures in American politics, but in the center between the poles of Stalinist communism and McCarthyism, broadly defined as "a campaign or practice that endorses the use of unfair allegations and investigations." Senator McCarthy's overzealous anticommunist campaign through the House Un-American Activities Committee (HUAC) that raged in the early 1950s was in fact halted by the senator's own colleagues in 1954, yet some on the Left continued to exploit its evil reputation to recast conservatives as protofascists and themselves as the firewall against tyranny. Irving was among them. While most of the others in his intellectual cohort shifted into the conservative wing of American politics, Irving sentimentalized the politics of his childhood. The kind of political revisionism I believed he practiced is what drew me to Mr. Sammler's teaching that all mapmakers avoid originality: "We cannot have the Mississippi flowing toward the Rockies for a change." The United States was wholesomely divided between liberals and conservatives, and to replace liberalism by socialism or conservatism by McCarthyism was to exchange the Mississippi for the Colorado.

But my friendship with Howe began without any such political component. Irving said he'd returned to the Yiddish of his immigrant upbringing when looking for solace at a time of political discouragement in the early 1950s. Whatever motivated him, he found in "Leyzer" Greenberg the ideal partner for a project that neither of them could have undertaken on his own. Until then, American Jewish writers in Yiddish and American Jewish writers in English had coexisted with almost no interaction between them. But when the Yiddish writer Greenberg came across a review by the English writer Howe of a book of Sholem Aleichem's stories in translation, it occurred to him that this man could help him introduce Yiddish literature to American readers. Their collaboration began at their first meeting.

Howe understood spoken Yiddish but read the language at only a beginner's level. In determining whether or not to include a given author, and if so, which stories, Greenberg would read aloud a selection of work and the two would then debate their way to a decision—an editorial process that Howe said made him much more familiar with the lesser writers than with the greats. This association was so satisfying that they followed up the first *Treasury* with another on Yiddish poetry.

In 1970, Howe asked me to translate an essay for their third anthology, *Voices from the Yiddish*. As translators were then in short supply, and as such an anthology would be useful in my own project of teaching Yiddish literature in English translation, our collaboration made perfect sense and was mutually beneficial. Correspondence with Irving about my assigned essay on the humor of Sholem Aleichem quickly moved to a first-name basis and into a working friendship that must have resembled his with Greenberg: he deferred to me on points of scholarship and I to him on most points of English style. In reading literature, he impressed me as having the literary equivalent of perfect pitch.

I also liked his idea that transposing from emotionally inflected Yiddish to English required "lowering the temperature," though it was clear that he felt free to make generalizations of this kind because he was uninhibited by too much knowledge. For example: speaking as a socialist, he would affectionately refer to Yiddish as "the literature of the little man" or, sometimes, "the little Jew" without considering the negative connotation of that phrase in Mendele Mokher Sforim's debut Yiddish novel, where it refers to a corrupt little schemer. Admiring the grand formulations in his own writings, I would have liked to split the difference between intellectuals who knew a little about a lot and scholars who knew a lot about a little.

As the two partners were preparing their fifth anthology, Greenberg suffered a stroke; Irving asked me to help him finish the book. Our work went so well that a few years later, when Irving was invited by Martin Peretz, publisher of the *New Republic*, to edit a collection of Sholem Aleichem stories for a new line of books under the magazine's imprint, he asked me again to be his partner. The introduction to *The Best of Sholem Aleichem* was written by us together in the form of an exchange of letters.

Martin Peretz, New York, 2015. In 1992, Marty endowed the Chair in Yiddish literature at Harvard that helped to stock the field of Yiddish studies in America.

Irving's industry amazed me. I once came to his apartment as he was going through the mail; he opened an envelope, glanced at the contents, wrote a reply when warranted on a prestamped postcard, then dropped the rest into the wastebasket and thereby disposed of the pile in a matter of minutes. He referred to his essays as *shtiklakh*, negligible piecework, yet could not seem to live without publishing.

As the junior partner in our association, I left entirely to him the negotiations for our Sholem Aleichem volume, without realizing that he might have regarded a simple request for payment as an unforgivable betrayal of his socialist principles. Agreeing to $2,000 for each of us, he forfeited royalties entirely, leaving us without recompense when the book received a front-page notice in the *New York Times Book Review* and proceeded to go through several editions. He did no better financially with our next project, the *Penguin Book of Modern Yiddish Verse*, on which we began work in the early 1980s and for which we recruited as coeditor Khone Shmeruk of the Hebrew University.

To be sure, financial profit was the last thing on our mind in that three-way New York-Montreal-Jerusalem partnership in which Irving recruited the translators, Khone and I made the first cut of poems, and Irving and I determined the final manuscript. What would have taken Khone and me a dozen years was managed by Irving in just two. Once we had decided on the contents, it was my job to provide our translators with literal prose renderings of the poems and to point out linguistic features or allusions they were likely to miss. Few of the translators had more than a basic knowledge of Yiddish; some had none at all. But we felt that in working with the last great living Yiddish writers we were performing a sacred act of cultural transmission, and were thrilled when poets John Hollander, Cynthia Ozick, Irving Feldman, Chana Bloch, Robert Friend, and others turned in poems as good as their own.

Only one of our problems proved insurmountable. Since (for reasons already explained) I was no longer in the good graces of the notoriously testy Chaim Grade, it was left to Irving to secure permission for the poem we intended to include. Grade agreed that Hillel Halkin would translate an excerpt from *Mussarists,* a narrative poem based on the author's youth in an exceptionally harsh Polish yeshiva.

Poet and novelist Chaim Grade, left, with Joseph Mlotek, writer, prominent figure in the Yiddish cultural world and managing editor of the Yiddish *Forward*. New York, December, 1978. (Gift of Harry Kronenberg)

But Grade died in April 1982, before giving us his written consent. We turned to his widow, Inna Hacker Grade, who replied by telegram: "CHAIM

GRADE'S INSTRUCTIONS WERE TO FORBID IRVING HOWE THE TRANSLATION AND/OR PUBLICATION OF ANY OF HIS WORKS. COPIES OF THIS TELEGRAM GO TO OUR LAWYERS." In what he would call one of his most masterful literary compositions, Irving replied tartly that the telegram was not really necessary—"a postcard would have had the same result"—and reminded her that her husband had actually given his verbal approval. "We all know the kinds and degrees of damage that have been done to literature by various agencies," he added, "ranging from state censorship to foolish advisers. But tell me—has anyone yet written a study of the damage done by widows?"

Although we did indeed suspect the widow of exerting her power less over us than over her deceased husband, Irving never wrote that study about this most intimate form of posthumous contention. As for our anthology, it featured only thirty-nine of our projected forty poets. At several points thereafter, this zealous widow sent lawyers' letters to my university, claiming that I had passed myself off as the author of her husband's work. These incidents were funnier in the telling than when they transpired.

∞

WHEN IRVING AND I BEGAN working together in the 1970s, his marriage to Ariel Mack was unraveling and he was recovering from a political hit. The socialist credentials that should have won him the respect of the then-flourishing New Left instead turned its members against him with the special venom reserved for closest rivals. He was older, respectable, and by their standards, neither culturally nor politically radical enough. He, for his part, was trained in ideas and committed to the democratic process. Inevitable clashes with activists like Tom Hayden alienated him from student revolutionaries who were using the war in Vietnam as a pretext to trash American institutions. As his former student and intellectual biographer Edward Alexander would later write, the "traditional university"—where from time to time Irving would find a home—was "the one institution that Howe very much wanted to *conserve*."

Irving's quarrel with the New Left was aggravated by his newfound attachment to Israel. Jewish political sovereignty in the Land of Israel had been a missing component in the intellectual and moral life of these Jewish intellectuals, who lacked the visceral attachment Ben and I had felt to the Jewish homeland. Educated in public schools with barely bar mitzvah exposure to Jewish sources, they retained warm feelings for their immigrant homes but developed their notion of "the learned American" largely ignorant of Jewish matters and without shared responsibility for the Jewish people. When my generation began reading them, we were amused by errors like Alfred Kazin's reference to *kosher—bosher* on the butcher shop window in his memoir, *A Walker in the City.* Any Jewish schoolchild knows that meat is *basar*, that the same Hebrew-Yiddish letter Shin turns to Sin when the dot is on the left, not the right. That manuscript must have passed through half a dozen Jewish hands before publication, yet no one had corrected this gaffe. The murder of Leon Trotsky in Mexico by Stalin's assassins absorbed them more than the massacres of Jews in Europe or the British blockade of Palestine.

In answer to my question many years later about the apparent indifference of his literary cohort to the fate of their fellow Jews, Saul Bellow said, "America wasn't a country to us. It was the world." To this Irving Howe might have added, it was the world some of us were in the process of turning socialist. The Left believed in an international order, and in its struggle for universal rights disdained what it considered the narrower fight for a Jewish homeland.

This changed with the war. Oddly enough, it was Jean-Paul Sartre's "discovery" of anti-Semitism under the Nazi occupation and his *Réflexions sur la question juive*, published in *Commentary* in 1948 as "Anti-Semite and Jew," that alerted them to their oversight. Sartre's intermittently brilliant and mistaken analysis of what makes the former anti-Jewish and what keeps the latter Jewish pricked their conscience and triggered their interest. They picked up on questions like what it meant to be a Jewish writer in the English language, the status of anti-Semitism in America, Jewish identity, Zionism, and the building of Israel. Irving Howe's recovery of his Jewishness began with Yiddish, but finally he, too, came to appreciate what the Jews had wrought. Admitting that he had never been among "those who danced in the streets when Ben-Gurion made his famous pronouncement that the Jews, like other peoples, now had a state of their own," he dropped his earlier indifference or hostility to Zionism when Arab armies encircled Israel in 1967, and later took his first trip to the Jewish state.

Irving's cultural investment in Jewishness and war with the New Left also drew him closer—temporarily—to the people around *Commentary*. He and I joked that we were now like the eponymous "neighbors" of a poem by Joseph Rolnick in our Penguin anthology. The poet feels that his earlier estrangement from a communist Yiddish writer matters less than their cultural affinities:

We talk like good old friends,
we talk plainly and honestly,
though he's left through and through
And I—just a bit to the right.

With political differences rendered almost irrelevant, I joined in celebrating the reception of Irving's most ambitious book, *World of Our Fathers* (1976), whose subtitle, "The Journey of the East European Jews to America and the Life They Found and Made"—aptly summarizes its contents and theme. He had been afraid that the influential *Times Book Review* would assign it to Harry Golden, the popular Jewish writer whose bestselling *Only in America* he had panned. Instead, he won the National Book Award, made the bestseller list, and enjoyed his first taste of celebrity.

Irving's wistful literary portrait of the Jewish immigrant generation as a socialist enclave on the banks of the Hudson turned out to have been propitiously timed. The socialist label that had been a liability in the 1950s, and was insufficiently radical for the revolutionists of the 1960s, became a badge of honor by the mid-'70s as anti-Western and anti-American attitudes took over universities, journalism, and Hollywood. Opposed as he was to some of these manifestations, Irving was also, as an author, their beneficiary.

He complained that the well-heeled bourgeois audiences that turned up to hear him at synagogues and Jewish community centers around the country no longer resembled the socialist garment workers and union organizers he had so lovingly written about. I sympathized with his nostalgia but pointed out that he was lucky. After all, in chronicling and celebrating those "little Jews" with their socialist dreams, his book had ignored the parts of the community that prospered and endured: the synagogue-goers, Zionists, and businesspeople who made good in capitalist America—and who were now the buyers of his book. Why begrudge them their success?

The irony of this reversal ought to have been cause for rejoicing—not for Irving, however. And it was not the only irony. His book owed a good part of its laudatory critical reception to a shift then underway in the higher reaches of the political culture. Where other New York intellectuals had been falling out of favor for turning "neoconservative," Irving was rewarded for remaining formally attached to his boyhood faith.

◌

THE UGLIEST ASPECT OF THE New Left was the embrace of the anti-Zionism that the Soviets had forged in the 1930s. This strain of venom originated with Karl Marx, who located political evil in the economic function of the Jews. "Money is the zealous one God of Israel, beside which no other God may stand," he wrote in an 1844 essay on the Jewish question. For many of his adherents, blaming the "Rothschilds" as capitalist demons remained a staple of socialist thought.

To this economic Jew-blame the Soviet Union added the accusation that Zionism, the Jews' recovery of their national sovereignty, stood in the way of international brotherhood. Stalin hailed the Mufti of Jerusalem's attacks on the Jews of Palestine as the start of the Arab communist revolution. He lumped the Jewish pioneers of the Yishuv with the British as imperialist invaders of the Middle East. Anti-Semitism had demonized the Jews in dispersion; Soviet-conceived anti-Zionism demonized the Jews in their homeland.

The New Left of the 1960s had only to dust off the old Soviet slogans. The groundwork had been laid by Arab leaders who, in a masterful stroke of inversion, transposed the Arab threat to "drive the Jews into the sea" into a claim that the Palestinians were the ones dispossessed by the Jews. Their alliance with the Soviet bloc allowed for the passage in 1975 of UN Resolution 3379 defining Zionism as racism, the evilest accusation in the liberal vocabulary.

It was shocking to see libelous representations of Jews as "colonizers" and "imperialist occupiers" taking hold not only at the UN but on American campuses and among media and cultural elites. But the maneuver succeeded, winning the sympathy of people on the lookout for certifiable victims of "racism and racial discrimination" (in the language of the UN resolution).

As in the past, these accusations also peeled off sectors of the *Jewish* left. I found this as predictable as any law of physics: the greater the pressure of anti-Jewish politics, the greater the number of Jews who would blame their fellow Jews for having caused it. They argued that the hostility would stop if only those other Jews were more working class, less ghettoized, more productive or more progressive, depending on the charges against them. Michael Lerner was soon to found the magazine *Tikkun* on the premise that if Israel yielded land to the Palestinians, the Arab war against the Jews would end. This version of blaming fellow Jews for anti-Zionism ideally suited the political climate in Berkeley, California, which had spearheaded the antiwar protests against American engagement in Vietnam. Such Jews could now attribute anti-Jewish aggression to the actions of the "Jewish Right," personified for them in *Commentary* and the 1977 electoral victory of Menachem Begin's Likud party over Israel's Labor party. The latter had been in power uninterruptedly since the founding of the state.

From the moment the UN passed its anti-Zionist resolution, I urged Irving to use his authority as editor of *Dissent* to speak out against it. Only the Left, I said, could effectively counter this attempt by parts of the Left to discredit Israel. He patted my shoulder and said, "Ruthie, no one pays any attention to the United Nations." This made me realize how out of touch *he* was.

Abby, Jacob, with the author on a visit to Hillel Halkin in Zichron Yaakov, 1987.

But he didn't stay detached for long: following his divorce from Ariel Mack, he married Ilana Weiner, an attractive Israeli who drew him into her literary circle on the far left of Israel's political spectrum and into the movement that had formed around the slogan *Shalom Achshav*. The movement was delighted to conscript this prominent American intellectual into its new American support group for Peace Now.

If Irving's elegiac lectures to Jewish audiences about American socialism's glory days were turning stale, the "peace movement" enlisted him in a new field of combat. To me, Israeli citizen-soldiers like Ezra Mendelsohn, whose involvement with Peace Now I've described in an earlier chapter, had an obvious right to endorse their nation's taking a risk on giving up strategic territory—even if I personally considered such a course suicidal. But those like Howe who toyed with Israel's security from abroad struck me more like spectators at Roman gladiatorial games turning thumbs down on their own brothers.

In a series of essays in *Commentary* I tracked these patterns of Jewish accommodation, and in 1992 I collected them in *If I Am Not for Myself: The Liberal Betrayal of the Jews*. Like two of my favorite Zionist polemics—Moses

Hess's *Rome and Jerusalem* and Hillel Halkin's *Letters to an American Jewish Friend*—mine was written in epistolary form. Hess writes to comfort a bereaved and troubled woman by showing her the healing powers of Jewish national sovereignty (before the term Zionism was conceived). Halkin seeks to persuade an American Jew that the better place for him is in Israel. My book took for granted that while the hub and heart of Jewish national life was henceforth Zion, some of us would continue to live abroad with responsibility for our common homeland.

My attachment to Zion being more passionate than friendship and less complete than marriage, I made my fictional interlocutor a married man who had moved to Israel with his wife and family. Briefly lovers, we had renounced that part of our attachment early on. This made it possible to correspond without deceit, fully loyal where our loyalties belonged, yet without giving up what we felt for one another. American Jews did not have divided loyalties. We were fully engaged in our land of citizenship and as fully attached to the Jewish homeland. Rabbi Nahman of Bratslav had said, "There is nothing as whole as a broken heart" (to which my mother added, "a broken Jewish heart"), and the same apparent paradox applied to our allegedly divided identity.

Even some people who liked the book felt uncomfortable with the "unnecessary" scaffolding. Admittedly, it was more important to me in writing the book than for its polemical content. I needed the framework of love and loyalty because I was writing about the most depressing feature of Jewish life: the capitulation and betrayal by Jews who prided themselves on their goodness and therefore had to hold other Jews responsible for the enmity that Jews aroused.

This pretended accommodation for the sake of "peace" demoralized the Jews from within their own ranks and undermined the ideal of justice. I concentrated on the evil closest to home, the tolerant liberals whose generosity extends to the perpetrators. My reading and experience in Jewish studies, debates with Irwin Cotler, Hillel and Ezra, Irving Howe, and so many others, went into the book. I learned from the New York Intellectuals and from my interlocutors how to think about politics and how not to.

෨

ONE DAY IN THE LATE 1980s, a friend alerted me to an unsigned boxed notice that had appeared in Irving's magazine *Dissent*. Its title was "Into the Depths":

Each issue of *Commentary* strikes a new low in intellectual vulgarity and political reaction. In the May 1988 issue there appears an article, "Israel and the Intellectuals," by Ruth R. Wisse, with the following sentences:

The obvious key to the success of Arab strategy is the presence, in the disputed territories of the Gaza Strip and the West Bank of the Jordan River, of Palestinian Arabs, people who breed and bleed and advertise their misery. Indeed, if we were to measure reality by the degree to which we are exposed to it, no people in the world today would appear of greater substance or in a graver predicament.

This remark, verging on or crossing into racism, is an instance of that dehumanization of the adversary that has been a curse of our century.

Dissent's smear itself marked a truly "new low in intellectual vulgarity." I did not deign to respond, but when, thanks to the internet, the quoted passage turned my allegedly dehumanizing phrase "breed and bleed" into a permanent *gotcha!* on my record, I was obliged to reconstruct its original context. Before Google (BG) no one but readers of *Dissent* and *Commentary* would have known of this altercation (anti-intellectual Woody Allen yoked and yakked them together as *Dissentary*). In the Google era when lazy folks linked to precisely this kind of schmutz, I turned to *Tablet*—the Jewish online magazine of news and culture that was run by people I knew and trusted—to expose the false accusers.

The context of that passage, as I explained in what would now likewise live on the internet, was my effort to distinguish the genuine suffering of Palestinians from the exploitation of that suffering by their fellow Arabs, and their real hardship from its phony attribution to Israel. My first draft had therefore represented Arab misery through Shylock's questions—"If you prick us, do we not bleed? . . . and if you wrong us, shall we not revenge?"— thinking to strengthen the point by associating the afflicted Arabs with Shakespeare's persecuted Jew. Whittled down through many revisions, the final version paired "bleed" with "breed." Guilty at most of sacrificing precision to compression, I never dreamed that "breed" was anything but a synonym for being fruitful and multiplying.

What sort of mind would accuse me of indulging in racist rhetoric for having traced Palestinian suffering to its source in Arab despotism? At first, I could not believe that Irving had authorized the slur. These were the kind of tactics I associated with the strong-arming culture of the 1930s, at which Irving had once excelled, not with the New York Intellectuals he had subsequently helped to define.

But later that year, I realized that I had underestimated his animus and failed to appreciate the change in political climate. The Communist Party itself was no longer active in America, and the Soviet Union was about to collapse, but rather than demolish the reputation of Marxism—as the defeat of Hitler had done to Fascism—the dissolution of the USSR gave the Left free rein to promote leftism without the devastating evidence of how it worked in practice.

Political correctness was back in fashion, including the Left's opposition to the Jewishness of Jews. The rise of Yasser Arafat's Palestine Liberation Organization promoted the newest form of warfare: terrorist attacks on behalf of states that could not be held responsible. Israel sounded the alarm, but some of the Jewish Left supported the justice of Arab claims (that allegedly drove them to embrace terrorism) or counselled appeasement as the "realistic" compromise and slandered supporters of Israel as enemies of peace. Howe, embracing Peace Now, was a darling of this movement, and I among the blackest of its villains.

In October 1988 we were both present at a three-day conference in Berkeley, California on "The Writer in the Jewish Community: An Israeli-North American Dialogue." I had looked forward to seeing Cynthia Ozick and several of the Israeli writers with whom we had once before attended a

Jewish literary conference in Bellagio, Italy. But that was in another country, another time, when a Jewish literary conference was devoted to the problems of Jewish writing. Irving's presence this time, alone from among the New York Intellectuals, as well as the almost exclusively leftist contingent of Israelis, signaled rather a political conference with literary trappings, which is how I described it in the account I felt compelled to write for *Commentary* in its aftermath. In addition to several talks on the sins of the Jewish "Right," we were treated to a lecture by the Arab-Hebrew writer Anton Shammas on the inherent racism of Zionism. Several of his fellow Israelis buttressed this with apologetics, self-recriminations, and revisionism to prove Israel's guilt for Arab crimes. Meir Shalev called Shamas "our fig leaf," to cover the embarrassment they felt for their country.

As though anticipating this degeneration, there awaited us on our arrival at the conference a letter from novelist Henry Roth expressing regret that he could not be present. Having gone through a long period of estrangement from his people, "and paid for it," he wanted to make clear that "the most pressing question to me at this time is whether the writers in the U.S. and those from Israel can reach some consensus with respect to Israel vis-a-vis the Palestinians:

> One has always to ask who's responsible for the Palestinian condition. It's the Arabs, it's Yasser Arafat. He, his kind and his terrorists will settle for nothing less than all of Israel, and they have said so in covenant. I take them at their word....Until the Palestinians put forward a leadership willing to coexist with Israel by recognizing Israel's existence, there can be no shrinking from the job of securing her safety, whether [or not] it takes occupation, ignoring queasy Jewish liberals and comfortable academic appeasers, and contending with the piranhas of the U.S. media. All these trials have to be borne. Israel has the means to bear them—and unlike the helpless, hapless, homeless creatures we've been for a couple of millennia, no matter what, every Jew has a land on which to rally and stand.

Henry Roth's fictional autobiography had not yet appeared, telling how he emerged from the modernist and communist labyrinth of his youth into this national clarity, but I kept the letter with me through the rest of the conference as a talisman against the rot I felt in too many of the sessions and conversations.

My article did not include the most discouraging episode of that conference when I asked a question from the floor at a panel Irving was chairing. Cynthia and I had by then been singled out for attack as the dreaded "right wing," and Irving took the occasion to hector me for my politics without addressing the question I had asked. Robert Alter, one of the panelists and hardly my ally, felt obliged to object that I had simply asked a question. He himself been a major figure in the Jewish intellectual wars when I started out, someone I had thought would do the writing that needed to be done; but in taking up a professorship at Berkeley he had avoided political engagement, bending carefully leftward whenever he did venture out. His uncharacteristic standing up for me meant that Irving's rudeness had disturbed even him.

"Try to understand," Irving wrote me afterward, "that I genuinely did not wish to get into a fight with you." His semiapology included a reminder of how "aggressive and combative and provoking" I had been, along with advice that I was not very good at political polemics, "certainly not as good as you are in literary discussions; I feel it's not your métier, that you force yourself to do it out of a sense of obligation (with attendant anxiety)." It was amusing to picture this veteran Trotskyist of City College polemics being put off by *my* combative style. Rather, Irving was relying on my side of our friendship, knowing that I would never attack him in kind. As frank as I was in our correspondence and conversations, I would not have insulted him in public. Did my gender play a part in his condescension? I took it as a lack of intellectual seriousness in one unprepared to debate me on the merits.

Lest this account seem merely an attempt at personal payback, a roster of Israeli writers had protested the selection of only leftists for participation in the conference, and the edition of the conference proceedings published five years later excised papers on "the interplay of literature and politics," explaining, "The conference was not intended to deal with this issue; in fact, it was designed to try to limit this discussion." Constructed as carefully as a Potemkin village, this doctored book bore no relation to the politicized conference any of us had actually attended. I was surprised that the group photo on the back cover did not crop out the offenders.

Whatever doubts I may have originally harbored about my fitness for political writing, I saw that neither Irving nor his political allies could lay a glove on me in the arguments I was setting out in successive articles. But I also understood that better arguments were not going to stop the Left or the Jewish Left from enabling anti-Zionism. Politics that claimed to transcend or improve on Judaism demoralized the Jews much quicker than the eliminationist kind. And sham neutrality like that of the conference proceedings merely signaled a willingness to let the Left carry the day.

Irving never dealt with any of this in his published writings, leaving me to figure out how he justified wanting to continue a friendship with the alleged racist of that boxed attack in *Dissent.* When he was awarded a MacArthur "Genius" grant, he called from New York to share the good news, assuming—correctly—that I would be happy for the financial security it brought him. After his daughter Nina settled in Montreal, he would sometimes drop by on his visits to her, to chat about family and such. I represented no danger to him. If anything, in protecting Israel, I made it easier for him to align himself with those exposing it to risk.

Irving's last letter to me was dated the day before he died on May 5, 1993. We'd been out of touch for a long time. He wrote to say that he had undergone several heart bypass operations but was now, for the time being, mended. Retired from the City University of New York, he had agreed to teach a course at Yale the following spring and asked how I was managing my first semester at Harvard.

Getting old was no fun, he said: "I sometimes ruefully think of Robert Frost's lines: 'No memory of having starred / Atones for later disregard / Or keeps the end from being hard.'" Since the letter arrived after his death, I could not properly thank him for our fruitful work together or hope for more honest exchanges in this world.

CR

In 1983, while I was teaching at Stanford for a semester, an appointment that had been suggested by my predecessor Lucy Dawidowicz, I met the master of all the New York polemicists, Sidney Hook, longtime professor philosophy at City College in New York and now a fellow at the Hoover Institution. Once the acknowledged American expert on Marxism, he had become its subtlest critic.

Aside from John Felstiner of the English department who had arranged my visit, Hook was the only one at Stanford who invited me to his home. We traded impressions about people we knew in common, and I mentioned a political attack on me—not Irving's—that I had chosen to ignore. Sidney reprimanded me, urging that I follow his example of never letting the slightest assault go unanswered, even if it appeared in some obscure midwestern newspaper.

The conversation stiffened slightly when, in answer to a question from his wife Ann, we began to talk about Jewish subjects. Although we were not talking personally, Sidney turned defensive and said about his Jewishness, "I was never untrue to my father." Without thinking I blurted out, "I don't care about your father. What did you do for your sons?" I regretted it instantly, but instead of the rebuke I deserved, Sidney and Ann exchanged a "significant look," as if this were a long-standing subject between them. But I was not going to pursue the subject, and they let it drop. Protecting Israel from its enemies was a political imperative, the prime test of good versus evil. Jewishness I considered a private matter, for each family to determine on its own.

CR

Irving Howe's renewed leftist opposition to Israel as a member of Peace Now had taken me by surprise because once he'd "discovered" the country after 1967, I assumed that he would fight for it as Henry Roth did, as I did. Yiddish was for me and my siblings—as for our parents and teachers—the vehicle not of socialism but of a Jewishness that naturally included Zionism, the organic connection of Jews to their homeland. Staving off the most lopsided war in history and one of the longest, still without basic recognition from a continent of enemies, Israel would have seemed to require from American Jews the most sustained political defense imaginable.

At home we learned from our mother the songs that she had learned from her mother, plaints about the neglected homeland and the call for national resurrection: "*Shtey oyf, mayn folk!* Arise, my people! You have slumbered for too long." In Jewish elementary school we sang the Zionides of Yehuda Halevi, whose journey to the Land of Israel inspired generations of poets including the German-Jewish Heinrich Heine. Once I began studying Yiddish at college, I discovered that Sholem Aleichem's 1898 Yiddish pamphlet, "Why Jews Need a Land," sold many times more copies than did Herzl's broadside *The Jewish State.* Yiddish-Hebrew, Jewish-Zionist, they were all of a piece.

Irving Howe at a Yiddish Conference at Columbia University, 1974. (Courtesy of YIVO)

In the course of my studies, I had also learned of Jewish opposition to Zionism, but the annihilation of European Jewry radically affected those views. Yiddish writers, no matter how pained by David Ben-Gurion's suppression of their language in favor of Hebrew, were among the most enthusiastic visitors to Israel after the establishment of the state.

Yiddish poets Itzik Manger (left) with I.J. (Yitzhak Yaakov) Segal during Manger's visit to Montreal, April 1951. (Courtesy Montreal Jewish Public Library Archives)

In 1958, several years after his Montreal visit, the self-advertised bad boy of Yiddish literature, Itzik Manger, immigrated from his temporary home in New York—after London, Paris, Warsaw and our native Czernowitz—to settle in Israel, where, like Heine and Bialik, he channeled Yehuda Halevi:

> For years I rambled in the world,
> Now I'm going home to ramble there.
> With a pair of shoes and the shirt on my back,
> And the stick in my hand that goes with me everywhere.
> I'll not kiss your dust as that great poet did,
> Though my heart, like his, fills with song and grief,
> How can I kiss your dust? I *am* your dust.
> And how, I ask you, can I kiss myself?

I associated that "rambling"—*valgern* in Yiddish (to roll around)—with the Rolling Stones' lead singer, Mick Jagger, who cultivated a similar image of dissipation. But Manger's rolling stone came to rest in Israel. On first arriving in the Land of Israel, many Jews kiss the ground; he already felt part of its soil.

Then there was Avrom Sutzkever, who, as I've told earlier, had brought me to the study of Yiddish literature. When he reached Israel in 1947, he wrote his own poem of thanksgiving:

> Were I not here with you,/ not breathing your joy and pain here—
> were I not afire with this land/ volcanic in its birth pangs;
> were I not, after my *akeydeh* [the biblical sacrifice of Isaac],/ not reborn with the land
> where every pebble is my *zeyde* [grandfather]—
> bread would not sate my hunger,/ nor water quench my thirst,
> till I would perish, Gentiled,
> and only my longing arrive on its own.

Modeled after the *Shehehiyanu* prayer that traditional Jews recite on first reaching the Land of Israel, his poem is cast in conditional form by someone who knows he might never have reached his destination. Along with gratitude for all he has attained, he gives thanks for all he has escaped. "Were I not here...." The word *not* appearing six times in eleven lines stresses the likelihood of not having arrived, in which case he would have died *fargoyt*, turned Gentile, a past participle invented by Sutzkever to capture the condition of being stripped of one's Jewishness.

I hope my clumsy translation conveys the poem's anxiety, not over what still awaited Jews in securing their homeland, but over what would have overtaken them had they failed. Speaking for the murdered millions, the poet avows that his yearnings would have arrived on their own, as Jewish yearnings had done since the Jews in Babylonian exile vowed, "If I forget thee, O Jerusalem...."

What Israel meant to Halevi, Manger, and Sutzkever also held true for me. I pinned my hopes for human civilization on the ability of Jews to maintain their national sovereignty. From the time that anti-Zionism began to make its way into America, I could not respect, much less befriend, anyone who joined the prosecution. Had he begun his work with Yiddish in the 1990s, Irving Howe would not have invited me to join him, and I could not have accepted. The answer to students' questions about the relation of friendship to politics lay with the man who, when asked how he became the best comedian in Poland, interrupts to say "T...t...t...timing." (If you don't know the joke, please ignore.)

CR

GIVEN THE POPULAR ASSOCIATION of Yiddish with Howe's world of immigrant peddlers, students enrolling in my classes could be forgiven for expecting to find in their classroom a customary liberal leftist. One of them was the young Aaron Lansky, today the wonderfully inventive and energetic founding director of the Yiddish Book Center in Amherst, Massachusetts. Aaron likes to tell of how, in the summer of 1977, he read *The Schlemiel as Modern Hero* while manning a fruit juice cart in Boston's Copley Square and decided to come to McGill for his graduate work.

I, too, had once decided no less impulsively on the same course of action, so we definitely had something in common. But politics was another matter. Attracted by my portrayal of the hapless schlemiel as a positive cultural type, Aaron (as he writes in his memoir, *Outwitting History*) was surprised to find instead:

> the most right-wing person—or at least the most right-wing rational person—I had ever met: an unyielding hawk on Israel; a critic of feminism who opposed the ordination of women rabbis; a fierce anti-Communist who championed American military strength to a degree that made Ronald Reagan look like a dove....

Aaron does grant that I was "unfailingly warm and generous" and my classes "intellectually exhilarating"—qualities presumably unexpected in your typical political conservative. But I was equally in danger of stereotyping him. His impish demeanor bespoke a Woodstock hippie who had drifted into grad school in order to escape whatever passed for "real life." It did not take more than a single class to recognize in him a keen student with a lively intelligence and the drive of a born entrepreneur.

Apart from his schoolwork, Aaron involved himself in the practical problems that beset me as a teacher. Montreal's only Yiddish bookstore had closed a decade before Yiddish studies were launched at McGill, and to equip my students I had to rustle up copies of the books on my syllabus from locals I knew who might have them. Poems I was able to circulate in mimeographed form, but photocopiers could not provide ten or twelve affordable copies of a Yiddish novel. This circumstance often determined what I could teach.

In addition, McGill's libraries had not yet acquired Yiddish books. To address that lacuna the administration allowed me to order a basic collection of literature and reference works from Vaxer's, a store advertised as the "last Yiddish bookseller on New York's Lower East Side." The promised date of delivery came and went before someone finally answered my calls and reported that the bookseller had died. My expression of condolence elicited further news: the contents of the store and warehouse were to be auctioned off as a single lot.

I flew into action, borrowed money from my older brother and sister-in-law, and, because I couldn't leave the children to attend the New York auction in person, asked my younger brother David, then a student at Brandeis University, to go and bid in my place. David gives the story a comic turn. Given an absolute limit of $2,000 as his highest bid, he listened as the bidding crept up into the hundreds and then called out, "Two thousand!" The auction came to a stunned stop.

Thus did I acquire many thousands of unsorted dusty volumes without having given a thought as to what I would do with them. Over subsequent years, the work of packing, hauling, storing, and sorting would cost me dearly—money being the least of it. My efforts were still in their early stage when Aaron arrived. Because the windfall still did not supply enough copies of the works we would be studying, he started canvassing local donors for disused Yiddish books. From this there evolved his idea of establishing a Yiddish book exchange. He went on to create the Yiddish Book Center, which he developed into one of the country's loveliest Jewish institutions.

To get back to politics: I think I've made it clear that no one in the academic field of Yiddish could avoid its historic connections with leftism. Indeed, even as Aaron's studies deepened his appreciation for the religious-national fusion of the Jewish way of life, support for his burgeoning institution often came from donors nostalgic for the progressivism they associated with the language. This bore no relation to the actual Yiddish-speaking communities, which remained what they had always been: outposts of Jewish separatism, consisting mainly of religiously observant Jews living culturally apart from the surrounding population. In the twentieth century, however, secular socialists had made the language the vessel for their movements, and though the movements themselves were gone, their construction of Yiddish lived on among social justice warriors of the next generation.

Young radicals, gays and lesbians, feminists, and others who felt marginalized sometimes found in what they regarded as the language of Jewish weakness—the language of Howe's "little Jews"—their ideal of moral purity. In the classroom I taught some of the texts infused with this ideology, while in my political writing I tried to expose some of its dangers. Students were never in doubt where I stood on the subject, though they were free to express strongly dissident views. Contention was a valued feature of Jewish and modern Yiddish culture.

ℭ

ON MOST JEWISH MATTERS, I felt comfortably aligned with my Montreal community, whose members joked that if they were ever stranded on a desert island, they could rest assured that the country's Combined Jewish Appeal would find and rescue them.

My first serious parting of ways with the community came over the issue of how to commemorate the Shoah. At about the same time that the United States Holocaust Memorial Museum was being built in Washington, DC, a local committee formed to consider establishing something similar in our city.

Commemoration of the martyred Jews of Europe had been part of my life since childhood and formed part of my teaching. My brother David gathered materials for an anthology, *The Literature of Destruction*, tracing how, from our beginnings as a people, successive catastrophes were integrated into collective memory and rites. Such a ritual was already being incorporated in Yom Hashoah, Israel's annual day of remembrance, in some synagogue services on Yom Kippur, and in family ceremonies like the one we include in our Passover seder.

I likewise greatly appreciated the research centers, including Yad Vashem in Jerusalem as well as those in America, Poland, and Germany that undertook to record every known detail about the process Hitler had called the Final Solution. Verification and preservation of evidence constituted an urgent international priority. Even if there were to be no more trials, no more punishment for unpardonable crimes, the facts had to be established and made known.

But I objected to putting the Holocaust on display. In my teens, the fate of the Jews in World War II came alive for me through *The Wall*, John Hersey's fictional account of the real-life historian Emanuel Ringelblum, who had set up a network of chroniclers in the Warsaw Ghetto. It was their sacred task to record every detail of every aspect of life under those unprecedented conditions and Hersey made it his literary task to convey their heroic efforts. In rallying the Jewish Fighting Organization (ZOB) for its final 1943 uprising against the Germans, the bookish Noach Levinson—Hersey's version of Ringelblum—quotes Y. L. Peretz:

> I am not advocating that we shut ourselves up in a spiritual ghetto. On the contrary, we should get out of such a ghetto. But we should get out as Jews, with our own spiritual treasures. We should interchange, give and take, but not beg.

The resistance of those starved and poorly armed Jews lasted longer than any other anti-German insurrection in Europe.

I was not surprised to learn that the historian Lucy Dawidowicz had done the research for Hersey's book, since her own book, *The War against the Jews 1933-45*, scrupulously documented both the German war against the Jews and the Jewish responses to it. Lucy had been a graduate student in New York in the late 1930s when she took the exceptional step of traveling to Vilna to study at the YIVO Institute and live at the heart of the Jewry she planned to make the subject of her scholarship. She returned to New York at the insistence of the American consulate shortly before the invasion of Poland in September 1939 with deepened knowledge and a lifelong sense of purpose. Like some others who had started on the political Left and felt its betrayal, she was tough minded about totalitarian aggressors.

Hersey's novel and Lucy's history emphasized the dignity of an unbroken people. By contrast, those who conceived the Holocaust museum in Washington and educational programs like "Facing History" wanted to turn the massacre into a universal redemptive story. They intended it to be a prophylactic tool against prejudice, as if learning about the atrocity would prevent its recurrence. Given that the Arab League's war against Israel had been launched the very year the Nazi genocide ended, and served some of those leaders as a *positive* model of what could be accomplished, I did not think the lesson would work as intended.

The idea that suffering could be made to seem redemptive was likely based more on Christian than on Jewish teaching. Jews had developed an entirely different idea of resurrection. Passover celebrates the passage from slavery to liberation. The Jews—who had lost one-third of their number— reenacted the same liberation in 1948. Moreover, Jews had readied the infrastructure of their newborn state in time to absorb the refugees of Europe and Arab lands.

There, in that stunning display of national resilience, was a story to inspire humankind! I believed—no, I was certain—that Holocaust museums and what cynics were already calling "Shoah business" would indelibly mark the Jews as targets and also invite imitation. If we were to insist that American curricula include a segment on the Jews, it should build instead on the Exodus example, ancient and modern.

Fortunately, our local Montreal committee declined to follow the American example, and the city's modest Holocaust center was incorporated within an existing Jewish institution. But there seemed no way of curbing the opposite trend. In many American cities, Jewish organizations insisted on teaching the Holocaust rather than the recovery of Jewish sovereignty in the Land of Israel, showing the mass murder of their people rather than the greatest comeback story on record. It was morally wrong and politically dumb to broadcast the triumph of anti-Jewish politics and the failure of Jewish political strategy. Worst of all, at the college level, where students are introduced to other cultures, courses on the Holocaust became the major draw of Jewish Studies while Zionism and Israel were almost never taught, except in the distorting Arab version of Near and Middle East departments.

People tired of hearing me go on about this at dinner parties, family gatherings, and in talks to Jewish groups: how could I oppose the community's commitment of resources to what others considered a sacred cause? Survivors wanted their stories told, and who could blame them for wanting to make known what others had tried to conceal?

Perhaps, in the end, nothing could have prevented Arab and Muslim propagandists from importing their anti-Semitic politics into North America—an effort whose late-ripening fruits are now all around us. But among the many factors contributing to the success of that effort, I remain convinced that the sustained public emphasis on the Holocaust as the prime marker of Jewish identity helped materially to obscure the issues at stake in the post-Holocaust era, to disarm American Jews and their friends, and to ease the way of their enemies.

This was my strongest point of contention with a majority of my fellow Jews, and the hardest to rally against.

12

LEADERSHIP

$\mathcal{M}$y father's parting words to me were peculiar. Seized by pain, he had been diagnosed with kidney stones and scheduled for emergency surgery on the first day of the Jewish New Year, Rosh Hashanah 1975. Because of his weak heart, his cardiologist was scheduled to be present as well. I accompanied our parents to the hospital and stayed in the room as the nurse poked needles into his veins. Everything happened so fast I was sure that after the operation I'd find him restored to health.

Thanks to sedatives, his pain must have subsided. Just before they transferred him to a gurney and wheeled him into surgery, he smiled at me and asked, "*Vos vet zayn mit di goldene keyt?*" The problem here is not merely translating from the Yiddish but straining to understand the point of the question, "What will happen to the Golden Chain?"

Di goldene keyt was the literary quarterly founded in Tel Aviv by Yiddish poet Avrom Sutzkever in 1949. My parents were among its original supporters. But *The Golden Chain* was also the title of a mighty drama by Y. L. Peretz that had brought the phrase into common use. Its three acts portrayed four generations of a rabbinic dynasty, each representing a different approach to leading the Jewish people in modern times. Sutzkever's appropriation of the term for his publication signified his intention of adding new links to that great Jewish chain of transmission.

Was Father asking about the fate of the journal, about the corresponding fate of the Jewish people, or about our own family? Why put this question to me when he was about to undergo surgery? Pricked to annoyance by this paternal appeal, his dim-witted daughter said: "If there's enough interest in the journal it will survive and if not, it will fail." I *could* have said, "If you're concerned, I'll write Sutzkever tomorrow assuring him of our continuing support." I *should* have stroked the hand that wasn't attached to the intravenous tube and reassured him that he could count on his children and grandchildren to preserve and strengthen the golden chain. But I declined to give more assurance than I could guarantee—maybe because I still wanted *him* to secure our future and balked at assuming the burdens his question implied. So the one time my father called me to duty, I failed to answer. He died during the operation.

On the anniversary of his death, a Canadian Yiddish paper referred to the late Leo Roskies as a *gezelshaftlekher tuer,* one active in community affairs. My mother, fierce guardian of language and reputation alike, reared up at the phrase without indicating what she would have liked in its stead. In fact, she had always encouraged us to learn from his example that a stellar reputation was superior to wealth. *Shem tov k'even tov* (a good name is a priceless gem).

My father had provided or found employment for refugees who arrived after the war, and anonymously funded people who needed his help. Thérèse Casgrain, a leading figure in the New Democratic party, attended his funeral to offer, on behalf of Quebec labor, appreciation for his management of Huntingdon Woolen Mills, which had never experienced a strike in the years he negotiated with the union. Representatives of the many charities and institutions he supported had similarly good reason to join us in mourning his passing. My brother David recalls that as the funeral procession drove past on its way to the cemetery, students of the Jewish People's School that we had all attended, and on whose board our father had been a permanent member, stood outside in tribute.

As our family was leaving the gravesite, I was motioned over by a wealthy member of the local Jewish community whom I had been surprised to see at the burial. He handed me a slip of paper and said, "You are chairman of McGill's Jewish studies program, and next week a building at the Hebrew

University is being dedicated in my name. Here is the tribute I want you to send." Vulgar as this was (if also a source of amusement to my colleagues), the incident remains my most vivid memory of the day. It bore in on me my inability to share it with Father, who would have reminded me of the man's philanthropy and urged me not to condemn him out of hand. Leo Roskies never needed to look down on another man in order to appear bigger than he himself was. Modesty was the cardinal feature of his authority and the quality I came to associate with true leadership.

◌◌

IN HIGH SCHOOL I HAD wanted to head every group of which I was a member. But over the years this ambition had subsided to the point that I became reluctant to assume any such tasks. A scholar-teacher had better things to do with her time than chairing a department, pleading with deans, and defending budgets. Although never temperamentally a follower, I was nonetheless happiest in an academic department with an entrepreneurial, ambitious chairman, in a synagogue with a strong congregational rabbi, and in a country headed by whoever most resembled Winston Churchill.

Still, if you tend to speak up forcefully, people assume you are a candidate for leadership. In the early 1970s, after attending the second annual conference of the Association for Jewish Studies (AJS), I was invited to join its board, and then, once it had run through likelier candidates, to chair the program committee for the annual conferences, and in time to preside over the organization itself. (Historian Jane Gerber had preceded me as the first female president.) Genuinely reluctant to assume administrative responsibility for anything more than my program at McGill, I nonetheless yielded to Arnold Band, a founder and former president of AJS who undertook to persuade me that (a) no one else could do the job and (b) it did not require much doing.

Since I had joined AJS only in its second year, I was not privy to what had gone into its creation. When asked, "Who is a Jewish studies scholar?" its founding president Leon Jick had apparently answered in a string of negatives: neither an anti-Semitic propagandist, nor a scholar without Hebrew language, nor a Bible teacher in a fundamentalist Christian seminary, nor a yeshiva rabbi whose "a priori commitments severely limit the range of problems or alternatives that [he is] able to consider."

The last was the real sticking point. Among the original members were former beneficiaries of a religious education who were eager to free academic Jewish studies from any association with the practice of Judaism. I thought this insecurity explained their eagerness to gain acceptance into the American Council of Learned Societies (ACLS). When our application was repeatedly turned down, their acute disappointment made me realize how much they still needed to prove their academic credentials.

Coming from Canada, I could not have cared less for acceptance by a body that was, to me, irrelevant. Having no exalted regard for universities in general, I did not crave any imprimatur. But in this I was shortsighted: the AJS was right to fight for inclusion among its peers. By the time this recognition finally arrived in 1985, the work we'd done to satisfy the criteria of ACLS had benefited us as an organization.

The only conflicts I recall from the early years were of the intramural kind. When it was proposed that an editorial board be formed for *AJS Review*, our newly founded annual journal, the list of recommended candidates included a professor notorious for his vendettas and abuses of influence. Almost all the other board members were either his friends or in some way at risk of his reprisal. With no such threat hanging over me, I strongly opposed giving him even a smidgen of authority. In vain: he was voted in over my objections. By the time I returned home from the conference, a letter had arrived from him comparing me with Hitler. It made me laugh. Less amusing was the realization that he'd had an informer at the meeting.

There were lighter occasions for laughter. Each annual conference in the early years honored a senior scholar who had taught one or more of the association's founders. These men tended to be as diminutive in height as they were mighty in knowledge. Until he spoke at the dinner in his honor, I had never encountered Harry Wolfson, Harvard's impressive, Lithuanian-born and Yiddish-accented authority in Jewish (and early Christian, and Islamic) philosophy. For most of his talk, I couldn't figure out who the *tchoitchfodders* were that he kept referring to. (See how well you do.) During another speaker's talk, I noticed some waiters behind the glass window gesturing others to come have a look at what was going on in the dining hall. Glancing around for the object of their amusement, I beheld a legion of academics asleep in their seats.

The first doctrinal issue I recall arising involved the Hanukkah candles that we would light collectively whenever the conference coincided with that holiday. The year a woman was asked to light them was the last time we ever did so together, or recited communally the blessing after meals. No one had ever considered Jewish studies the exclusive preserve of Jewish males, or for that matter of Jews, and as I've noted, the founders were determined to distinguish themselves from ex-seminarians. Still, the almost uniform profile of the membership in its early years was what made it natural to include certain Jewish rituals. Rather than debating the issue, eliminating these rituals had now become the simplest way to prevent the emergence of factionalism. Thereafter, adherence to kosher food remained the only institutional vestige of Jewishness.

I regretted the lost warmth of communal blessings. Like the AJS founders, I had considered the introduction of Jewish studies into higher education to be a final step in the normalization of Jews in America. That this was becoming a reality was confirmed when Charles Berlin, the executive director who ran the AJS singlehandedly, concluded that our annual conference had outgrown the facilities of Brandeis and Harvard and approached Boston's Copley Plaza to explore the benefits of a multiyear contract. The hotel manager, in making his pitch to our board, explained that they were renovating its rooms with high-quality products—from ashtrays to curtains—and were looking for "your kind of people."

The irony was not lost on those around the table, several wearing skullcaps, who knew that the hotel had once altogether excluded "our kind of people." But the management was as good as its word. Though the conference was held every year from Sunday to Tuesday in the week before Christmas, only at its conclusion was the decorated seasonal tree set up in the lobby. Whenever I saw that tree being installed at checkout time, I took it as silent acknowledgement of our welcome as valued guests: normalization had made us commercially viable.

As in all such conferences, the quality at ours was uneven. But these Sunday through Tuesday gatherings were also a time for seeing old friends, talking with colleagues and students late into the night, and, in later years, enjoying the presentations given by my own graduate students. One regular pleasure was the Montreal-to-Boston drive with my friend Gita Rotenberg. Gita would show up at my house after the end of what was invariably the shortest Sabbath of the year with sandwiches for the 250-mile trip that it was my job to complete before her mandatory viewing of *Saturday Night Live*.

A rabbi's daughter who had grown up in the Conservative Movement, Gita knew many of the conference attendees since childhood, so on the return trip we would review what we had learned, struggling to curtail *l'shon ha-ra*—defined as "scandal mongering." We would also indulge in some private Christmas caroling, courtesy of Gita's American public schooling and mine in a Montreal Protestant high school. One year we were joined by a scholar-rabbi who objected to our Christian songfest; it may have been the last time we offered anyone a ride.

At first, I experienced no tension between the typical elements of a Jewish studies program or conference and those of other disciplines. I simply assumed that relevant aspects of Jewish history, such as Jewish religion and thought or Jewish languages and culture, would be and were already being integrated without difficulty into the sphere of the humanities and social sciences.

Some of my interventions as president worked well, as when I corrected the underrepresentation of history at the annual conferences by asking several senior scholars to organize panels in this area. I made no headway, however, in promoting greater use of Hebrew or getting scholars to send complimentary copies of their books to the National Library of Israel, both of which would advance our field of research. Nor did I realize how quickly changes in the rest of the academy would affect our corner of it.

When a group of feminist professors wanted to organize a breakfast caucus, I was unable to dissuade them from promoting the women's movement within the AJS. I had entered the academy to function as an academic, "irrespective of race, creed, or gender," and regarded this Little Girls' Club as both a retreat from maturity and a bid for collective power. Even the concept of "women's studies" seemed to limit our scope, since unlike national or religious groups that developed their own culture, women were always in interaction with others and could best be studied in a holistic framework whether in literature, history, sociology, or religion.

But at least women's studies undertook academic research within an academic framework. The women's caucus made it less likely that these women would collaborate with their male colleagues in serious scholarship.

The caucus organized by Americans for Peace Now went farther in changing the pattern of association from scholarship to politics. I was delighted when Irving Howe agreed to participate in the AJS for the first time until I learned that he had joined a panel so that he could simultaneously lend prestige to the Peace Now group. It quickly followed that when I tried to stop this politicization, I was accused of engaging in politics. Once the founding generation passed from the scene, it was only a matter of time before the organization would trend with the rest of the academy.

The AJS was still in its infancy when Arab anti-Zionism began penetrating the universities in the mid-1970s. As the trickle of Palestinian protesters became a well-funded initiative that would eventually give birth to the movement for "Boycott, Divestment, and Sanctions" (BDS) and then merge with the grievance coalition of "intersectionality," Jews ceased to be a neutral constituency on campus, and Jewish studies came under strain. The organization did not acquit it itself well once Jews (and males) came under assault.

∽

I NEVER LIKED THEORY, THE elevation of the particular to a level of abstraction, and therefore chose literature over philosophy, at first simply by instinct. That resistance to theory is what appealed to me when I heard David Hartman contrast Greek philosophy and the Talmud, which will not even distinguish between legal principle and anecdote, between the rules governing the high priest and placement of privies in the Temple. My preference was by no means anti-intellectual, but I trusted the mind that made distinctions more than the kind that tried to homogenize and combine. I considered the former to be harder and sounder.

This discomfort with theory did not extend to comprehending the laws of nature, meaning the findings of science. If I prayed, I would have included the benefits of medicine and technology in my daily blessings. But science stays humbled through controlled experiments whereas social and cultural theory remains impervious to disproof. People worry me when they think they can fathom humankind better than God does. I don't know how else to put it. Give me Dostoevsky over Karl Marx, Kafka over Walter Benjamin.

This explains my compounded alarm at the rise of postcolonialism, the application of already disproven Marxist and Leninist theory to European imperialism—theories that arose in the academy when colonial powers were already withdrawing or being repelled. Yet Frantz Fanon attributed the wretchedness of once-colonized populations to the continuing aftereffects of subjugation on every aspect of life. Enlisting the British term for junior officer, Gayatri Spivak created the category of "subaltern" for women and colonized people who could not speak for themselves owing to their systematic suppression by those in power. Suddenly, papers in the humanities and social sciences felt obliged to include these theories which inveighed against Western democracies, reduced critical thinking to power arrangements, encouraged victimhood while discouraging agency, and required dishonesty of everyone—tokenism on the part of those intelligent enough to realize the fallacy of these ideas and corroboration from those who obediently applied them.

The most influential among the founders of postcolonial theory was Edward Said, the Palestinian scholar-activist who launched an anti-Zionist offensive that almost singlehandedly won the war against the Jews in the academy. A former student of Lionel Trilling, who had subordinated his

Jewishness to what he considered the larger claims of Western civilization, Said had no compunctions about doing the reverse. He used the skills and status he had acquired in his Western education to accuse its scholarship of "Orientalism," or prejudicially patronizing the Arabs and other "Eastern" cultures it studied. In his bestselling book on the subject, Said charged Western scholars, Jews prominent among them, with intellectual imperialism for laboring to understand cultures other than their own. His inversion was straight out of the anti-Semitic arsenal that attacked Jews for conspiring to conquer the societies they had been trying to serve and improve.

Said's accusation complemented postcolonial grievance, with the added frisson of blaming the Jews. Said himself personified the case against Israel in a narrative designed to delegitimate the Jewish state. Born in Jerusalem during a visit to relatives by his parents, who were actually living comfortably in Cairo, and raised in Egypt (his father was also an American citizen), he claimed that he grew up in Jerusalem and was "expelled" from his home there. His biographical makeover won him canonical status as a member of the Palestine National Council, and the corrected actual account by Justus Weiner in 1999 did not appear to damage Said's reputation.

At Columbia University, Said came to dominate not only the Middle East Institute—which controlled appointments in Hebrew—but all the humanities. After the fall of the Soviet Union in 1989, postcolonialism replaced communism as the theoretical framework of choice for the academic left, and Palestinians were touted as prime examples of the "subalterns," the oppressed. These postmodern locutions cloaked their radical intentions and added an air of mystique and authority to their war against the civilization that the university claimed to transmit.

It was depressing to see this kind of Orwellian double-speak infect student papers and classroom discussion and to recognize the many Jewish professors signed on to Said's anti-Israel petitions. Even after Said's death in 2003, his legacy remained at Columbia through appointments he had arranged for his protégés.

I expected Jewish academics to provide an intellectual and academic framework for explicating and defending the Jewish people's connection to the Land of Israel. The growing campus assault called for rebuttal and correction, with Jewish studies leading the way. After all, virtually every academic discipline—archaeology, cartography, economics, geography, history, linguistics, literature, politics, psychology, religion, sociology, theology—possessed tools for substantiating the Jewish right to the Jewish homeland and, conversely, for demonstrating the falsity of its denial.

Instead, Jewish academics began caving to the anti-Zionist assault from Port Said. The situation at that heavily Jewish endowed and populated university brought to mind a favorite anecdote of Avrom Sutzkever's about the rabbi and his students who take a summer stroll outside town and all come back running for their lives. Fearing a pogrom, the townspeople ask what happened. The rabbi gasps, "A *sheygetzl* came toward us and there we were, the ten of us, all alone." The comedy of Jewish cowardice expressed through the diminutive of being "all alone"—*zalbetsent, eyninke aleyn*—against a lone gentile boy became my image of the postmodern academy.

The few who immediately countered the attacks, like Alvin Rosenfeld at the University of Indiana or Tammi Rossman-Benjamin and Leila Beckwith in the University of California system, showed that effective leadership could straighten the record—and the Jewish backbone. They called out this defamation and insisted the school administrators deal with it as firmly as they opposed all other campus aggression. As anti-Jewish animus spread, academic groups like Scholars for Peace in the Middle East (SPME) and Academic Engagement Network (AEN) formed to expose the anti-Jewish propaganda, provide factual information about Israel, and protect professors and students who were being personally attacked. The representative organization of Jewish Studies, however, acquiesced in silence, and professors who did finally start to organize for Israel came mostly from outside the AJS.

And so, instead of advancing Jewish civilization, as I had expected, the expansion of Jewish studies accompanied a decline in Jewish moral confidence. Though the AJS never responded to attacks on Israel, some hundred and seventy members later signed a petition objecting when President Trump moved the American embassy to Jerusalem. For the most part, younger scholars followed academic trends, including those openly hostile to Judaism, while senior scholars shirked their duty behind the excuse of academic neutrality.

In my active years I had tried to lure senior professors to AJS conferences for the luster conferred by their presence. Once it hurt to attend, I joined the ranks of absentees, and I was not missed.

CR

ONE MORNING IN 1992, THE phone rang in Montreal and on the line was a stranger's voice saying (I am transcribing from vivid memory): "This is Zalman Bernstein and I'm speaking from Jerusalem. You don't know me. I want to talk to you, but this call is costing me a fucking fortune and I can't stand being overcharged. I'll give you my number. Call me back, I'll reimburse you."

Naturally, I dialed the number. For this call I was to be compensated beyond reckoning.

Zalman, né Sanford, was unlike anyone I knew. My family was in textiles, some of our friends were in business; but financial services—making money by investing money profitably—was as strange to me as alchemy, and Zalman was unusual even among his peers. He had launched his investment firm with full-page ads in the *New York Times* and *Wall Street Journal* that featured the single word **Bernstein** in the center of an otherwise blank page. Everyone had stories to tell about this man whose intelligence and brashness had earned him a fortune while providing ample returns to his clients.

The legend really took off in the late 1970s when Sanford himself underwent a transformation. In one of many versions, he had gone one afternoon to Lincoln Square Synagogue near his office to say Kaddish, the memorial prayer, for his recently deceased father. He was then Sandy to his friends, a man about town. After the service, being a pay-as-you-go kind of guy, he asked the rabbi how much he owed. Rabbi Shlomo Riskin, himself no shrinking violet, replied, "You don't have enough money to pay what you owe." Bernstein: "Do you know who I am?" The rabbi said he didn't, but did Zalman know what a synagogue was?

The upshot of this showdown was that Sandy began studying privately with Riskin, and because the rabbi would not tolerate the obscenities that his pupil could not suppress, they settled on a $180 fine for every verbal offense. A different variant of this urban legend by Riskin himself sets the initial encounter in a crowded lecture hall where Sandy stood up and, as a sign of his bona fides, opened his shirt to reveal his late father's ritual fringes. But all end with Sanford becoming Zalman and thenceforth living in accordance with Jewish religious law. Such a Jew is known as a *ba'al t'shuvah,* one who has returned to Judaism and to active membership in the Jewish people.

I was drawn to this man from the moment I heard his raspy voice. Without exaggeration, I had never met anyone so focused on results and so little concerned about the impression he made in achieving them. His red suspenders, habitual profanity, and impatience with anyone who underperformed were foreign to the religious community he joined. But he did not expect to lead by example; he expected to lead so effectively that people would overlook or excuse his example.

A half-dozen years after that first visit to Rabbi Riskin's synagogue, Zalman brought together several distinguished business friends to establish a foundation he called Avi Chai, My Father Lives (an allusion to Genesis 45:3). Handing over control of his company to trusted associates, he conducted his philanthropy by the same standards that had made him his fortune. Rabbi David Hartman once complained that men headed organizations so that they could make the mistakes they could not afford to make in their businesses; Zalman brought the best investment practices to his philanthropic ventures. Rather than soliciting applications, his "trustee-driven" foundation identified and vetted the projects it intended to support and the persons who might carry them out. Trustees were expected to drive themselves almost as hard as the founder drove himself.

Zalman never told me what prompted him to invite me to join the Avi Chai board as its sixth inductee. My own hope was that, after too many years of idly worrying about the Jews and Israel, I would now in my fifties have a chance to "get something done." The mission of Avi Chai was to perpetuate (I would have said reinforce) the Jewish people, Judaism, and the centrality of the state of Israel. To achieve this in North America, the foundation promoted "understanding, appreciation, and practice of Jewish traditions, customs, and laws." In Israel, it encouraged Jews from different backgrounds and dispositions to understand and appreciate each other. The initials LRP, shorthand for literacy, religious purposefulness, and peoplehood, became the standard for assessing how well we were advancing our aims.

The first thing I learned was that financial support, even when rooted in solid intentions and combined with genuine effort, did not necessarily produce good results. One challenge was pointed out to me by Roger Hertog, who was Zalman's closest business associate and who, after the latter's death, would become chairman of the Tikvah Fund, another of the foundations he established. American philanthropy, Roger said, was essentially liberal in its assumptions of how a society could be changed through, in effect, strategic engineering. Foundations like Ford and MacArthur had actually reversed the intentions of their conservative benefactors. The traditionalist objectives of our venture were thus at odds with the conventional methods of achieving them.

In fact, at the time I joined the board, Zalman and I were the only ones who voted for conservative political candidates, and I'm not even certain about him. Of course, charitable foundations were prevented by law from directly engaging in politics, but somehow, of the two political directions, only conservatism was deemed to be "political" while liberal causes were perceived to be just benevolent. We were moving against a powerful current.

A trustee-driven foundation meant that all the initiatives came from the board. Here was one of them in the early years of experimentation: it seemed a good idea to pursue our aims by "promoting awareness of Jewish holidays and rituals through advertising in the Jewish and general media." We enlisted the help of an advertising executive who shared our goals, and he invited several young Jews in his firm to brainstorm with us. After we had outlined the general concept, I asked them to tell us which holidays or items of Jewish practice *they* thought could be effectively promoted in a broad campaign.

Instead of answering, they balked at the very notion that there was anything in Jewishness they would *endorse*, that is, designate as a value. In other words, they responded not as professionals to a client but as Jews who could not accept any normative, much less prescriptive, goal. "Choice" was the ultimate modern value, and here we were suggesting that it was *better* for Jews to live as Jews! Too late, we realized that we would have done better with a Gentile and conservative firm.

The reaction of these staffers persuaded me that our campaign would probably be perceived by the Jews we were trying to reach—liberal people just like them—as unwelcome coercion. Thankfully, Zalman applied measurements of outcome that shut down projects like this one as soon as they fell short of their stated aims.

Sooner or later, everyone in advocacy thinks of persuading filmmakers to take up their cause. When it was proposed at Avi Chai, I thought of David Brandes, who had written and produced a fine Jewish film, *The Quarrel,* based on a story by the Yiddish writer Chaim Grade. Grade was the poet whose work Irving Howe and I had been unable to include in our Yiddish poetry anthology, but after the war he had also become a writer of prose. In this story two former yeshiva classmates, estranged when Chaim (the implied author) quits the yeshiva to become a secular Yiddish poet, meet up in Paris after the war that had destroyed their entire former world, including their families. Rather than reminisce or exchange experiences or engage in any dramatic action like getting drunk together, the religious Jew and the secular Jew pick up the argument where they left off nine years earlier. Their argument aired competing challenges of faith in Man and faith in God.

That Brandes had managed to make an affecting film from this philosophic material made me confident that he could lead our effort. We invited him to organize a study group of Jews in film who wanted to learn more about their heritage with an eye to incorporating parts of it in their own creative work. He organized one group of well-established writers and another more socially oriented group for younger people in movies and television. The expectations were unusually modest: a local rabbi or scholar would lead monthly discussions about Jewish sources in the hope that deeper knowledge would create greater Jewish self-confidence. The reports were good. I led a session about Sholem Aleichem and found the groups interesting and responsive. But the study circles continued for only so long as we supplied the resources, and as far as I know, not a single project ever came of them.

By contrast, when Avi Chai then undertook similar initiatives in Israel, they resulted in high-quality films. Among the most successful have been those that humanize the image of Ḥaredim, the so-called ultra-Orthodox whom many Israelis, religious and secular alike, have long resented for their low participation rates in the workforce and the exemption they enjoy from national service. Israeli productions funded by Avi Chai, like the film *Ushpizin* and the television series *Shtisel*, were eventually imported into America. We learned that creators in their sovereign country may have the cultural confidence that American Jewish filmmakers have rarely shown.

After several years of launching such projects, the board determined we could best achieve our aims in North America by investing primarily in Jewish elementary and high schools. Reliable data showed that students attending such schools were also likeliest to continue Jewish practice. Similar claims for the lasting influence of Jewish camping were also confirmed by the data, and in this area as well, Avi Chai invested significantly.

Education had long been the mainstay of Jewish life in the Diaspora, but the high cost of American day school tuition had made it, in one wag's formula, "the most effective form of Jewish birth control." Cost was only part of the problem of sustaining high-quality Jewish education in an open, culturally competitive society. Once we concentrated on this area, the staff, headed by Yossi Prager, initiated programs of matching grants and loans for the construction or expansion of buildings, training principals and mentoring new teachers, setting standards for various subjects and improving curricular materials, and encouraging modest experiments in online and distance learning.

Henry Taub, a successful entrepreneur who headed the International Board of the Technion Institute in Haifa, was the logical choice to lead the effort when we looked for ways of sustaining Jewish schools on a permanent basis. Henry was a lifelong Democrat, member of a Reform synagogue, and liberal in his instincts. His children had not attended Jewish schools and his politics favored the teachers' unions. It was all the more sobering when he reported back that Jewish schooling could not flourish in the long run without government support. Neither his political inclinations nor any false optimism prevented him from honestly assessing the data.

Active in Israel and America, the foundation sometimes had to work toward a common goal in opposite ways. In education, for example, we in America needed financial support from government for the general studies part of the curriculum while Israelis tried to get government to stop calling the tune. In other areas, the incredible lightness of being a Jew in North America contrasted brutally with Israeli exigencies of self-defense.

A brand-new set of challenges opened when trustee George Rohr urged us to extend our work to the world's third-largest Jewish community in the former Soviet Union. New initiatives had to be designed for a population that had been forcibly deprived of Jewish culture for seventy years.

A sovereign country may occasionally elect a strong and wise leader, whereas Diaspora Jews are led by whoever seizes the reins. This randomness made me grateful for Zalman's leadership and fearful when he was diagnosed with lymphoma. All I could think of was what my mother said when I fell sick: "*Mir zol zayn far dir,*" would that I could endure this in your stead.

But his genius proved itself then above all. He had appointed philanthropic heirs—Arthur Fried, Mem Bernstein, and Roger Hertog—who were able to continue and expand his work. They established a permanent Avi Chai Center in Jerusalem, and through the Keren Keshet Foundation and Tikvah Fund cultivated new cultural centers in North America, the latter fostering a new amalgam of Jewish conservatism.

These three custodians and the professionals they hired stimulated Jewish culture and strengthened Jewish life. Their efforts could not make up for the collapse of Jewish morale in the universities, but they created alternatives. When I retired from the university, I continued to enjoy teaching through the seminars and online courses of the Tikvah Fund.

THE LESS I WANTED TO take on organizational leadership, the more I honored those who did. I knew people who had founded magazines, schools, and philanthropies. But in 1981, Midge Decter founded a new organization, Committee for the Free World, to fight for political and economic freedom at home and abroad. She drew up a statement and invited intellectuals and academics to sign it: signing made you a member. The Committee published a monthly bulletin, *Contentions,* and sponsored an annual conference in New York or Washington, and as far as I know that was the sum of its political action. But what a boon it was for this Montreal provincial to attend those gatherings and mingle with the people who were fighting communism, which I considered the most urgent international threat.

Contentions specialized in skewering fashionable anti-American writing and scholarship. In one of the issues making fun of recent literary prizes, Midge exposed the anti-Americanism of Gore Vidal, an icon of the literary Left. To my unpleasant surprise, Saul Bellow, who until then had his name on the masthead, withdrew from the board and wrote in pique that he could not allow others to speak in his name about writers and literature. "Where there are enemies to be made, I prefer to make them myself, on my own grounds and in my own language."

News of his resignation reached me just when he was coming to Montreal for celebrations in his honor. I was to be one of the speakers. Saul was my most beloved and *necessary* writer and thanks to his visits to Montreal we had even struck up the beginnings of a friendship. All this I put at risk when I slipped him a note saying how disappointed I was that he could have put any consideration ahead of fighting for America and against the Soviet Union.

He chose to take no offense, and in fact, asked Len and me to invite Louis Dudek, another of Saul's local admirers, to join the three of us the next night for dinner. It was a great evening. Len and Saul traded stories about local politics and Louis admitted that Saul had done better to stick with his Jewishness than he had done in abandoning his Polish roots. As for *Contentions,* I saw that Saul and I could only be friends if I was prepared to

283

accept that as between literary politics and real politics, Saul and I had different priorities.

When the Soviet Union unexpectedly crumbled in 1991, I happened to be in Russia at a training program for young European Jewish leaders. At dinner, I proposed a toast to President Reagan and to the Committee for the Free World for helping to bring down "the evil empire." Once that blessed event occurred, Midge, defying every convention of foundation life, declared "mission accomplished" and shut down the operation.

CR

No such definitive victories could be claimed in the ongoing Arab war against Israel. CAMERA—the Committee for Accuracy in Middle East Reporting in America—was founded in 1982 by Winifred Meiselman to expose the *Washington Post*'s distorting coverage of Israel. I learned of it and joined the board when Andrea Levin, head of its Boston chapter, took charge several years after.

Israel's incursion into Lebanon to try to eliminate the terrorist attacks of the PLO became the excuse for unrelenting negative coverage. The well-staffed Jerusalem bureau of the *New York Times*, to cite just the clearest example, used Israel's democratic press to publish the Left's attacks on the government, while kowtowing to censorship on the Arab side and publishing its verifiably false reports. CAMERA organized a team to monitor the media and correct disinformation on a daily basis. In 1989, I was one of the speakers at what was until then the most ambitious conference on the media's treatment of Israel. The draw of over one thousand people gave the momentary impression of a movement that could actually correct the problem.

As I was then doing my own tracking of media coverage of Israel and often writing and lecturing on anti-Jewish propaganda, I knew how grim this labor could be. Above my desk I pasted the Polish proverb, "It is a terrible thing to swim upstream in a filthy river." Since someone had to do it, I could not thank Andrea enough for building this indispensable organization. The same held true for other remarkable women and men who in the following years created political, legal, media, and eventually, even the aforementioned academic organizations to counter the multipronged war against Israel and the Jews.

In 1991, on one of my trips to New York, Lucy Dawidowicz introduced me to Seth Lipsky, who had recently become the editor of the English-language *Forward*. (The paper was originally founded in 1897 as the Yiddish-socialist *Forverts* by the renowned editor Abraham Cahan.) Lucy had already established the Fund for the Translation of Jewish Literature to help me put out a series of Yiddish classics, and she kept me up to date on what was going in New York. What Midge Decter did through her organization, Lucy did informally by bringing like-minded people together. Through her I met Irving Kristol and his wife, the formidable historian Bea Himmelfarb. Now she thought it would be fruitful for Seth and me to know one another.

Seth was a newspaperman of genius. After working for twenty years at the *Wall Street Journal*, he wanted to run his own paper, and with the backing of some bold investors he assumed leadership of this Jewish weekly, determined to dwarf the coverage of the *New York Times* on everything concerning the Jews, which happened to include much that went on in the world.

The *Times* was not ideologically anti-Semitic in fascist or Soviet terms, and it still did reliable reporting on other issues—but not on the Jews. Its liberal opposition to Jewish religious civilization and to the political sovereignty of the Jewish people actually dated from the same year that Cahan started up the *Forverts*, when Adolph Ochs bought the *Times* and imbued it with his own German-Jewish antagonism to Jewish peoplehood. Ochs was closely aligned with the Reform Movement that tried to redefine Judaism as a religion like Protestantism, an ethical code of conduct without a national biblical foundation. A newspaper that enjoyed succession through several family members (including through marriage) and employed hundreds of editors over twelve decades cannot be defined monolithically except as politically Democrat and traditionally anti-Zionist. It opposed anti-Semitism when it threatened Jews—including the owners—but downplayed anything that promoted Jewish self-emancipation, gave notoriously low coverage to Hitler's Final Solution, and kept pace with anti-Zionism in its coverage of

Israel. In monitoring the media for accuracy and bias, CAMERA could have used a full-time employee for *Times* coverage alone. One year, it posted a billboard opposite the *Times* building that juxtaposed a pointed missile and a pointed pen with the message: "HAMAS attacks Israel, not surprising. *New York Times* attacks Israel, also not surprising."

Lucy, Seth, and I, proud Jews all, felt that standing up for the Jews and America went hand in hand, not least because they faced the same assailants and stood for the same democratic values. Seth intended his paper to provide an antidote to the daily diet of corruption that *Times* readers were being fed. As a means of supplying readers with a crash course in modern and American Jewish history, Lucy undertook to cull from the archives of the Yiddish daily *Forverts* a pick of "what happened this day fifty and seventy-five years ago." Cahan's socialist leanings had evolved greatly over the decades. Though the ears of the paper--on either side of the masthead--continued to carry the Marxist slogan, "Workers of the world unite: You have nothing to lose but your chains," the paper mostly familiarized readers with modern America and tracked dangers to the Jews of Europe. Cahan was an early anticommunist back when socialists were among the fiercest opponents of Sovietization, and in 1921, when the Soviet Union established the Yiddish daily *Freiheit* as its American beachhead, Cahan was its fiercest opponent. Cahan also visited Palestine for himself in 1926, and what he witnessed there made him drop his earlier hostility to the Zionist project.

Cahan's *Forverts* indisputably slowed the drift of American Jews into pro-Soviet ranks, and Seth intended to do the same against the leftism of his day. He hired young writers and created a culture of muscular journalism that I doubt any professional school ever rivaled. At one time or another his staffers included Jeffrey Goldberg, Ben Smith, Ira Stoll, Jonathan Rosen, Alana Newhouse, Jonathan Mahler, and Philip Gourevitch, to name only those who then forged their own careers in journalism. For a time, I submitted a bimonthly column that ran simultaneously in the *Canadian Jewish News*.

Seth's long-term intention was to turn the paper back into a daily. But in 2000 he was outmaneuvered by those who embraced a sodden version of the leftism that Cahan had outgrown eight decades earlier. This deprived

Jewish journalism of the best paper it had ever fielded and came just before the internet had begun to kill off print journalism. Seth himself went on to found the New York daily *Sun*, and, when that proved unsustainable, a pared-down version as an editorial website.

At media conference of the Committee for Middle East Reporting in America, (CAMERA) New York. April 1999. With Len, executive director Andrea Levin, writer Cynthia Ozick, and her husband Bernard Hallote.

Ever since Seth's ouster at the *Forward*, I've called it the *Backward*. (The online Yiddish *Forverts*, by contrast, stayed somewhat lighter on political provocation.) In 2018, the *Forward* editor boasted in the same breath of the publication's "fearless" independence and of being personally congratulated for her editorial achievements by the *New York Times*. She was soon replaced by an editor *from* the *Times!*

ॐ

WHEN THE IDEOLOGICAL WAR AGAINST the Jews was launched through the Zionism-Racism resolution at the United Nations in 1975, the man who led the charge against it was not a Jew, though he acknowledged the help of his good friend Norman Podhoretz. Daniel Patrick Moynihan, then U.S.

Ambassador to the UN, could not prevent the Soviet-Arab bloc from pushing through the resolution in the General Assembly but rose immediately after its passage to declare, "A great evil has been loosed upon the world." He denounced the resolution's misuse of Nazism's racist language to slander Zionism as successor of Nazism and accused it of contravening the very purpose of the United Nations, of corrupting the organization and the idea of human rights it was created to enshrine. Since the House of Representatives had voted to condemn the resolution by a vote of 436 to one, Moynihan could truly say, "The United States of America declares that it does not acknowledge, it will not abide by, it will never acquiesce in this infamous act." Channeling Roosevelt, he called it a day that "will live in infamy."

But Moynihan did not represent all Americans after all. As this ideological assault on Israel intensified, it soon swept with it the academy, parts of the media, the Democratic Party, and the liberal Jews among them, as had formerly happened in the face of Marxist accusations. The self-proclaimed idealists in each instance promoted perversions they should have led the fight to oppose. Individual anti-Zionists like Noam Chomsky quickly bourgeoned into groups like J-Street, Bending the Curve, Jewish Students for Peace, and Students for Justice (actually, Jew killing) in Palestine, that masked their hostility in benevolent concern for the real aggressors just as their forebears—with far greater risk to themselves—had once sacrificed their fellow Jews to the cause of peasants and proletariat. Amazing how the study of Yiddish literature had educated me in politics. In sour moments I said that I had been teaching the history of Jewish mistakes.

Literature was both my instructor in politics and its elevation to a timeless, more commodious sphere. Y. L. Peretz—author and welder of *The Golden Chain*—wrote this story on the predicament of Jewish leadership as he experienced it:

Rabbi Naḥman of Bratslav has just been "revealed." In Hasidic idiom, this means he has been recognized by his followers as their leader. But as they prepare to celebrate his assumption of authority, he abruptly leaves their company and when discovered, he is in a state of dejection. They urge him to rejoin them, and in yielding to their entreaty—it is the Sabbath, after all, when gloom is prohibited—he offers them this "Tale of the Billy Goat."

Our goat feeds on a special plot of grass that makes its horns grow so luxuriant and strong that when unfurled they reach the moon. The goat does this periodically, hooking its horns over the lower tip of the moon's crescent to ask, "Isn't it time for the messiah to come?" The moon relays this question to a star, which passes it to another, and so on all the way to the Throne of Glory. The only response ever heard from the heights is a sigh, but the goat perseveres because "such questionings can cumulatively have their effect...." Peretz loved to trail off his sentences with ellipses.

One day, a Jew strolling on the outskirts of town catches sight of the well-endowed goat and asks for a sliver of the splendid horns to carve himself a snuff box. The goat obligingly bends down, and the resulting box becomes the envy of the synagogue. One after another, Jews come asking the goat for a piece of its horns and the goat obliges them all, with the obvious consequence.... The story saddens the Ḥasidim, but in the spirit of Rabbi Naḥman himself, Peretz assures his listeners that it all ended well. The Jews shall have their leader but not their redemption; in this golden chain of storytelling, the teller will comfort his readers without achieving the sublime.

Peretz, Rabbi Naḥman, and the parabolic Billy Goat are all at the service of the Jewish people. Each might prefer to advance his claims in inspirational spurts of genius, but a people needs plainer satisfaction of the kind that comes though snuff boxes or reassuring tales. Rare and precious are the writer-intellectuals and those who lead the Jews without yielding to despair. Peretz reminds us of our divine mission and of all the good that is already within our grasp.

13

ARRIVAL

On January 1, 1993, I arrived at Harvard to take up a newly endowed professorship in Yiddish literature. It seemed preposterous: me at Harvard, Yiddish at Harvard. But as the taxi deposited me at the entrance to Lowell House, a new chapter of my life began in pretty much the way new chapters begin in some of the novels I teach.

The temperature was in the midfifties, which, coming from snow-bound Montreal, I took as a splendid omen. A student resident of the house who introduced himself as Shai Held (later to become a noted rabbi and author) directed me to the apartment I was renting. It was more than ample for my needs: bedroom with desk, cupboard, lamp; sparsely furnished living and eating area; smaller second bedroom in case one of the children came to visit; galley kitchen; bathroom with shower. Len would not be joining me for several months, so I did not expect to entertain. The ground-floor apartment looked out on the courtyard, which, being winter break, was wonderfully still.

Harvard had never figured in my aspirations. Several years earlier, I had received a phone call from Lucy Dawidowicz, saying that a position in Yiddish literature was being set up at Harvard and that I would likely become its first incumbent. I laughed, asking whether she was exchanging history for prophecy. This may have discouraged her from saying any more about it.

Lucy died on December 5, 1990, scant weeks after learning that she had cancer of the liver, and thus was not around when Harvard announced that

Martin Peretz, publisher of the *New Republic* and a former lecturer at the university, had endowed a chair in Yiddish. Had I asked Lucy to explain herself instead of advertising my indifference, I might have learned how the initiative came about. But I disregarded Lucy's augury, and, likewise, when the new position was announced, I ignored Harvard's call for applications and never looked at the job description.

In truth, I felt very much at home at McGill, where I had worked hard to establish the program in Jewish studies. I also appreciated how attached Len was to his birthplace and his father's before him. We had a good life in Montreal with family, friends, and colleagues.

Yet by the 1990s things were not so straightforward. I had been appointed to McGill's first named chair in Jewish studies; but since the university funded no graduate fellowships in our field, I would miss the chance to prepare future scholars of Yiddish.

Moreover, our own children had joined the exodus of English-speaking youth from Montreal. Billy was working at the quiz show *Jeopardy!* in Los Angeles; Jacob was studying art history in New York; and Abby, in Israel, was employed at the *Jerusalem Report*. Apart from my job at McGill, almost everything else in my working life—publishing, lecturing, participating in the Boston-based Association for Jewish Studies—was situated in the United States.

Thus, when biblical scholar James Kugel, heading Harvard's search committee, invited me to be considered for the new position, I did not immediately decline. I asked what the process required, and he replied, not much: I was to submit my curriculum vitae, deliver a seminar-style lecture, and meet informally with faculty and students.

Len urged me on, saying I had nothing to lose, which, except for the tranquility of a predictable future, was true enough. In the years that followed, when people asked, "How do you like Harvard?" my mind would slip back to my exploratory visits when I repeatedly asked myself the very same question. Harvard subsumes those in its orbit. No one had ever asked me how I liked McGill.

Ꮗ

CROSS HARVARD YARD ANY DAY of the week, and you have to skirt clusters of tourists photographing the statue titled *John Harvard, Founder, 1638,* that stands outside the administration building. Campus guides enjoy pointing out that the statue is "a trio of lies." John Harvard was a mere contributor to the college; the college was founded in 1636; and the statue is actually a likeness of someone else. Yet these fictions have become part of the school's mystique.

So, too, as I came to know the place, any weaknesses I discovered made me feel duty-bound to help correct them. When I was already teaching there, an exchange student from China told me she had sought me out because I was the world's expert on American Jewish literature. Refusing to accept my demurral, she insisted that it must be so or I would not be at Harvard. This being the case, the credit she was conferring on me would redound to her as well, and to the Chinese institution that she would return to serve back home. There is no discounting presumed value, and it is not *always* groundless.

My impressions of Harvard had been formed mostly from what I knew of its program in Jewish studies. Harry Austryn Wolfson, the first tenured professor in this field in the United States, who taught philosophy there from 1915 to 1958, was world-renowned for his erudition. He was said to have been the first to enter and the last to leave Widener Library every single day of the week. Some of his repute devolved upon his successor, Isadore Twersky, who received his PhD from Wolfson and then built a program in classical and medieval Jewish studies that was labeled, only half in jest, Harvard's "yeshiva."

I had a taste of this atmosphere several years earlier during a week of research on Y. L. Peretz. Widener's entire Yiddish collection was still on open shelves, and the scholarly part of my soul delighted in the monastic stillness of the lamp-lit cubicle assigned to me in a corner of the stacks. In my otherwise favorite place of study, the Judaica reading room at the National Library in Jerusalem, half a dozen colleagues might intercept you as you tried to find a place at a table. Depending on how many of them were grabbing a smoke in the foyer, a trip to the restroom could cost you an hour's reading.

Twersky's chilly authority garnered respect for Jewish studies at Harvard. Of the other ordained rabbis who were then teaching in universities, he was probably the most demanding and certainly the most intriguing. Scion of the Talner Hasidic dynasty that dated from the mid-eighteenth century, he inherited his father's position as spiritual leader of the Talner congregation in Brookline, where in addition to his full-time Harvard position he carried out the duties of teacher, pastor, and religious authority. Somehow, Rabbi Professor Twersky managed to satisfy both of his constituencies, while simultaneously setting a standard for expertise in primary Jewish sources that made the Harvard program preeminent in scholarship.

Though I admired the Twersky academic model, the search committee for the Yiddish chair was looking for something else. In endowing it, Marty Peretz had wanted to moderate what he considered the rigidity of Jewish studies with its overemphasis on medieval texts. The introduction of Yiddish and its modern secular literature would shift the academic stress from rabbinic high culture to the everyday life of the Jews of Eastern Europe and their American descendants. Marty had been raised in the socialist branch of that culture and valued the part of Jewish heritage that rose through language, literature, and folklore from the bottom up rather than through Talmudic learning from the top down.

Some of my prospective colleagues, similarly eager for more modern subjects, also thought that my administrative experience at McGill and the Association for Jewish Studies would qualify me to succeed Twersky as director of Harvard's Center for Jewish Studies. And my gender—ah, my gender! Let's just say that by the 1990s, an all-male program in the almost exclusively male Department of Near Eastern Languages and Civilizations felt obliged to appoint a female. That is how the female for whom Harvard's "yeshiva" had been her ideal of Jewish studies became a shoo-in for the position in a program she was loath to change.

The ironies did not end there. The Department of Comparative Literature, where I was to hold a joint appointment, was undergoing its own transformation. Founded by polyglot scholars who enjoyed investigating the creative interplay among literatures, the department was now moving in the direction of literary theory and interdisciplinary approaches described to me by one student as "making ingenious connections among the least likely subjects."

This quip reminded me of Dr. Johnson's unflattering verdict on the metaphysical poets, in whose verses "the most heterogeneous ideas are yoked by violence together." But those were ideas, not ideological theories. By 1993, no self-styled academic conservative like me—who taught literature old style, one text at a time, reading along the grain rather than against it, with appreciation for its texture and its historical, cultural, and linguistic contexts—could have won the vote of some of the department's trendsetters had I not been a woman. In yet another irony, these progressive members of the committee did not know that I had opposed affirmative action for women at McGill.

In short, I was appointed at least in part on the basis of a policy I deplored. "Tits and ass," I would occasionally mutter to myself in the years that followed, quoting one of the most cynical songs in the Broadway musical *A Chorus Line.*

The interview process proved almost as easygoing as Jim Kugel had promised. I enjoyed it immensely, inured against failure by not having sought the job in the first place. In his memoir, *Making It,* Norman Podhoretz writes that not wanting a job is a reliable way of getting it. While I would probably have felt some disappointment had the position gone to someone else, part of me wished to be spared the decision that would be required if I were offered it.

Because I did have misgivings. About a decade earlier, Twersky had invited me to Harvard to speak at a symposium on modern Jewish studies. On the appointed afternoon, I'd made my way to a hall where the sun shone in on almost empty rows. No one approached to greet me. I went up to the front to thank our host for having invited me and took my seat on the platform with him and the other three speakers, all of whom were from the Hebrew University.

Without preamble, Twersky read off our names and topics, adding that the four of us would present our papers in sequence, with discussion reserved for the end. A half hour into the program, I had already lowered any expectations of a lively give-and-take when a female student suddenly appeared at the back of the hall and began to shout, "You should be teaching love, not spreading hate! You're preaching hate! Hate!" Our chairman did not react. Taking their cue from him, the other participants tried to continue as if nothing were amiss. But the screaming girl was not to be ignored, and the lack of a response only induced her to yell louder.

Finally stepping down from the speakers' platform, I asked her to join me in the hall outside. There she began to lay out her Palestinian grievances against Israel and the Jews. Resisting the urge to reeducate her on the sources of aggression—with herself as exhibit A—I said merely that her interference was inappropriate in an academic gathering on subjects far removed from those that were concerning her, and that she had no business harassing Jewish-studies scholars.

The young woman appeared to accept my objections and took off without another word. I returned to the hall, where there had been no pause in the proceedings. At the close, in saying our goodbyes, Twersky thanked me so obliquely that I was not sure whether he was alluding to my participation in the event or to my intervention with the protester. But the awkwardness inside the room and the assault from outside hardly endeared the place to me.

When I met again with Twersky as part of the interview process, he again set me a little on edge by probing for my weaknesses rather than discussing subjects of mutual interest. The more he probed, the less I tried to impress him—I was not, after all, his graduate student—leaving him obviously disappointed with me. Quoting his predecessor, Harry Wolfson, he said, "Scholarship is not writing everything you know about a subject, but *knowing* everything that is to be known about a subject." I replied, "That's very wise," wondering whether his teacher might have once wounded him as he was now trying to wound me.

CR

GREATER THAN MY DOUBTS ABOUT fitting into the quasi-rabbinic culture of the Harvard department was my growing discomfort at the prevailing groupthink already palpable in the rest of the university. If I were to leave Canada for the land of the free, I didn't wish to be mired in political correctness. Being out of the mainstream had never bothered me. Friends sometimes accused me of cultivating opposition for its own sake. But I wanted to be among at least some independent thinkers.

In Montreal, I had only to drop into the kosher bakery to be among fellow Jews who were feistier than anyone I knew in the academy. Where around Harvard would I find such uplift? Cambridge was so politically hegemonic it had not fielded even a Republican *candidate* for Congress since the early 1950s. William Kristol, who had lived in Cambridge while studying and then teaching at Harvard, recounted that in one election he had checked the box for the only alternative candidate, thinking he was voting Republican, only to discover from the next day's paper that he had cast his ballot for a communist.

The Kristols—Irving, Gertrude, and Bill—were intellectuals of the order I aspired to, and though they intermittently taught at universities, they found their intellectual homes in magazines or think tanks. Harvard had no such conservative-tending center, not at the Kennedy School of Government, the Weatherhead Center for International Affairs, nor anywhere else as far as I could tell. Whatever hopes I nurtured for academic fellowship, I foresaw little chance for political give-and-take.

At one point in the interview process, I shared my concerns with Phyllis Keller, Harvard's associate dean for academic affairs, who seemed to be running the university from behind the scenes. One of her close faculty friends, the historian Stephan Thernstrom, had lately been accused by students of "racial insensitivity" for his failure to include slave narratives in the curriculum for his course on American history. Though his tenure at the university was not threatened, he was bitter at the lack of departmental support.

In relating this story, Phyllis was claiming me as an ally. As she escorted me from one administrative interview to another, she paused in the stairwell to say, "You know, we read you in *Commentary*." The intimation that some at Harvard would welcome me into their company became an incentive for taking the job. It did not occur to me to ask how many others were included in her "we." Len and I would soon befriend all five couples.

Interviews over, I returned home and went on with my life, which included an annual trip to Israel at the end of the school year. I was in Jerusalem, hurrying to my cousins' for Sabbath dinner, when I heard my name called by the literary scholar Dan Laor, who lived on the neighboring street. Catching up with me, he seized my hand and congratulated me on having gotten the job. A sometime visiting fellow at Harvard's Center for Jewish Studies, he had more direct sources than any available to me.

I accepted the position and the following year I was made the Center's director in turn. Jacob Katz, one of the shrewdest professors at the Hebrew University, having been asked by anxious colleagues how this change at Harvard would affect their future sabbatical rotations, advised them, "*Mi-kan v'hal'ah tsarikh l'haḥanif et rut vays*," from now on you'll have to butter up Ruth Wisse. He shared this witticism with Neal Kozodoy at *Commentary*, who cheerfully shared it with me.

But things had changed. Eager to avoid Twersky's (undoubtedly judicious) exercise of power, my new colleagues and I instituted a formal, competitive application process for a subsidized annual seminar on varying research topics. When the academic market later took a sharp downturn, we alternated this with a postdoctoral seminar to help recent PhD graduates jumpstart their career. I considered this open process a definite improvement, but the rest of the picture is murkier. It would prove easier to bring down the "yeshiva" than to replace it with anything sounder.

◌

Among Harvard's blessings—Widener Library foremost among them—are its limitless opportunities. Having been assured that my chair would be accompanied by a lectureship in Yiddish language, I set up a full ladder: language instruction, undergraduate courses, and a track for graduate students supported by generous stipends.

Seated between President of Israel Ezer Weizmann and historian Yehuda Reinharz at the President's reception for the Conference on the Centenary of Zionism, co-sponsored by Harvard University, May 1998. We were listening to remarks by historian Anita Shapira who co-chaired the conference with Reinharz and the author. At left, Shlomo Hillel, speaker of 11th Knesset.

Once I settled in, I also organized a conference in 1995 to mark the fiftieth anniversary of *Commentary* and a much larger one in 1997 on the centenary of the founding of the Zionist movement. For the latter I partnered with two eminent historians, Jehuda Reinharz of Brandeis University and Anita Shapira, representing the Hebrew University and Tel Aviv University, and raised funds from private donors for a gathering at Harvard in the fall and then again in Jerusalem the following spring. We planned this academic gathering on a grand scale, bringing in a range of speakers that included Conor Cruise O'Brien, the feisty Irish writer-politician who wrote the popular history of Israel, *The Siege,* and David Vital, one of the senior historians of Zionism, no less iconoclastic a thinker or personality from *inside* the Zionist camp. The contingent of Israelis included Ezra Mendelsohn, who studiously tried to keep his personality and his politics out of his scholarship, and Benny Morris, at that time more ideological journalist than historian, whose 1988 book, *The Birth of the Palestinian Refugee Problem, 1947-49,* accused Israel of atrocities and a policy of "ethnic cleansing" that he subsequently revisited and revised. Still very much the old-fashioned professors who believed in airing "all sides of an issue," we had included him in the program. I did not yet realize that the academic and media atmosphere was hardening into a policy of righteous unilateralism. What little coverage we got featured one inflammatory Benny Morris over all the rest.

After a well-attended session, Daniel Pipes, a Harvard graduate and by then a recognized scholar of Middle East studies, told me he had not imagined it would be possible to hold such a conference at Harvard. That was for me one of its high points. One of the low points came at the session on the aftermath of the Oslo Accords in which I was a panelist. The failure of that ostensible peace agreement to encourage responsible Palestinian self-government and the inverse escalation it had brought of anti-Israel violence was already beyond dispute: the one hundred lethal terrorist attacks within Israel since the signing of the treaty had killed more Jews than in the fifteen years preceding it. My prepared remarks included that putting Yasser Arafat in charge of the Palestinians was the first—and only—time Israel had wronged that Arab population. My fellow panelist, the distinguished Israeli political scientist Shlomo Avineri, accused me of perpetrating a blood libel against his countrymen.

Several weeks later, crossing the campus in the evening on my way home, I heard someone calling, "Professor Wisse" and stopped for a student I did not recognize who had hailed me. He said he had attended that public session of the conference and wanted to know: "Did that Israeli professor really accuse you of perpetrating a blood libel?!" This student's evidence that "attention was paid" momentarily displaced my simmering concern that Israel's "peace camp" was doubling down on rather than confronting its error. Happily, none of that contentiousness surfaced the following spring in the Israeli part of the conference, whose opening event was hosted by President Ezer Weizman at the presidential residence in Jerusalem, and where cordial relations with Shlomo Avineri were resumed.

In retrospect, I should not have kept a low profile for these conferences but instead tried to win them the broadest possible coverage in the *Harvard Crimson,* the *Boston Globe,* and beyond. Theodor Herzl had understood that

Zionism had to stand tall and proudly announce its presence. A century after his mission was accomplished in Israel, the reputation of Zionism was back on trial, and I had not done enough to prosecute those who were still intent on undoing the realized dream.

CR

To back up a little, a few months before my move to Cambridge, Marty Peretz called to say he was organizing a party for the inauguration of the chair and could I please supply a list of invitees. In the early years of our marriage, Len and I used to throw exuberant New Year parties. There were always too many people for the available space, and I imagined Marty's "party" as some such rollicking reception with a couple of toasts and abundant hors d'oeuvres.

But I did not know my man. He was planning an elegant sit-down dinner, and rather than telling me to trim my large list by two-thirds, he moved the event from the smaller venue he'd reserved to the grand foyer of Harvard's Fogg Museum. A week before the event, he dropped by my Lowell House apartment to arrange the seating—which is when I first took in the enormity of my mistake, and the additional costs he must have incurred to accommodate it.

He waved off my apology and said he enjoyed organizing this kind of event. Indeed, the evening would be a tribute to his skills. I knew nothing of his negotiations with Harvard for the space, but I saw how much care he would, as impresario and heart of the proceedings, lavish on the comfort of his guests.

The February evening of the dinner was intensely cold. But my guests and I were thoroughly warmed by the grandeur of the room, the excellence of the food, and the spirit of the welcome. The evening had some of the amiable excitement of a bar mitzvah reception. It may well have been Marty who invoked the bar mitzvah analogy. To him, Harvard's reception of Yiddish, that lowly vernacular, ought to be marked in style, like my mother's dictum that Yiddish, meaning its representatives, must be well dressed. The university had been offering courses on the Hebrew Bible and medieval Jewish philosophy, but Yiddish was the argot of the immigrants whom Henry Adams and his fellow "bourgeois-Bostonian" Henry James feared as they beheld the jabberers corrupting their English language.

In his remarks, Marty jovially observed that Harvard president A. Lawrence Lowell, who in the 1920s had instituted Jewish quotas, must be turning in his grave. His sentiment was echoed by the *New Republic*'s literary editor Leon Wieseltier, who had studied under Twersky as a postgraduate member of the august Society of Fellows. Most of the evening's remarks—by Jeremy Knowles, dean of the faculty of arts and sciences, Henry Rosovsky, its former dean, the writer Cynthia Ozick, Marty, and me—were celebratory, splendidly topped off by Marty's friend, cellist Yo-Yo Ma, playing Bach.

Between speeches I spoke mostly with my tablemates: Neil Rudenstine, Harvard's president, and his wife Angelica, née Zander, an art historian. I happened to know a little about her family because at the home of my Jerusalem cousins we had met her brother, the orchestral conductor Benjamin Zander. In 1937, their father had fled from Berlin to London, where he was interned at the beginning of the war as an enemy alien. A passionate Zionist and founding secretary of the British Friends of the Hebrew University, Walter Zander was also passionate in his belief that conflict with the Arabs in Palestine could be avoided.

I was curious to know what Angelica knew and felt about her father's life and politics, but interruptions kept sending our conversation off its path so that we found ourselves talking instead about the father of her friend and fellow art historian Leo Steinberg. Both their fathers had left Berlin for London, but of the two Leo's was the more famous. Didn't I know about Isaac Steinberg, who was associated with Yiddish?

I certainly did know about I. N. Shteynberg, founder and theoretician of the *Frayland ligeh*—the Freeland League for Jewish Territorial Colonization—but it had not occurred to me to associate him with the Leo Steinberg whose writings on art I had read alongside those of his American counterparts Meyer Schapiro and Harold Rosenberg. Were Shteynberg and Steinberg truly father and son? The father had led a double or triple life:

justice minister in the first Soviet government, founder of the Territorialist movement to promote the establishment of semiautonomous Yiddish-speaking Jewish communities wherever Jews gathered in sufficient numbers, and an Orthodox Jew. Anticipating the implementation of minority rights for Poland's three million Jews, Shteynberg had envisioned a secular culture that could sustain limited Jewish sovereignty without doing battle for it.

This was the bond between the two parents: Angelica's father had harbored *within* the Zionist movement a belief, similar to Shteynberg's *outside* the movement, that Jews would not have to engage in military self-defense. She also seemed to imply that Leo was as removed from his father's idea of Jewish peoplehood as she was from her father's Zionism, and that the two of them had taken the bloodless Jewish nationalism of their parents a giant step further by abandoning Judaism for art.

Our conversation was of special interest to me since our son Jacob was studying to become an art historian and curator. With his attentiveness to detail, Marty had seated Jacob at the table of Joseph Koerner, another son of refugees (from Vienna rather than Berlin) who had become an art historian and was teaching at Harvard. Bernard Berenson, the Jewish boy from Lithuania who remade himself as the world's greatest connoisseur of Renaissance painting, remains the most spectacular example of such self-transformation, but how many more Jews had followed his lead in turning from Judaism to the religion of art?

Not long before this, Jacob and I had been at dinner in New York with some friends, including Cynthia Ozick. When Jacob said he was studying artists of the Northern Renaissance, Cynthia leaned across the table—she was sitting at the opposite end—and asked: "How can you specialize in Christian art!?" I saw that Jacob was puzzled. My mother—his grandmother, to whom he dedicated his doctoral thesis—had a houseful of paintings and artwork, much of it of no obvious ethnic or religious derivation. The subjects of his dissertation were fifteenth-century city painters of the Burgundian Netherlands. They did not function under the aegis of the Church, so he did not necessarily identify the art of Christian Europe as inherently Christian.

Cynthia was not being provincial. She knew full well that many Jewish students of art had left the tribe without a formal conversion to Christianity, dubbed by Heinrich Heine the "ticket of admission to European culture." The protagonist of her novel *The Cannibal Galaxy* is a European Jew who survives World War II and expects to escape cultural conflict by designing a "dual curriculum" of Jewish and secular studies. The book can be read as a cautionary tale about even the best-intentioned program of cultural amalgamation. Small wonder she might worry about a Jew specializing in European art.

Here was something strange. In coming to Harvard to teach Yiddish literature, I had not considered Jewishness a matter of concern. There had been little anti-Israel agitation or Jewish discomfort at McGill, and I'd expected even less of it at Harvard. Yet there was palpable unease at our head table. Neil Rudenstine spoke of his Jewish father who had run off at fifteen to join the army where he served for twelve years. This severed ties with his Jewish family, and he subsequently remarried an Italian Catholic, so that Neil grew up culturally Italian. However, once this Jewish family opened its arms to them, Neil's younger brother considered himself Jewish. Neil had recently attended the bar mitzvah of his nephew who read fluently in Hebrew.

All this emerged because Neil had evidently been rattled by Marty and Leon's references to Harvard's history of anti-Jewish discrimination. When his turn came to speak, he set aside his prepared remarks and instead offered an impromptu defense of President Lowell (dead since 1943) with a weird account of how Lowell had once come to the rescue of his sister, the poet Amy Lowell. Maybe he was reaching for the only redemptive detail about Lowell that came to mind. But more peculiar was his attempt to justify his precursor as though his own reputation were at stake.

This improvised talk raised eyebrows. One of our invited friends— Anglican, as it happens—asked me why President Rudenstine had "lost it." Why didn't he just say he was glad that the prejudices of Lowell's day had since then been overcome?

I opened my own prepared thanks that evening with the Yiddish quip, "If a Jew eats a chicken, one of them must be sick," intending by this to demonstrate the joke's obsolescence. The dinner was so elegant, most people had not noticed that the food was kosher. The security of Jews, which I took, and still take, as the barometer of a morally and politically secure society, seemed assured by the satisfactory condition of Jews and chickens alike. Yet the tremors of unease I sensed at our table were about to cause a tectonic shift.

The genteel discrimination of Lowell's generation had apparently given way to a generation of Jews who were uncomfortable with the label and wary of those who wore it proudly. The likes of Columbia's Professor N., who had tried to keep my Jewish scholarship out of the academy, were none too pleased about its presence there. University culture was becoming less tolerant of Jewishness, not more, quite as though it had expected Jews to shed it in return for being admitted. Once made aware of it, I noticed that some Jews in attendance that evening were discomfited by seeing elements of tribalism openly affirmed.

There would never be another such evening during my tenure, or in any foreseeable future. The percentage of Jewish students probably peaked about the time I came to Harvard and dropped precipitously with the boost of affirmative action into virtual quotas.

Meanwhile, that lone Palestinian student in the '80s shouting "Hate!" at the back of the hall was about to be joined by others whom Harvard did nothing to disabuse of their conviction that Israel was to blame for the Arab and Muslim aggression against it.

CR

WHEN I TOOK UP MY position at Harvard, most of my colleagues were traditional scholars, having been hired--as my Chinese exchange student would assure me--because they were considered "best in the world," a ludicrous standard to my way of thinking but one that, in emphasizing academic excellence, underscored what was expected of us.

I was not involved in undergraduate admissions, but in my first years where I was at the graduate level, I saw only academic criteria being applied.

Affirmative action in faculty appointments was only creeping in when I arrived and there were no administrative bureaucrats to monitor ideological and political compliance. Enforcers in any system know that their job depends on proving the need for it, which means finding an ever-increasing number of infractions and then passing more rules that guarantee further infractions. In this way a policy introduced in the name of greater fairness, equality, social justice, and other such virtues can quickly destroy the institution that tries to impose it.

The school I entered was still pretty feisty. "Every tub on its own bottom"—a puzzling motto the first time I heard it—described the university's highly decentralized authority that allowed independent fiefdoms to flourish. The Center for Jewish Studies (one of dozens such) had been founded to supplement the academic teaching of Jewish studies through conferences, scholarships and prizes, fellowships for visiting academics, intramural and intermural publications, and town-and-gown community outreach. This kind of academic entrepreneurship made for a lively campus, with seriously competing attractions on any given day. No matter how carefully I checked the university calendar, any event we scheduled was bound to coincide with others of comparable merit.

As for the students, I had been warned that the ambitious ones who came to Harvard tended to be docile, reluctant to challenge those from whom they wanted less to learn than to earn an A. When I sat in on an art history class that my son Jacob was teaching at Stern College in New York, I envied him the hands that shot up for questions. Our students seemed to fear that asking questions betrayed their ignorance.

But they delighted me when they pushed back. Once, invoking a work that had been written inside the ghetto under harrowing conditions, I mocked the luxury of Virginia Woolf's complaint about lacking "A Room of One's Own." A student beside me said, in a very low voice for my hearing alone, "Oh, that's not fair!" I was so enchanted that I took up his objection to explain why my comment had indeed been unfair, given the difference in the two writers' circumstances.

Then there was the day, during a seminar on the New York Intellectuals—Robert Warshow, Delmore Schwartz, Irving Kristol, Norman Podhoretz, Irving Howe, Saul Bellow, and others—when I saw my student Sue Kahn, subsequently a fine anthropologist, sadly shaking her head. I asked what troubled her. She said, "We will never be able to write like that, never, never...." That was exactly why I'd wanted to teach their work in the first place.

By temperament I was still the same *Fräulein Hoffentlich* who had left Czernowitz in 1940. If the natural hopefulness of the four-year-old had been somewhat tempered by aging, it was also reinforced by good fortune beyond anything that a European-born Jewish child had any reason to expect. My friends and I grew up confident that the worst was behind us and the best was yet to come. This was how I experienced growing up, raising a family, building a life and a career. It had not occurred to me that there could be systemic failure in the world around me.

Teaching at Harvard was a rare pleasure and one for which I would have wanted to express only the gratitude I continue to feel. Yet I am now faced with the need to describe the academic decline I would witness over the next twenty-one years: a decline I was powerless to arrest and see no immediate prospect of being reversed.

14

RECKONING

$\mathcal{B}$y the early 1990s, when I moved from Montreal to take up my new position at Harvard, I was able to participate in campus life more than I could in the years when I was raising a family. At McGill I had scheduled classes and office hours to coincide with our children's school day; now I was freer to behave more like your typical male—or at least that's what feminists might say, except that almost none of the male members of my Department of Near Eastern Languages and Literatures showed any interest in campus affairs.

Many if not most university professors function strictly within their own departments, leaving faculty-wide policy to be made by those who regularly show up to make it. It would not have occurred to me to attend my first meeting of the Faculty of Arts and Sciences (FAS) had Charles Berlin not insisted that I appear in person to receive my new degree. I had gotten to know Charlie as Harvard's head Judaica librarian and the founding executive director of the Association for Jewish Studies, and he had always given me excellent advice.

It seems that Harvard requires every tenured professor to be a graduate of the university; those without its degree are therefore granted a Harvard MA upon assuming their role. This little ceremony eased me into the faculty, so that a half year later, when I became director of the Center for Jewish Studies and was thus expected to attend faculty meetings, I was familiar with the protocol.

The spacious, high-domed room in the administration building where FAS holds its monthly meetings, lined with portraits of past dignitaries, guarantees a formal air to the proceedings. After a quarter-hour "tea" plus mingling, the university president, at this time Neil Rudenstine, took his chair at the front, flanked by the faculty dean and secretary, and the meeting was called to order. I asked why Rudenstine presided at ours when he surely did not for other faculties and was told that he did so as the head of the undergraduate college, the whole of which was under the aegis of FAS.

My favorite part of these meetings came right at the start with the "memorial minute" for recently deceased members. These testimonials were prepared by a committee of colleagues and read aloud, sometimes in the invited presence of the departed's family. I had not been at Harvard long enough to know the people being eulogized, but I relished hearing their accomplishments, which in addition to academic feats often included military service. Behind the standard items of praise, one caught glimpses of the kindly teacher-shepherd, the genius with irrepressible humor, the occasional curmudgeon who had outlived his welcome, and the thoroughly decent colleague who assumed the bulk of administrative duties.

Most of these obituaries bespoke a very high standard of mind and spirit that we, their heirs, were expected to uphold. I was sorry when, by the end of my tenure, the time allotted to reading them aloud was curtailed and the full texts were instead made available online.

CR

I HAD BEEN DELIGHTED WHEN Dean Jeremy Knowles asked me during our first interview whether I would be prepared to teach in Harvard's version of the "Core." I assumed that professors in various disciplines were covering a curriculum like the compulsory survey course I had taught when starting out at McGill. It turned out to be a very different thing.

While acknowledging that students did need *some* guidance in their pursuit of knowledge, the Harvard program merely offered a grid of subject areas from which undergraduates were obliged to select ten courses over their four years. The prescribed areas included foreign cultures, historical study, moral reasoning, quantitative reasoning, science, social analysis, and so forth. Mine was to be a sub-division of literature and arts that focused on critical approaches to literature through questions like "How does literature function?" and "How are literary genres and traditions constituted and transformed?" In other words, there were no required foundational texts like the Bible, Homer, Shakespeare, the Federalist Papers, and other sources constituting (in Matthew Arnold's famous phrase) "the best that has been thought and said." Courses were vetted to ensure more or less equal levels of difficulty but were otherwise as individualist as the instructor's design.

Nonetheless, I planned what was in effect a "great Jewish books course" featuring Sholem Aleichem (Yiddish), Franz Kafka (German), Isaac Babel (Russian), Isaac Bashevis Singer (Yiddish), Shmuel Yosef Agnon (Hebrew), Primo Levi (Italian), and Saul Bellow (English), thus including major works written in at least six languages to represent the multilingual quality of modern Jewish literature. We would track the experience of Jews in the twentieth century in the various ways that fiction interpreted history.

When I submitted my course proposal, the Core supervisor said, "I see that you assume students will not know what a *shtetl* is, but you think they will understand the term 'tsarist Russia.' Actually, half our incoming students have not taken a history course since ninth grade." So I added more historical background to the literary analysis, enjoying the challenge of engaging students from across the disciplines, including those who may have registered only because they had to fulfill a requirement.

I appreciated having students from the former Soviet Union in the class when I taught Isaac Babel's *Red Cavalry*, which they read in its original Russian. They gently corrected mistakes in the pronunciation of Russian names, but some were also deeply and justifiably concerned about the stories themselves. The greatest moral challenge in teaching modern Jewish literature arose from this autobiographical fiction by a Jewish writer embedded in a Cossack regiment of the Soviet army in 1920 during its first war—a war that was being fought against Poland over Jewish-populated territory, whose unarmed civilians were easy pickings for both armies. Some students felt I was condoning the author's immorality when I highlighted examples of his literary genius in describing brutal acts. As casualties of the Soviet experiment, my students found it hard to appreciate Babel's sympathetic treatment of Cossack brutality and ironic deprecation of his Jewish self. They were making their way back to Jewish life in a free country, and here I was trying to get them to appreciate a Jew who tried to do aesthetic justice to the equally murderous Cossacks and communists. Babel was challenging for everyone; for them it was personal.

At the start of one semester, I noticed a girl wearing a hooded sweatshirt so low over her forehead one could scarcely see she was African American. She turned up during my first office hours, still hooded, to say she was stymied by the first assigned text: Sholem Aleichem's *Tevye the Dairyman* in a translation generously sprinkled with transliterated Hebrew quotations. I assured her that almost everyone in the class would need to resort to the glossary provided at the back of the book, and then tried to show her that the game might prove worthwhile if she could just relax and enjoy it. From then on, she came to see me almost weekly and was soon doing most of the talking.

Thanking me for the course at the end of the semester, my student surprised me by singling out the aforementioned novel *Mr. Sammler's Planet,* Saul Bellow's demanding indictment of the counterculture and permissiveness of the 1960s. The book's protagonist is a European Holocaust survivor living on New York's Upper West Side. "Like many people who had seen the world collapse once, Mr. Sammler entertained the possibility it might collapse twice. He did not agree with refugee friends that this doom was inevitable, but liberal beliefs did not seem capable of self-defense, and you could smell decay." Through Sammler, the author calls out the ruinous consequences of sexual freedom, relaxed policing, radical ideas, and abandonment of civilizing norms. It was not a young person's book, but it had had its effect. "When I arrived here," the student said, "I was the you-go girl! I was going to change everything. I was going to change the world. Well, this book showed me that I could also change it for the worse." She articulated better than I had done what a course on modern Jewish fiction could hope to transmit.

I had the opposite experience with a Muslim student from Pakistan who refused to deal with Agnon's Hebrew novella, *In the Heart of Seas*, because he deemed it racist. This tale of a group of pious Jews, ten men and seven women, who journey to the Land of Israel in the early nineteenth century was the most affirmative work in the course. The travelers must overcome many human and natural obstacles and wrestle with inner difficulties in reaching their destination, but there is one in their company who reaches Zion before them, borne on a handkerchief that is Agnon's symbol for faith.

Writing when Hitler had come to power in Germany, Agnon drew on the whole of Jewish learning and liturgy to ensure that the contemporary Zionist story include the traditions that inspired it. The travelers experience their adventures in terms of the texts that they have studied, the prayers they have recited, and the longing they have absorbed from countless generations before them. The supernatural accompanies the natural, the narrator accompanies these travelers of the previous century, and humor blends with tragedy very much in the Jewish folk tradition. This book was as complexly "modern" as the others on the course, and morally as difficult but straightforward as the voyage it described.

A Muslim student could only find this "racist" if he was raised to *disbelieve* in the Bible's formation of the Jewish people and the natural right of the Jews to their homeland. The Arab and Soviet coalition had rammed through the villainous resolution equating Zionism with racism at the United Nations, but this young man took that equation as much on faith as Agnon's travelers believed in their return to Zion. Who knows how early it might have begun in his schooling; the United States had the resolution revoked after the fall of the Soviet Union in 1991, too late to limit its damage.

The student was highly intelligent and had until then been doing very well. It being too late to withdraw from the course, he demanded to complete it without having to deal with this book. This was technically possible since assignments and exams left him enough to choose from without it. I discussed it with Dara Horn, the teaching assistant of his section, and we decided to accede to his request. We had by then experienced enough of Harvard's swelling bureaucracy to know what it would cost in time and energy if we were to refuse his petition.

I have always regretted taking the easy way out. It was obvious that Agnon's novella had as much to teach this student as *Mr. Sammler's Planet* had educated the other. He might have realized that it was in many ways closer to his own cultural tradition than other books in the course. If there was any truth to the claim that college exposed students to diversity or offered any hope of undoing anti-Jewish prejudice, here was an opportunity. Instead, after an unsuccessful attempt at persuading him to deal with the book, I allowed a member of Harvard's "educated elite" to have his prejudices confirmed.

I don't blame the college bureaucracy for that retreat, but let me offer an example of what I was up against. One year when my Core class had a larger than expected registration, I put out a call for additional teaching assistants; these are graduate students who after two years of classwork were expected to teach weekly sections of the large undergraduate courses as part of their responsibilities. Good teaching assistants were at least as important as the quality of the professor, so there was a scramble for suitable match-ups at the start of each semester. After briefly considering one applicant, I had to turn her down when I learned that she was scheduled for surgery in the final weeks of the course. Days after I informed her, I received a letter of reprimand saying that the student had protested my discrimination against her disability and was requiring me to employ her. I was certain that the administration had not understood that she could not see the students through to their examinations, so I wrote explaining the situation. I was then summoned to a meeting. I refused, and said that if there was any pressure to hire a teaching assistant who would be absent when she was most needed, I wanted the home addresses of the registered students, as I intended to write to the parents, letting them know that the school had required me to jeopardize their child's experience of my course. The issue was dropped and I heard nothing more about it, but would I have done this had I not been tenured?

The university was rapidly shifting its educational priorities toward grievance compliance. Additional administrators began slowing every interaction so that one could no longer see a dean without passing through assistants who were not themselves academics. They did much to dampen the tremendous sense of possibility I had felt when starting out.

CR

SOON AFTER MY ARRIVAL AT Harvard I received a call from a gentleman introducing himself as Harvey Mansfield, professor of political philosophy in the Department of Government, inviting me to lunch. The name was unfamiliar, and I had no idea why he'd sought me out. The only other person who'd invited me for coffee that first semester was a young professor about to come up for tenure who was eager to secure my departmental vote.

Though seemingly shy, Harvey was delightful company. Toward the end of our lunch, he mentioned that he ran a program on constitutional government that regularly brought visiting speakers to campus. Would I care to attend? Thrilled by the sound of the thing but afraid he had made a mistake, I asked, "Are you sure you have the right person?" I think he smiled. "I know who you are. I read you in *Commentary*." Although I hadn't quite realized it myself, by then I was writing as much about politics as literature—the fate of Yiddish having impelled me to figure out why its speakers had become the no-fail targets of European anti-Semites. He recognized me as a fellow conservative before I had applied the term to myself.

Harvey's relation to the university was at once intimate and estranged. One day, walking through campus, he pointed out to me the window of his freshman dorm, and I think he still attended every home football game. At the same time, even some of his colleagues seemed to fear him. After one of my first faculty meetings, I was told that if a dozen people were prepared to vote for a proposed measure and Harvey rose in support of it, there wouldn't be two yea votes left by the count.

An admirer of Leo Strauss, Harvey wore with a lighter air the intellectual mantle of the University of Chicago where Strauss had taught. The brightest students sought him out and I realized why when I sat in one of the courses that he was coteaching with Peter Berkowitz. He was an elegant lecturer and original thinker. His friendship helped to offset the isolation I would otherwise have experienced in a political climate that reminded me of Flaubert's *Dictionary of Received Ideas. Nature:* "How beautiful is Nature!" To be repeated every time you are in the countryside; *Republicans:* Republicans are not all scoundrels, but all scoundrels are Republicans. (Flaubert, to be sure, meant something different by the term.)

As I write now, by the beginning of the third decade of the twenty-first century, "political correctness" on campus is taken for granted. But what I experienced was less the direct coercive tyranny of leftism than a pervasive culture of capitulation and pusillanimity, with everyone from administrators to deans and professors to students and even the campus police looking over his or her shoulder in fear of censure by others. When Peter Berkowitz came up for tenure, he fell victim to the hardening dogma. He went on to become one of America's most distinguished interpreters of liberal philosophy and American politics, but no conservative-liberal scholar was ever hired to replace him, gutting Harvard's offerings in political thought. What a relief it was to attend Harvey's regularly scheduled events amid congenial company and hear speakers like Charles Murray, Camille Paglia, James Q. Wilson, and Ayaan Hirsi Ali, the last of whom required stricter security arrangements than did many heads of state.

Once I had the unique experience of hearing the economist Glenn Loury literally "take the words out of my mouth" and say exactly what I had intended to say, only better. (Sadly, he soon stopped attending.) I also enjoyed the biannual postelection analyses conducted jointly by the two Williams, Kristol (conservative) and Galston (liberal).

As the university's most prominent conservative, Harvey functioned like the lone sheriff of a disoriented town, trying to uphold standards that had prevailed when he first arrived there as an undergraduate in 1949. He offended even some potential allies in his crusade against grade inflation when he attributed the practice to instructors adjusting upward the grades of students admitted through affirmative action. He solved his own problem by giving his students the grade he thought they had earned alongside the usually higher grade he submitted. They rewarded him with the title, Harvey "C minus" Mansfield.

Opposing the introduction of gender studies at Harvard on the grounds that it was not a legitimate discipline, Harvey explained some of his objections in his book *Manliness* that included a trenchant critique of feminist orthodoxy. One never knew when he would rise at a faculty meeting to challenge a resolution. Once, during a discussion of guidelines governing behavior between professors and students, he impishly asked whether the new policy would include a "grandfather clause." Most of us knew that his then-wife Delba Winthrop had been a graduate student of his.

Though I sometimes felt like Harvey's deputy sheriff, I had my own issues. At a faculty meeting in the spring of 1996, President Rudenstine presented a congratulatory report on the implementation of "diversity at Harvard." I provoked him to what the next day's *Crimson* called "an uncharacteristic display of emotion" by warning against the political consequences of ethnic/racial classification, and insisted we speak honestly of "group preferences" rather than euphemistically about "affirmative action." The person beside me whispered: "This is the first time I ever saw him lose his temper!"

I hadn't meant to irritate the president, but I was no less indignant than he. A society trying to correct past injustice ought to offer special encouragement and assistance to those whom it or its precursors had damaged. But a public policy of reverse favoritism based on color and ethnicity could only deepen the insecurities and disparities one was trying to overcome.

Raised on the biblical model of the freed slaves who needed the disciplining laws of Sinai to transform them from a rabble into a self-accountable people, I felt that condescension to the disadvantaged implied contempt rather than reciprocal trust. It troubled me that that a university would undertake a social experiment of such importance without establishing benchmarks to check on whether its good intentions were actually producing the intended improvements. I was certain that this cosmetic approach to profound social issues would damage far more than the university itself.

When the question of "diversity" later resurfaced under the presidency of Drew Faust, I suggested that the faculty test the correlation between the introduction of group preferences and the decline of intellectual-political diversity. Faust—Harvard's first female president—had been appointed to replace Lawrence Summers in a process I will shortly recount. She was expected to avoid public controversy, which could only be done by appeasing the faculty leftists.

It seemed obvious to me that once the contested principle of group preferences was made sacrosanct, it *had* to shut down the diversity of viewpoints, since everyone appointed according to those guidelines would naturally want to reinforce them. President Faust mocked my suggestion by pointing to the women and dark-skinned individuals in the rows in front of her as evidence that diversity, plain and simple, had been attained. I doubt she realized that she had proved my point: counting heads by gender and race had replaced the diversity of the ideas inside them. I only erred in underestimating the speed with which political-intellectual uniformity would set in.

Student groups, with greater presence of mind than their teachers, organized a campus debate on affirmative action with Professors Cornel West and Michael Sandel speaking for it, and Harvey and me against. (I'd been approached after several others declined.) Turning up outside the hall on the designated evening, I found the line already stretching far back into the campus. The organizers, taken unawares by the size of the crowd, soon had us running to the Science Center, and when that proved inadequate, to Sanders Theatre, which was then crammed with a thousand students.

Cornel West, whom I had never met before and who disarmingly called me "Sister Ruth," tried to preempt our arguments by rejecting as "myths" the idea that racism no longer existed in America, and that it was un-American to consider the group ahead of the individual. West was a superb showman, but I think Harvey bested him on these very points by exposing the harm done by reverse discrimination. I "won" my side of the argument because I was the only one talking about gender quotas while the others talked about race. We all held our ground before an appreciative and by no means homogeneous crowd.

In truth, affirmative action required lying. Departments looking for the "best" person to fill a position were obliged to demonstrate, not that they had conducted a fair and open search, but rather that they had interviewed an appropriate percentage of women and other "minorities." Since individual merit and group diversity are contradictory goals, the entire process was corrupt irrespective of outcome. At one departmental meeting, when the chair asked us to supply evidence of a member's candidacy for promotion, someone at the table hooted, "Why bother with all this? He's Hispanic!" I was the only one who laughed at this eruption of suppressed truth.

When I arrived at Harvard, I enjoyed the friendship of a number of conservatively inclined faculty members. By the time I left in 2014, almost all were gone. One could be certain that no strictly meritorious appointees had replaced them.

At the same time, being visibly conservative was a personal advantage. I was a sounding board for students who wanted to affirm but not advertise a similar orientation or were just intellectually curious. In my capacity of faculty adviser, I came to know the feisty students of the Republican Club, the conservative campus newspaper *The Salient*, clubs associated with the military, Students for a Safe Israel, and the Stand-Up Comedy Association.

One day I was visited by several girls who asked me to become faculty adviser to a new right-wing Catholic club. They brushed aside that I was neither Christian nor a categorical opponent of abortion, their main driving issue; on a hegemonic campus it was enough that I supported their *group's* right to life. I suggested they try harder to find someone who could more truly represent them. But I had gotten to the point of welcoming almost any challenge to liberal pieties and was very pleased that they considered me an ally.

CR

MORE TROUBLING EVEN THAN AFFIRMATIVE action was the exclusion from campus of the Reserve Officers Training Corps. During the Vietnam War, Harvard's faculty had objected to any form of campus military training that either provided (or implicitly denied) exemptions to the draft. But once conscription was repealed in 1973, rather than encouraging students to join what were now the voluntary reserves, the faculty found a new pretext for banning ROTC in the military's "don't ask, don't tell" policy regarding homosexuals, declaring sweepingly that *any* form of discrimination "unrelated to course requirements is contrary to the principles and policies of Harvard University."

This excuse was disingenuous. Opposition to the military was a faculty obsession.

After ROTC was banished from campus, Harvard's administration arranged to reimburse the neighboring Massachusetts Institute of Technology for absorbing the few annual Harvard recruits. This backdoor channel made it possible to accommodate the "need-based" students on ROTC scholarships whom the faculty presumably wanted to help, while burdening them with the need for predawn travel back and forth to MIT.

Then, in 1995, in an upsurge of Pecksniffian preening, FAS declared that even this arm's length arrangement implied collaboration with the armed forces. What to do? Rather than risk a confrontation with the faculty activists, the administration asked sympathetic alumni to defray the costs for the handful of students annually enrolled in the program. Call it Harvard's version of money laundering. And when the student body, to its credit, voted in 1999 to reinstate ROTC, the faculty refused to change its previous position. Needless to say, all this time Harvard was accepting grants from the government whose policies it selectively opposed.

Mere hypocrisy is not enough to get under my skin. I teach nineteenth-century satire, which excoriates religion and traditional morality for preaching standards to which their followers do not adhere; their mockery made me equally distrustful of reformers who failed to rise to the moral standards of those they mocked. Like political theorist Judith Shklar—who died before I got to Harvard—in her book *Ordinary Vices*, I defended old-fashioned hypocrisy against the nihilistic alternative of renouncing all aspirations to a higher morality.

The campaign against the military, however, went far beyond hypocrisy. A country's protection depends on soldiers of college age. On a campus studded with memorials to students who had died serving their country, the faculty congratulated undergraduates for evading this highest responsibility, and for forty years strutted its moral superiority to the students who actually served. By now, a much-weakened ROTC has been readmitted to campus, with no apology and no renewed call for student enlistment.

At many universities, the same faculty cohort that expelled ROTC and took up so-called progressive causes was also becoming increasingly anti-Israel. In 2002, Harvard's English department invited to the campus the poet and Oxford lecturer Tom Paulin, best known for writing a poem in response to the first intifada accusing Israel of gunning down "another little Palestinian boy/ in trainers, jeans, and a white teeshirt." In 2003, Yale's Afro-American Cultural Center joined the Black Student Alliance in hosting Amiri Baraka, formerly LeRoi Jones, and cheered when he read his loony conspiratorial poem about 9/11, asking, "Who told 4,000 Israeli workers at the Twin Towers/ To stay home that day/ Why did Sharon stay away?" In 2006, a faculty group at Brandeis University invited former President Jimmy Carter to speak upon the publication of his malignant book *Palestine: Peace Not Apartheid.*

Each of these cases followed what I had come to call the three-step: (1) An avowedly anti-Israel event generates (2) a protest against it, which then triggers (3) a counter-protest against the alleged attempt by the protesters to suppress free speech. The initiators of the event thereby outmaneuver defenders of the Jews by appealing to the forces of law and order to punish those engaged in the perfectly legal act of protesting an aggression that is in fact being perpetrated against them.

ॐ

FOR ALL THESE REASONS I was hopeful when, in the summer of 2001, Lawrence Summers became president of Harvard. Even before the attacks of September 11, he had addressed the need for military service and made the point explicit by personally attending ROTC commissioning ceremonies. I had never met the man (it seemed natural to refer to him as Larry) and knew only that he had taught in the Economics department and served as President Clinton's secretary of the treasury. But I liked him the first time I saw him in action, chairing the faculty meeting as though he were performing a minor duty not to be confused with the serious business of running the university.

Summers was born into economics royalty. The son of two economists, he was also the nephew of economists Paul Samuelson and Kenneth Arrow. It was hardly surprising that he should have switched to the study of economics during his studies at MIT. But his appointment to Harvard in 1983 as its youngest tenured professor at twenty-eight was obviously on his own merits. It was this aura of competence and willingness to wield authority that I felt when he assumed the presidency of Harvard. For the first time, I felt that the university might reverse the downhill drift that I had sensed since I came on board.

Most importantly, Summers seemed to take charge by monitoring academic performance itself and by holding the professoriate to a meaningful standard of excellence. I also saw his concern for the undergraduates under his charge. He organized a welcoming picnic for the freshmen that he clearly *enjoyed* attending, and he dropped in for visits in each of the student residences. Students found his concern for them genuine and made him by far the most popular president of the four I saw in action.

Popular, that is, among students. Not so among professors. A few whom he called in for private discussions welcomed his interest in their discipline, and one told me he appreciated being reminded of the school's high expectations. But others had a different agenda. Cornel West, who had apparently already negotiated a transfer to Princeton, went public with the president's alleged complaints against him: namely, that he was busy cutting rap records instead of pursuing serious scholarship, that he had headed a political committee for Al Sharpton as president, and that he inflated student grades. West implied that these criticisms were racially charged, knowing that, unlike himself, the president would feel obliged to maintain the confidentiality of their meeting. His was the first shot across the presidential bow.

Around the time of Larry's appointment, some seventy faculty members from Harvard and MIT petitioned their universities to divest from Israel and from companies that sell arms to Israel. Led by MIT Professor Noam Chomsky, the petition intended to stoke opposition to Israel whether or not it achieved its stated goal. The fact that Larry was Jewish had until then been as irrelevant as the fact that Neil Rudenstine identified as an Anglican-Episcopalian. But once Israel became a campus issue, the Jewishness of the president came under scrutiny.

Of course, Chomsky was also a Jew. His reputation as a pioneer in linguistics made him the most prominent anti-Zionist in America, and his being Jewish was used to preclude the possibility that his opposition to Israel was anti-Semitic. Tackling that apparent contradiction had become one of my preoccupations in the study of Yiddish literature, and now here it was surfacing in my backyard. The contradiction was only *apparent* because the ferocity of anti-Jewish assault had always turned some Jews against their fellow Jews. My personal experience of this began back in graduate school, but the pattern had emerged at the beginning of Jewish history, and even without statistical data I was certain of the correlation between anti-Jewish venom and the rush of some Jews to avoid it. Such avoidance included joining the opposition, or finding reasons to hold fellow Jews responsible for the war against them. And leftism allowed Jews to become anti-Jews without the necessity of formal baptism.

Chomsky was no mere socialist, but a radical anti-capitalist who blamed Western imperialism for the evils of the world, and opposed Israel, its alleged imperialist proxy, with the same anti-Zionist animus that made Stalin support the original Arab assaults on Jews in Palestine.

Saul Bellow puzzled over this phenomenon in his 1976 treatise on Israel, *To Jerusalem and Back*, noting that for American radicals, all evils flowed from Washington, but mocking the idea that "state capitalism" could really be as diabolical, conspiratorial, and all-powerful as Chomsky said it was. "Much clearer than the shadowy workings of centralized state capitalism is the fact that young men, mere boys of twelve and fourteen, carry automatic weapons in the streets of Beirut, and that they murder with perfect impunity, and that close to thirty thousand persons have been killed in Lebanon in little more than a year." Bellow redirected the blame for Middle East violence back to its proper Arab sources. Nonetheless, in the intervening quarter century, Chomsky's anti-Israel crusade had gained ground in the universities and consolidated in the Boycott, Divestment, and Sanctions movement, whose acronym was soon as familiar as CBS or NBC.

I was therefore thrilled when Larry Summers added his prestige to a boycott counterpetition that gathered more than ten times the number of original signatories, and when he said in his maiden address at Memorial Church that anti-Jewish politics did not end with the Holocaust but rather morphed into attacks on Israel. Academic communities, he said, were obliged to admit expression of all viewpoints, and "there is much in Israel's foreign and defense policy that can be and should be vigorously challenged." But, he added, "[serious] and thoughtful people are advocating and taking actions that are *anti-Semitic in their effect if not their intent.*"

This gracious phrasing that I have emphasized did not deter the predictable three-step. At the next faculty meeting, with an open bellicosity that I had never before witnessed in that room, Summers was accused of stifling free expression. His accuser, J. Lorand Matory, a professor of anthropology and African and African American studies, was backed up by a chorus of obviously orchestrated supporters. Although the press was excluded from faculty meetings, the next day's *Boston Globe* carried a front-page item reporting the charge. Within a year of his arrival, two professors of African and African American studies had labeled the president a racist and a Zionist-racist opponent of free speech.

This offensive should have come as no surprise. In the summer of 1992, just before I was to begin teaching at the university, Harvard's chair of African and African American studies, Henry Louis Gates Jr., known as "Skip," had published in the *New York Times* an article entitled "Black Demagogues and Pseudo-Scholars," advising that while anti-Semitism was generally declining, it was on the rise among black Americans, especially the younger and more educated. Earlier that year Harvard's Black Student Association had hosted Leonard Jeffries, a notorious professor of black studies who denounced Jews for running the slave trade, and Conrad Muhammad of the Nation of Islam, who blamed Jews for "despoiling the environment and destroying the ozone layer." Clearly troubled by these and other "crackpot" theories circulating on his watch, Gates cautioned that this was anti-Semitism from the top down, "engineered and promoted by leaders who affect to be speaking for a larger resentment."

But now Gates said nothing in defense of the president, and Larry, instead of calling out Matory and his supporters as he had the Chomsky petition, tried to ignore the attacks against him. Having placed my hopes on Larry's leadership, I watched the unraveling of his authority with real horror. His temperamental mildness, perceived as timidity, inspired disaffected corners of the university to rise against him. The keenest students were as troubled as I was. "I watched him closely," said a student of economics who had enjoyed his classes and was distressed by his inability to confront his attackers. "I think he is autistic." She was referring to the perceptible gap between his intelligence and his ability to read people.

Though the term "intersectionality," coined in 1989 by black feminist Kimberlé Williams Crenshaw, had not yet come into common use, the campus grievance coalition made Larry Summers its first target. Campus feminists administered the coup de grâce after a small private conference on "Diversifying the Science and Engineering Workforce" to which Summers had been invited. Asked to provoke discussion of why, although more women than men now attended university, women did not enter fields like mathematics, engineering, and the physical sciences in the same proportions, Larry offered a range of ideas, starting with the general fact that certain groups are "underrepresented" in certain activities. He tentatively asked whether the discrepancy might be due—in declining order of importance—to female choices, unequal distribution of cognitive skills across the sexes, or discrimination:

So my best guess, to provoke you, of what's behind all of this is that the largest phenomenon, by far, is the general clash between people's legitimate family desires and employers' current desire for high power and high intensity, that in the special case of science and engineering there are issues of intrinsic aptitude, and particularly of the variability of aptitude, and that those considerations are reinforced by what are in fact lesser factors involving socialization and continuing discrimination.

Finally, he wished "nothing better than to be proved wrong," because he would have liked the problem to find a better solution.

Summers had been ambushed. MIT professor of biology Nancy Hopkins stormed out of the hall telling reporters (but where had *they* come from?), "This kind of bias makes me physically sick." The *Boston Globe* obliged her by reporting that the number of tenured job offers to women had "dropped dramatically since Summers took office," implying the correlation without any attempt at proof. Falsely accused of sexism and of calling women innately inferior to men, he yielded to a caucus of senior women faculty complaining of discrimination against them and created a task force to address the charge. The leftist-feminist-anti-Zionist coalition was now drawing blood.

Once again, students aired what faculty members had tried to squelch. At a quickly organized graduate students' forum on women's careers, most of the young women spoke, just as Larry had conjectured, about the difficulty of balancing family life with the demands of the hard sciences. One had already switched to a career path that did not require open-ended laboratory experimentation; others described trying to figure out how to combine family with work.

In addressing this forum, I made my usual pitch for gratitude over grievance—gratitude to science for having given us so much better control over the age-old concerns of women: conception, childbirth, and infant mortality. I was furious with the women's movement for politicizing womanhood rather than facing up to the anxieties that quite naturally accompanied their freedoms, and I aired these ideas in a *Commentary* article in the form of a letter to a student like the ones who had organized the forum. "Dear Ellen; or, Sexual Correctness at Harvard" drew a range of thoughtful responses, mostly dissenting, but in a spirit of open debate altogether absent from the faculty.

Summers failed to shore up his authority. Though he and I had never spoken, I requested a meeting to urge him to fight for his position. Did he not understand that "blood in the water" attracts sharks? Why did he not rally his supporters—including students—against those trying to shut him down? Those of us who had counted on his leadership to protect critical inquiry, the pursuit of truth, equality irrespective of race, gender, color or creed, and a return to teaching the best of Western civilization were prepared to stand up for him. Alas, he submitted to my reproach as meekly as he had to the others.

By speaking out as one of the few vocal "defenders of Summers," I got a taste of media frenzy. I normally received no more than a couple of phone messages a week. Now a dozen or more awaited me between classes. Reporters with an otherwise dull academic beat saw their chance for bylines on a story that would stay hot for only so long as the president could be kept on the ropes. Since it was easier to go back to the same people for statements than to find new ones, I could have been talking to reporters all day. The publicity I would rather have sought to promote one of my books was now mine—only for supporting a leader who was not speaking up for himself.

The end came fast: at a special open meeting of FAS, J. Lorand Matory, who had made ousting Summers his special cause, introduced a motion of no confidence that passed by a vote of 218 to 185 with eighteen abstentions. On the way to the meeting, held at the American Repertory Theater—the regular venue being too small to contain this spectacle—two junior faculty members told me they were coming to vote against the president. They stood to lose nothing because neither of their appointments had been renewed, but they enjoyed the prospect of bringing Larry down.

That spring, after the last faculty meeting that he chaired as president, I ran into Larry as I was leaving the building. As though continuing our conversation in his office, he said that I had not taken into account the pressure he was under from the Harvard Corporation, which had hired him and had the power to fire him. I answered, with less sympathy than I felt, that this should have made him fight even harder. He was correct that I did not know all the facts. But I did know the stakes, and I had the impression that his defeat may have meant more to me that it did to him.

History rarely issues us a red alert. But the surrender by America's premier university to its anti-intellectual assailants marked a point of no return. Responsibility was so equally distributed among the administration, Board of Governors, Faculty of Arts and Sciences, and the main players that I saw no way the damage could be repaired. Students had been the driving force behind the leftism of the sixties, but current students who wanted a better education were unlikely to mount a response. The most independent among them simply stayed independent of the university, and almost none intended to remain stifled in its repressive atmosphere by becoming professors themselves. Larry was justly disappointed that the Board of Governors did not support their appointee, but it would have made a difference had the president of Harvard led a public fight on his own behalf.

CR

THINGS QUICKLY DETERIORATED. FIVE YEARS later, apparently not satisfied with his earlier triumph, Matory resumed his campaign, now aimed not only at the already deposed Summers but at the other most prominent Jewish defenders of Israel: the law school's Alan Dershowitz and me. In an opinion piece in the *Crimson*, he charged that through the enforcement powers wielded by the three of us, the state of Israel was making people like him "tremble in the fear of losing their friends, jobs, advertising revenues, campaign contributions, and alumni donations if they question Zionism or Israeli policy."

There was something crackpot about the letter, so that in addition to my usual reluctance to respond to unprovoked attacks, I did not want to grant him the notoriety he sought: I refused to dance the three-step. After several weeks of quiet, which seemed to confirm my strategy, the agenda for the upcoming FAS meeting contained the following proposed resolution:

"That this faculty commits itself to fostering civil dialogue in which people with a broad range of perspectives feel safe and are encouraged to express their reasoned and evidence-based ideas." Attached was a note explaining that the context for this motion was Matory's opinion piece in the *Crimson*, with the entire document appended to the faculty agenda. That undigested mess of vitriol began:

> Since Vietnam, Israel has become the heartbeat of U.S. foreign policy and a litmus test of what can be debated—and even of who will be allowed to speak—on university campuses.

Where would one even start to separate the freakish from the vicious in that charge, or from the paranoid projections that inspired it? Did he intend to say that debate over Vietnam had once been muzzled because of American involvement in its war, and that debate over Israel was being stifled for similar reasons? But incitement against Israel *bourgeoned* in 1975, the same year as the fall of Saigon, when the passage of the UN resolution defining Zionism as racism turned the world organization into the largest ever platform for anti-Jewish politics. What was the "heartbeat of foreign policy" anyway in Secretaries of State Cyrus Vance, Edmund Muskie, Alexander Haig, George Shultz, James Baker, Lawrence Eagleburger, Warren Christopher, and Madeleine Albright?

His account of history alleges that Israel was the chief preoccupation of American foreign policy in both parties and all administrations, and that Jews controlled the universities as well. Yet the Middle East Studies Association actually fell so thoroughly under the sway of academics opposed to Israel that two of its members, Bernard Lewis and Fouad Ajami, felt compelled to establish an alternative association. Harvard's Center for Middle East Studies was unabashedly and culpably anti-Israel, while Harvard's historian of the Middle East claimed that the creation of Israel was a mistake. And here was the man who had brought down President Summers presenting himself as a victim of the prosecution he initiated, summoning a trumped-up trial on the charge that he was being silenced.

Had a student submitted this, I would have sent it back for a rewrite. Far more troubling than the letter itself was that our colleagues had included it on the agenda, and without first informing Alan and me. Matory had actually told an interviewer that he had no academic credentials or knowledge of the subject, and no special reason to go after Israel beyond what he had gleaned from the "international press." Yet the faculty council admitted his spurious call for free speech—speech already guaranteed by existing guidelines—and gave this mugger the attention I had refused him.

His letter supplied no context or evidence, made no reasoned connections between one allegation and another. It read:

> This year, the Congress of the University and College Union—the British lecturers' union—proposed a boycott of Israeli universities and academics for what it regards as their complicity in 40 years of Israeli occupation of Palestinian lands. This boycott has its counterpart in a decades-old U.S. practice of threatening, defaming, or censoring scholars who dare to criticize Israel.

The obvious counterpart of the British boycott movement of Israel was the boycott movement in America, and they were the ones doing the threatening. The author projects his own malice onto some imagined "decades-old U.S. practice," and defines any *defense* of Zionism as an attack on haters of Israel like him.

Matory felt no inhibition either about launching an ad hominem attack. He conflated Summers, my support for Summers, and Dershowitz's defense of Israel as an assault on the defenseless Palestinians, which he likewise experienced as an attack on his defenseless self.

> In a 2006 faculty meeting, Peretz Professor of Yiddish Literature Ruth R. Wisse vocalized the underlying rationale of such censorship as few other professors have dared. Denying that anti-Zionism and anti-Semitism are separate phenomena, she declared anti-Zionism-that is, the rejection of the racially-based claim that Jewish people have a collective right to Palestine-the worst kind of

anti-Semitism. For such defenders of Israel, any acknowledgment that Zionism in principle and in practice violates Palestinian rights is tantamount to an endorsement of the Holocaust.

But is it anti-Semitic to ask why the Palestinians should pay the price for the ghastly crime of the Germans? Why were the property rights of the German perpetrators sacrosanct and those of the guiltless Palestinians adjudged an acceptable casualty? In U.S. foreign policy, not all racial groups are guaranteed the same rights and protections. Otherwise, why does the U.S. rightly defend Jewish people's claims on European bank accounts, property, and compensation for labor expropriated during the 1930s and 1940s, while quashing the rights of millions of Palestinians refugees to lands, houses, and goods stolen as a condition of Israel's founding in the late 1940s? As a nation we seem unconscious of the hypocrisy. The convention that persecuted Europeans had the right to safe havens on lands stolen from non-Europeans was, by the mid-20th century, as outmoded as the Confederacy's defense of slavery in the mid-19th.

The inversions here are breathtaking. What I had "dared" to do was defend Israel against the boycott movement—because no one else stood up to do it. I had indeed shown that anti-Zionism was a more advanced form of anti-Semitism, the former launched against the Jews in dispersion and the latter at Jews in their homeland. Matory's definition of anti-Zionism as "the rejection of the *racially-based claim* that Jewish people have a collective right to Palestine" slips in that insinuating phrase and thereby turns a signpost around to send the reader off in the false direction. Zionism resembled dozens of contemporaneous movements of national self-liberation and the Jews' indigenous right to the Land of Israel is as solid as the claim of the Chinese to China.

How could Harvard faculty members in good standing have submitted this anti-Jewish tirade as an example of free speech that was ostensibly being *denied?* In *Jews and Power*, published in 2007, I defined some of the methods of anti-Jewish politics of which inversion was the simplest and hardest to undo. In the quoted passage, to correct the reversals one would have to rehearse the "ghastly" crimes of the Arabs against the Jews, beginning with the Mufti of Jerusalem's organized pogroms against the unarmed Jews of Palestine and his collusion with Hitler to leave no Jewish child alive, and provide details of the decades-long criminal refusal of Arab leaders to accept the idea of coexistence.

The American political columnist and my Montreal landsman Charles Krauthammer described Israel as the only nation that inhabits the same land, bears the same name, speaks the same language, and worships the same God that it did 3,000 years ago. If reparations were due, then the hundreds of thousands of Jews who fled Arab lands after 1948 deserved compensation for infinitely more wealth and property than those Arabs who fled during Israel's War of Independence. The facts are all there out in the open, but the sheer indignity and mind-numbing effort of untangling the lies almost ensures that they remain unchallenged.

I linger over this model of paranoid politics because it demonstrates why assault is so much more fun than cleaning up. Larry, Ruth, and Alan— Matory's designated three stooges—had to do a garbage detail of clean-up because their colleagues had accepted a screed defaming the Jewish state and Jewish professors as its example of "reasoned and evidence-based ideas," and devoted two full meetings to this mischief. With the wasted effort I also lost my last traces of respect for these professors. However, Harvard lost more. Members of his anthropology department spoke up for Matory's proposal, and not a word was heard from his second home department, African and African American studies, whose chairman had once warned against the anti-Jewish animus we were witnessing. The identity politics Skip Gates had deplored in 1992 had since then turned respectable and what he once feared might discredit his department now underwrote it instead.

Soon after the sordid second meeting at which the resolution was defeated it was announced that Professor Matory would be leaving Harvard for a position at Duke University. A friendly colleague sent me a message of good cheer, but Matory was only the mouthpiece for others with greater ideological sophistication who knew that every such skirmish cleared the road for future victories. Blaming Israel and its Jewish supporters was taking over the culture and a large swath of the Democratic Party, with the leftists of Harvard leading the way.

What had popped into my head during the worst of that time was watching on television the scene of Soviet dissident Natan Sharansky in 1986 being set free at Berlin's Glienicke Bridge. Told to walk straight across to the American side, he zigzagged his way across instead. In retrospect, we defenders of Israel ought to have turned our backs on the faculty of a distinguished and venerable institution and said, "Such crap will not be tolerated." We should not have dignified the meetings with our presence.

Even more than Sharansky's defiance I was haunted by the book of my beloved teacher Max Weinreich that I had simply skimmed when I first acquired it, thinking it a weird, if understandable, deviation from his Yiddish scholarship. During the Second World War Weinreich had taken time off from his usual subjects as research director of the YIVO Institute to research and write *Hitler's Professors: The Part of Scholarship in Germany's Crimes Against the Jewish People.* Hard as it was to assemble this information while the war was still in progress, he meticulously documented the role of serious scholars in developing Aryan theories about the Jew as demon and justification for their elimination. One of the book's carefully footnoted citations is the declaration by Professor Max Clara: "Today we can proudly state that scholarship contributed its share to the success of the Fuhrer's great plans." Hitler's men rose not from the gutter but from the university. The book was Weinreich's contribution to the prosecution.

Some of Germany's scholars, like many around me at Harvard, were otherwise decent people. But how they both enjoyed inverting anti-Jewish aggressors and their Jewish targets! It was an intellectual sport like no other.

It all went hand in hand—abandonment of a common curriculum to reinforce the foundations of our hard-won liberal democracy; replacement of equal opportunity by a competing idea of enforced egalitarianism that led to equalized outcome; politicization of gender with women as the new proletariat; indulgence of racialism as a corrective to alleged white supremacy; and a culture of institutional cowardice. For every self-respecting Jew and honest liberal prepared to resist this deterioration, there were ten ready and willing to allow it, and several to fire it up in hopes of reaping its rewards.

CR

THOUGH MARTY PERETZ HAD ENDOWED a chair in Jewish studies, his longer-standing association with the university was through its Committee on Degrees in Social Studies, a program he helped to found and where he had taught hundreds of undergraduates, including senator and vice president Al Gore. He had also hosted dozens of gatherings in his home for visiting professors, graduating students, and other university occasions. He loved the college.

It was therefore fitting that in the fall of 2010, to commemorate the program's fiftieth anniversary, a group of his former students announced a new research fund in his honor. Marty was to be one of the speakers as well as an honoree. If he himself bore any responsibility for the ensuing ugliness, it lay in an item he had published the previous month in his blog, *The Spine*, his remaining connection to the *New Republic*, the magazine he'd once owned.

Plans were then afoot by imam Feisal Abdul Rauf to build a mosque abutting the site of the former Twin Towers in lower Manhattan. Objections to the project included its insensitive proximity to the target of Islamist attack, the imam's favorable view of Iran's terrorist proxy Hamas, and his creeping reputation as a slumlord. Marty's objection to the project included this intemperate passage:

> Muslim life is cheap, most notably to Muslims. And among those Muslims led by the Imam Rauf there is hardly one who has raised a fuss about the routine and random bloodshed that defines their brotherhood. So, yes, I wonder whether I need honor these people and pretend that they are worthy of the privileges of the First Amendment which I have in my gut the sense that they will abuse.

His speedy apology for these remarks—inflammatory only by Jewish, not by anti-Jewish standards—did not stop his political antagonists on campus from using his words as a pretext for their ambush. Muslim and Arab student groups protested the honor being done him, and general emails were sent through some of the undergraduate dorms inciting students to "Party with Marty." As he emerged from the event, he was met by a phalanx of jeering students and had to be conducted through their gauntlet under police watch, accompanied by professors Michael Walzer and Charles Maier, two old friends and fellow members of the program's committee. Its current faculty, by contrast, supported the protest, and one declared that everyone "was—without exception—appalled by Peretz's comments."

This ugly and unpunished assault on one of Harvard's staunchest supporters and friends completed the arc that had begun with my arrival. How much had changed in the interim! Xeroxing had gone the way of spats, *The Social Network* had replaced *Love Story* as Hollywood's idea of Harvard, and a wonderful new cadre of Harvard-trained academics was out there teaching Yiddish literature. I took more satisfaction than credit for the last of these. My advisees were usually as independent-minded as I was. I loved my own freedom so very much that I wanted to extend it to others and was delighted when each student veered off in a slightly different direction. The best advice I had for them was to find some true way of getting to the heart of every work they intended to teach.

Once again at Harvard, just as in my childhood, I felt my private fate diverging from the arc of history. In 2007, in a lovely ceremony at the White House, I was awarded the National Humanities Medal from President George W. Bush for "scholarship and teaching that have illuminated Jewish literary traditions." It cited my writings on Yiddish literature and Jewish culture. On the flight to Washington for the occasion with Len and me were my fellow honoree, professor Richard Pipes and his wife Irene, and among the others who joined us in the ceremony were author Cynthia Ozick, historian Victor Davis Hanson, Stephen Balch who founded the National Association of Scholars, and philanthropist Roger Hertog. Their distinguished company made it hard for me to dismiss the award as purely the outcome of the kind of academic horse trading that typically determines such things.

Receiving the National Humanities Medal from President George W. Bush at the White House, November 15, 2007. The citation reads, "for scholarship and teaching that have illuminated Jewish literary traditions. Her insightful writings have enriched our understanding of Yiddish literature and Jewish culture in the modern world." (White House photo by Eric Draper)

I had been fortunate in the timing of my career, but in fairness to the idea of the university, I end this chapter of my life testifying to its undeniable decline. The previous year after a faculty meeting, Professor of Religion Diana L. Eck, who had earlier been awarded the Humanities Medal by President Clinton, told the Harvard *Crimson*, "Wisse's remarks 'don't make much of an impression on the Faculty' because of their 'extreme nature.'" Her attack I did not leave unanswered:

> This, in a nutshell, is the tactic of political correctness, never to confront the content of a divergent opinion, but to dismiss it as "extreme" or out of bounds. Through their attacks on me, my colleagues during the meeting and after were warning others not to step out of line lest they invite the same contempt. Imagine the fate of any junior faculty member who might share my point of view on such issues as the importance of ROTC on campus, the pernicious effects of group preferences for women in hiring, or the dangers of anti-Semitism in its latest anti-Zionist manifestation....

My colleagues claimed they wanted to put the expulsion of President Summers behind them in order to get on with the curricular reform they had neglected, but the most crucial reform would have required ensuring greater intellectual diversity among the faculty, and I saw no sign of that happening. The absence of conservative views, most of which were classical liberal views when I was an undergraduate, meant that students were being shortchanged and poorly served by teachers who lacked the moral confidence to transmit the foundational texts and ideas of America and Western civilization.

I had made a practice of going to see every newly appointed FAS dean and university president to describe faculty-propelled anti-Semitism and how it would have to be confronted. At each appointed half-hour meeting over the years, the administrator dutifully took notes as I spoke. A friend of ours liked to tell of the CEO of an airline company who wrote a personal reply to the complaint of a first-class passenger about the cockroach he had found in his meal. On the back of the letter was scrawled in pencil, "Send this guy the cockroach letter." That was just how I felt after my every such warning about anti-Jewish infestation.

Unbearable that this was the academy I left to my students.

15

RESOLVE

The term *closure* suggests that we can bring human experience, especially of the unpleasant kind, to some resolution. I appreciate the wisdom of the Jewish schedule of mourning that releases grief in descending order of intensity from the first week of shiva, to the first month, to the first year, setting out appropriate practices for each stage, so that when children stop reciting Kaddish for a deceased parent after eleven months, they may experience closure. I did not achieve such calm over anyone I've lost, and certainly not for my brother Benjamin, and yet recently, life, in its unexpected way, did try to provide resolution for our family.

On the first of April 2016, I found the following message in my inbox addressed to my brother David and me:

> My name is Saule Valiunaite, I am from Vilne and I work as a historian in Jewish Museum here. This week I found information about amazing project by International Litvak Photography Center based in Kovne. The director of this center is Richard Schofield, he will also be getting a copy of this email, so if you would like to contact him, you will see his email address…

Attached to this message was a file of 112 digitized photographs that Schofield had posted under the cutline "A Lost and Forgotten Family," asking for help in identifying its members. Saule had taken up the challenge and was writing to say that she had identified the family and its living relatives "who, I know, will also be very happy to get this unexpected news." Indeed, about half the images in the attachment seemed to come from our mother's album—pictures we had often leafed through of her siblings, their family reunions and holiday excursions, and actors and actresses of the Yiddish theater that she had befriended. There were also two pictures of me, aged two and four.

I was at first so disoriented that I had to remind myself that Mother's album had been in my sister Eva's possession in Montreal since our mother died there in 1999. It took some time before I brought myself to understand that this must be the album of Mother's beloved sister Annushka Warshavski, deported from the Kovno Ghetto on October 26, 1943. Sisters with sister albums—what could be more natural?

Vilna and Kovno (Saule had used the Yiddish form, *Vilne* and *Kovne*) are the Litvak heartland of Mother's family. Between the two world wars, Vilna was in Poland and Kovno in Lithuania, but today both cities are again part of the latter, or what Yiddish called *Liteh*. I had been to Poland several times before I was able to take my first trip to Lithuania in September 1997 as part of a study tour with professors of the Hebrew University. By day we traveled to the many sites where Jews had once flourished and to the places nearby where they were murdered, and evenings we supped like regular tourists, once even accepting the hotel's invitation to entertainment that turned out to be an in-house striptease. The evening we spent in Kovno was exceptionally mild, and as others strolled along a lovely boulevard, I decided to phone my mother from there rather than, as originally intended, the next day from her native Vilna.

"*Mamale*," I said when I reached her in Montreal in mid-afternoon: "*Veyst vu ikh bin?* Do you know where I am? I am in Kovno."

"Are you going to see Annushka?" she asked.

I glanced down at my watch. It was already nine o'clock. "I think it's too late," I said, meaning too late in the evening to pay someone a visit. It even ran through my mind that I did not have my aunt's current address. We hung up without alluding to our shared lapse of memory and never spoke of that conversation again, just as we had never spoken of Anna's fate. As far as Mother was concerned, her siblings were still alive, and she had apparently raised me under the same illusion.

So my first reaction to the recovery of our aunt's album was not joy but shock at this ratification of her death. In the following hours and days, as our family pieced together the information supplied by the remarkable Richard and Saule, I burned with rage at the Germans who had rounded up and murdered our family. By what right?! Who had given them the unspeakable idea of forcing Jews into a ghetto and the power to deport them to their deaths? The photographs of my never-met Warshavski cousins Fifa and Ella celebrating their birthdays, of my splendid aunt decked out for her professional photographs, of these passionate, talented, vibrant people in the full bloom of their complicated lives, ignited the fury I had never before *felt*, let alone expressed. How quickly we had all, in good Jewish fashion, channeled our energies into whatever had been salvaged. We let public commemoration of the khurbn, Shoah, and Holocaust absorb our grief.

Mother had done well to redirect mourning into the more creative prolongation of Jewish Vilna through its Yiddish language and culture, but nothing had kept the Germans from their sport. For much of our family it had always been too late.

We had been raised on stories of Mother's family. She grew up as the youngest child and half sister of ten siblings: Alexander, Helena, Mina, Rosa, Nyonya (Benjamin), Anna, Lisa, Maria, Grisha, and Nathan, whose name she never mentioned until she was in her nineties. All the time I was growing up, I tried to avoid her family reminiscences that fell on me like a tarpaulin, covering up my life with hers. Even in my fifties I had too little patience for her stories, but when Zoloft began to soften her as she approached her nineties, I reciprocated by sometimes drawing her out.

Once I asked her about a town in a Yiddish story that I was reading: Had she ever been to Kaidonov, not far from Vilna? No, she said, it was Annushka's responsibility to take care of Nathan who was billeted in Kaidonov. That was the first any of us had ever heard of an Uncle Nathan whose mental or other disability was such that the family maintained him in a town that apparently functioned like a psychiatric facility. Anna was the go-between who delivered the payments and kept up contact with the patient. Mother mentioned Nathan as matter-of-factly as earlier she had asked me about dropping in on my aunt.

Anna Warshavski, née Matz, was Mother's favorite sister, ten years her senior and her surrogate mother after theirs died of tuberculosis in 1921. Unlike me, who tried to avoid her stories, my younger brother David became our mother's amanuensis, and in a memoir called *Yiddishlands* he has described the complicated Matz clan, lingering on the romantic exploits of Anna that were no less intricate than her mother Fradl's. Anna's name in the index of his book is the clue that helped Saule locate us: a Polish scholar who specialized in Jewish history, she was familiar with the way first and last names took on varied spellings and pronunciation in Lithuanian, Russian, Polish, and Yiddish, and thus recognized that Sara Varšauskienė (Lithuanian) was actually Anna Varšavskiai (Polish), or Warshavski or Vashavski in Yiddish/English transcription. From the dedications and messages on the backs of the photos that Richard had posted along with the album's pictures, she also figured out that Anna and her husband Lyova spent time in the resort town Birštonas not far from Kaunas (Kovne) where the album was found:

> After that I was looking through a virtual exhibition about Jewish community in Kaunas and noticed that description of Engel choir photograph mentions Leiba [Lyova] and Ona (Lithuanian form of name Anna) Varšavskiai….Finding out that Anna Varshavski was one of the leaders of the Engel choir helped me to find out about her musical career. So at this point I knew that the pictures belonged to Anna (Sara) and Leiba Varshavski, who lived in Kaunas and also owned a villa in Birštonas which was used as children's sanatorium. It also became obvious that Anna was a singer who was one of the main soloists at Engel choir.

Masza with her beloved sister Anna Warshavski on her visit to Czernowitz, 1938.

Clearly, without Saule's sleuthing we would never have recovered the album, and Annushka, though never forgotten, would have remained forever lost to us. But ours was a tunnel dug from both ends, and had Mother not done her share of the work there would have been no family to return the album *to*. She had told us all about Anna's musical career; we even knew the song about the ever-turning wheel of fortune that she had learned from Anna during her sister's 1938 visit to Czernowitz. David and I had recorded that song in a video presentation of our mother's repertoire, *Daughter of Vilna*, and it was a photograph of Annushka, featured in that video, that made Saule positive she had identified the family.

But how did the album survive in the first place?

I began this memoir with our flight from Romania in the summer of 1940. As we made our way westward, the Warshavskis were trapped, first by the Soviet annexation of that part of Lithuania, then by the Nazi invasion in June 1941. A year later they were herded into the ghetto among the city's thirty thousand Jews. The album was apparently one of the items Anna brought with her into the ghetto. Sometime before she and her daughters were deported to Klooga concentration camp in Estonia, she smuggled it out to the Lithuanian woman who operated a butcher shop from her home less than twenty yards from the ghetto fence. That house is still in the family's possession, passed down to her son and from him to a nephew. The butcher was Therese Fedaraviciene, whose actions began to be pieced together when Richard Schofield discovered the album in 2016. About Lyova Warshavski's fate we have learned nothing at all.

Since it is unlikely that the album was all that Anna brought with her into the ghetto, she may have found a way of trading other items with the butcher for the food that grew scarcer from day to day. The album had no commercial value and its possession could have cost Therese her life, maybe even at the hands of Lithuanian neighbors who joined the German efforts to rid the city of Jews. We shall never know what transpired between these two women. They took their secrets to the grave—a merely fanciful expression since Anna does not have one. Mother would have the names of all her murdered siblings inscribed on her tombstone in the Montreal cemetery on De la Savane. We do not know either whether Therese ever told her family about the album or stored it in the attic, hiding its provenance even from them.

The image that originally caught photographer Richard Schofield's attention of the Warshavski family—Anna, Lyova, and their daughters, Fifa and Ella—from the album astonishingly preserved.

None of this could have been brought to light had Richard Schofield not moved from his native Britain to pursue his interest in Lithuanian Jews, known as Litvaks. In Kovno Richard set up his Institute for Litvak Photography, and one day while photographing an item in the city's Sugihara House Museum he was captivated by some unusual family photographs. He learned that they came from an album deposited in the museum by Alvydas Malinauskas, a local politician with an interest in the history of the Slobodka area where the Kovno Ghetto once stood, and who had acquired the object on condition of anonymity from Juozas Fedaravicius, Therese's grandson. Upon discovering the album with these unrecognizable photographs in the house he had inherited from his uncle, Juozas later told Richard he had intended to burn it with the rest of the attic junk. "It must have been the hand of God that intervened," he said, meaning the staying hand of his wife, who objected to destroying photos of people so young, handsome, and prosperous. Anna's personality and prosperity had not saved her life, but it saved this record of her existence.

Our judgment of humanity depends, I suppose, on the relative weight we ascribe to the murderers and to those who withstood them. The return of Annushka's photographs reminded our family of the threads of decency that can exist in coats of mail. Persuaded not to destroy the album, Juozas got rid of it to avoid trouble. Communist rule was no gentler to the Lithuanians than the Germans it replaced, and under it you never knew what constituted a crime until the arrest. But Lithuania was freer now, and acknowledging local Jewish history was one sign of that freedom. The museum is named for the building's former occupant, the Japanese consul Chiune Sugihara, who in 1939 to 1940 wrote out several thousand visas to Japan that enabled Jewish families to escape the fate that awaited them had they stayed in Kovno. Perhaps our aunt failed to take advantage of this escape route because she hoped that rescue would come from us—us her relatives, us our countries—in the west.

Now that Richard's "lost and forgotten family" had become found and remembered, we matched the album photos with Mother's and tried to reconstruct what we could of their contents. As the director of the Yeshiva

University Museum in New York, our son Jacob conceived an exhibition of what the photographs brought to life: the passion of these young people for travel, theater, music, photography, and their practice of what other cultures have called *noblesse oblige*. Many of the photos are of children in the sanatorium Anna and her husband established and helped to run, and since they made no separation in taking the pictures, we sometimes can't tell our cousins from those youngsters.

A chasm separates people like my aunt from her murderers. The moral refinement of millennia had gone into the making of people like Anna who studied music in Berlin so that she could return to teach schoolchildren in Vilna. She surely believed that when her album reached her sister in Montreal, we would replant her memory in the living heart of the Jewish people. This was the Jewish way of life I had felt it necessary to include in my university's teaching about Western culture, lest the erasure of Jews from the curriculum leave Nazism and communism as the culmination and fulfillment of what Europe had wrought.

The Matz-Welczer-Roskies family tree that Jacob featured in the exhibition was unbearably precise about the price Jews had paid for their way of life. The top row of Mother's siblings stretched across the wall with her photo and Father's on the extreme right. A huge blank space over nine-tenths of the canvas covers all the missing branches of the family, as ours tumbles down the far side and spreads ever wider across the bottom. Ben's daughter Jennifer moved to Jerusalem in 1995. We do not count her grandchildren lest an envious evil spirit snatch one of their number, which you might consider a crude superstition until you have seen those evil spirits assume their human form.

❧

MY FRIEND GITA ONCE TOLD me she had ended a squabble among her children over which one was getting favored treatment with the declaration, "Life is not fair." I must have tried that out at home as a mollifying factor because many years later, when I once apologized to Abby for something

I had done, she blurted out, "No, the only thing I can't forgive is your once telling me that life was not fair." Why ever would her own mother have tried to *reconcile* her to the fact of injustice?

Long before the return of Annushka's album I had struggled with the questions forced on us by the massacre of six million Jews in five years. In truth, the twentieth century had rendered the question of "why bad things happen to good people" far too innocent, too childlike. The more pertinent situation has been the political one, in which *bad ideas are mobilized against good people.* To ask the question "why" is therefore to call for political analysis. Becoming impatient with the use of theological or moral-ethical language in analyzing or explaining political warfare, I began instead to concentrate on the functions of anti-Semitism—to see how and why it works and where it succeeds.

Jews were innocent of all they were accused of, but by attending to self-improvement without commensurate care for self-protection, they had created a political vacuum and for others a political opportunity. The Jewish combination of prowess and powerlessness worked as predictably in politics as do the laws of solubility in chemistry—a comparison suggested to me by the Polish thinker Aleksander Świętochowski, who started out in the latter part of the nineteenth century as an exemplary liberal, a Positivist who looked for practical solutions to social challenges, convinced that "the Jewish problem does not exist" and that Poles and Jews were equally in need of rational enlightenment. But when he then veered into a more defensive Polish nationalism that could no longer accept the prominent Jewish presence in Polish society, the same logical reasoning brought him to anti-Semitic conclusions. It was he who compared the irritant Jews with the salt in Polish water, arguing that too much salt could no longer be dissolved and would have to be expelled. As for the anti-liberals of neighboring Germany, far less elegant in their logic, they simply accused the Jews of contaminating their country "from within" and gave that reason for having to cleanse Germany of Jews.

At the Lost and Found Exhibition of the Yeshiva University Museum, 2018-19, featuring the album of Anna Warashavski, some of the great-grandchildren of Masza and Leo Roskies sit under their side of the family tree. From left, Maddy and Camilla Lieberman-Wisse; Sonia, Theresa, and Pearl Schachter; Lilly and Elisha Halperin. Nine-tenths of the wall is bare.

Cousins on the porch at Loon Lake cottage in the Adirondacks, summer 2019. From left, Camilla, Theresa, Pearl, Isaiah, Maddy, Claire, Nate, Sonia. Camilla and Maddy are the children of Jacob Wisse and Rebecca Lieberman; Theresa, Pearl, Isaiah, and Sonia of Abby (Wisse) and Ben Schachter; Claire and Nate of Billy and Suzanne (Jack) Wisse.

Once such propositions became politically plausible, the fires of grievance had only to be stoked for the pillage to begin, spontaneous in some
societies, highly organized in others. How so, and what accounts for that
difference? It is meaningless and all too easy to end the discussion with sympathetic references to the Jews as "canaries in a coal mine"—that is, sacrificial
signals of a lurking society-wide poison. The analytical task is to isolate the
political variables on the sides of the victims and the perpetrators and to
identify how and why the political behavior of Jews permitted—or invited—
such a pattern of aggression. As a general rule, a self-reliant community that
fails to protect that which it creates, and that cannot threaten reprisal in
kind, will fall prey to the resentment or ambition of others.

My interest in the organization of politics against the Jews turned into
a book, *Jews and Power*, or, in its Hebrew translation, *The Paradox of Jewish
Politics*. But what was one to do with this thesis? Once I asked a visiting group
of Israeli school principals at what age or in what grade they considered it
appropriate to discuss Arab warfare against their country. The head of an
elementary school in Judea laughed and said, "The kindergarten children are
already way ahead of us"; the principal of a secular high school in the north
answered, "Never!" These ideologically divided educators understood their
tasks in opposite ways. Nevertheless, and despite his reluctance, the principal in the north would prepare each year's graduating students for their
approaching military service, and his students, in turn, would fight as hard
as those in Judea to protect their common home. No such enmity surrounds
the United States of America, stretching as it does from sea to shining sea
with pacific Canadians on the north and would-be immigrants to the south.
That is why Israelis are currently more politically realistic than Americans,
though, as with recovering alcoholics, one should never take the political
sobriety of Jews for granted.

America's most recent political reckoning came on September 11, 2001
when a group of al-Qaeda terrorists brought down the World Trade Center
in New York, damaged the Pentagon, and almost struck the White House.
That Tuesday morning, I was at home in Cambridge when Abby called from
her office in New York to tell me to turn on the television. By our second

call, when it was clear that this was a terrorist attack, Abby said, "Mom, no one here has seen anything like it before." During her own four years in Israel, suicide bombings had sometimes been daily fare; along with the sheer enormity of the 9/11 assault, she was shocked by the incomprehension among those around her.

As for Israel's most serious political reckoning, it had come on September 13, 1993, the day its leaders signed the Oslo Accords, putting Yasir Arafat, then the world's leading terrorist, in charge of the Palestinian Authority. On a late afternoon of the previous week, when I happened to be in Jerusalem, I received a phone call from Richard Bernstein of the *New York Times* asking me to comment on the agreement that had just been scheduled to be signed. It surprised me that a reporter would have taken the trouble to track me down in Israel to solicit my view on something happening back in Washington. If Bernstein had to go so far afield, I thought, he must have been having trouble finding a dissenting voice. But he had now found it. Pacing back and forth, holding nothing back, I argued against the agreement as though he, on the phone, had the power to abrogate it.

About an hour later, Bernstein called back to confirm the words that would appear in the morning paper:

> "I think that the Jews think that they can solve the Arab problem and I think that that is a terrible mistake." Ms. Wisse's concern is that in dealing with Mr. Arafat, the Israelis are, in effect, intervening in Arab politics, choosing the PLO chief, whom she called "a killer," to be the leader of the Palestinians in the West Bank and the Gaza Strip.
>
> If things go wrong—and she believes there is a good chance they will—it is Israel that will bear responsibility, she said. "It's the first time that an Israeli government is doing something for which I, as an American Jew, would not like to bear moral responsibility."

Although Bernstein had turned my certainty that things *would* "go wrong" into a mere belief, the words, however clumsy, were mine. But then he surprised me again by giving me his number and saying he would wait another half-hour in case I wanted to change the thoughts I had put on record. Before or since, no interviewer has ever made me such an offer. What impelled him? It may have been the same thing that kept my heart pounding after I'd put down the phone: how could I renounce the dream of peace, of toleration, of recognition, of hope for a saner world, the hope that had eluded the Jews since almost their beginnings in history?

Writing many years later, Michael Oren, an American who had moved to Israel with his family and later returned to his native land (minus the citizenship he had to sacrifice) as the Israeli Ambassador, explains that though he doubted that peace was actually in reach, for reasons both moral and political he supported the peace *process* itself, and endorsed Prime Minister Yitzhak Rabin's decision to enter into the agreement:

> Even if we could not immediately achieve peace, we were morally bound to lay its foundations. We had to convince the world and, more importantly, our own children that Israel had done its utmost to avoid confrontation. Hundreds of thousands of Russian and Ethiopian Jews were arriving in Israel, and absorbing them required beating some swords into plowshares. So, too, did transforming our economy, long girded for war, into a global, high-tech contender. And while the land of Israel—including the West Bank [of the Jordan River]—remained our birthright, sustaining it came at a rising international price.

Moving words. Yet I found better grounds for saying that Jews were "morally bound" to *resist* the obvious self-delusion of a unilateral peace process. Yasser Arafat was more than a "killer": he was the original and archetypal Arab-Muslim terrorist, backed by regimes that did not want to take the risk of violent action against Israel for fear of retaliation but were eager to direct against the Jewish state the festering discontent of their own populaces that might otherwise be directed against themselves. This was the new form of warfare by terrorist proxy.

Had there ever been any real prospect of peace with Israel, negotiations with Arafat would have been conducted by legitimate representatives of Israel, and not, as was the case here, by self-appointed, unelected, and gullible Jews who convened meetings in secret—in Norway!—with PLO men who bore no accountability to any public. The Jews who organized these meetings, not all of them Israelis, subverted the will of the citizenry that had elected Rabin on the strength of his promise that no such negotiations would take place. No nation had ever armed its self-declared enemy with the expectation of gaining security. Once Israel did that, granting Arafat the legitimacy that no Arab state would ever have given him, he predictably suppressed his Arab subjects and organized an armed force to conduct anti-Israel terrorism at close range.

While I had often feared for the safety of Israel, this time I was in despair. I doubted that any people—much less Jews with their bad political record—could survive so stupid a political move. After my phone call with Richard Bernstein, I composed a letter of apology to a man I felt I had wronged for fifty years. In 1943, when Shmuel Zygielbojm had learned of the deportations and mass killings of the Jews of Europe and knew he had failed to persuade those around him in London to act in time, he committed suicide, writing: "Perhaps my death will achieve what I was unable to achieve with my life, and concrete action will be taken to rescue at least the few hundred-thousand Jews who remain out of three-and-a-half million."

The latter number referred to the Jews of Poland; he did not know about Russia, and Hungary was still to come. I had hated Zygielbojm's desperate act from the moment I heard about it at my Jewish school assembly, but that night in 1993 I fully sympathized with his motive. In 1943, the world had failed the Jews; in 1993, the Jews had failed themselves.

Inevitably, as soon as he was installed, Arafat declared open season, killing Jews in buses and at bus stops, in discotheques, cafes, and restaurants, at street markets and in family homes. Abroad, those who had invested in the peace process drove the propaganda on his behalf, blaming Zionists for the war against Jews, because to blame Arafat would have required acknowledging their own indefensible mistake.

I would turn Michael Oren's moral calculus on its head. Even if Israelis could not immediately achieve peace, they were morally bound to lay its foundations by persuading the world of what? That they were prepared to hold out against their enemies until they were granted the unconditional acceptance that had been their due since 1948. Israel was not, in Saul Bellow's memorable phrase, the "moral playground" of its moral inferiors.

But in thus despairing over the Oslo Accords, I also came to realize why it was foolish and wrong to compare my fears, real as they were, with those of the man who had learned that his wife and child had been killed in the Warsaw Ghetto. Convinced that the Jewish people would not prevail, Zygielbojm did not want to outlive them. I dared not compare my situation to his. Our family was thankfully growing, and Israel was strong despite this lapse of judgment. Had Yigal Amir not assassinated Yitzhak Rabin, the prime minister would have been defeated at the polls. It was now time to save America from the same political vulnerability that had repeatedly doomed the Jews. Democratic societies are open to similar temptations, and what can be learned from the experience of one may help protect another.

I CANNOT RECALL WHO fIRST urged me to read "Why We Remain Jews," the talk that philosopher Leo Strauss gave at the University of Chicago Hillel in 1962, but I can still feel the shock of coming upon this passage:

> The root of injustice...is not in God, but in the free acts of His crea-
> tures—in sin. The Jewish people and their fate are the living witness
> for the absence of redemption. This, one could say, is the meaning
> of the chosen people; the Jews are chosen to prove the absence of
> redemption.

Though I was by then in my sixties, already a conservative, an admirer of the Bible's emphasis on human imperfection and on the tough moral reckoning it demanded of the Jewish people, I was awed by this summation of our political function among the nations. Some Jews probably left the tribe because they did *not* want to be the living witnesses to the absence of redemption, but Strauss unflinchingly rooted his insight in the *Aleinu* prayer that, he said, "surpasses everything that any present-day man could write":

> It is our duty to praise the Lord of all things, to ascribe greatness to Him who formed the world in the beginning, since He has not made us like the nation as of other lands, and He has not placed us like other families of the earth, since He has not assigned to us a portion as to them, nor a lot as to all their multitude....

Jews are accustomed to praising God in many forms—the Almighty of the Psalms, Benefactor of the Liturgy, Glorious Creator of the Kaddish that is recited over the dead—but here was Strauss, praising God for the precarious role He assigned us in history. Yiddish speakers who had borne the full brunt of that history quipped, "*Thou hast chosen us from among the nations*: why did you have to pick on the Jews?" or, "Thanks for nothing," or, "No wonder the whole world envies us!" I adored that humor of point/counterpoint, with skepticism tweaking faith, but I liked Strauss better, interpreting him in my own way to mean that the absence of redemption has so far been demonstrated by the inability of other peoples to accept our civilizing presence in the world, and that therefore we dare not falter until they do. I accept our assignment—and am prepared to give thanks for the privilege.

Came Annushka's album to remind me yet again of how unfairly that privilege had been allotted, and to revive doubts about the high cost of Jewish survival. While here I sit writing about them, my cousins' flesh and bones have been rotting in conditions that make me ashamed to use the word "redemption," even in order to deny its presence. The Germans went out of their way to dehumanize the inmates of the death camps, deliberately meting out arbitrary punishments and in every way teaching Jews that here your fabled logic and humanity will be turned into the shit you will drown in, should you be pushed—on our whim—into those stinking pits. Burdens always fall unfairly, in families, communities, nations, and generations, but the Nazis pushed unfairness beyond any limit, determined to crush every last intimation of Jewish justice, conscience, and sanity. By these actions, they intended to destroy the idea of man forged in the image of God, for how could one ever erase from collective memory this subhuman depravity?

In teaching and writing I never get away from these questions. Primo Levi, who survived the Auschwitz death camp, thought it immoral to pray to God for personal salvation. He came to Auschwitz a nonbeliever, and his experience compounded his disdain for the idea of a divinely ordained humanity. When a Jew prayed after having been spared selection for the gas chambers, Levi wrote, if he were God he would spit on that prayer. I have taught his views, but continue to believe that he got the message backwards. The God of the Jews had always known about the degeneracy of Sodom. Judaism had come to repudiate Nazism before the fact, to keep a people morally strong and psychologically vibrant despite what they were made to endure and could neither prevent nor avenge. The *Aleinu* prayer trusts us to *ensure* that Sinai will prevail over Auschwitz.

Jean-Paul Sartre in Vichy, France, believed that Jews had an existential duty to remain Jews in defiance of those who came to annihilate them. The only Jews whom Sartre knew were leftists like himself, thoroughly assimilated individuals who were forced back into their Jewishness by Christian opposition and Hitler's racial laws. From a psychological-philosophical viewpoint, he thought it shameful for these Jews to try to escape their responsibility, and urged them to resist the anti-Jews by affirming their Jewishness. As though they were characters in a Sartre drama, he insisted they remain Jews because Jewishness was being denied.

Strauss saw it differently, as do I. Jewish faithfulness was not a reaction to enmity, but to the people's own experience of slavery in Egypt and of the demoralization that followed their release. The Bible's account of Exodus shows them forged as a people by the law through Moses, and history confirms how generations of exegetes instilled respect for the Torah as the civilizing alternative to undisciplined freedom. Perhaps, as I argue in *Jews and Power*, Jews succeeded too well, concentrating on their own decency without paying enough attention to the villainy around them. Yet just as the released slaves in the desert became the nation worthy of entering the promised Land of Israel, so the Jewish survivors of Europe and the Arab Middle East in the twentieth century learned to rebuild and then to protect their recovered state. Jews are not the reaction to barbarity: they are its eternal autonomous alternative.

In her Jewish school in Vilna my mother learned to sing the first poem published (in 1891) by the then-eighteen-year-old Chaim Nahman Bialik, destined to become the towering figure of modern Hebrew poetry. In this eight-stanza verse, the speaker welcomes back to his East European windowpane the lovely bird—*tsiporoh nekhmedes*—on her annual return from more temperate lands. The bird's presence, heralding the change of seasons, makes the young man painfully aware of the wintry life he leads among people who resent his presence and wish him gone. He asks his visitor whether she might be bringing greetings from his brothers in Zion to lift his spirits. This apparently simple, childlike poem, in a Hebrew that Bialik was already fashioning into an old-new Jewish literary vernacular, enveloped all the suffering of exile in the hopeful augury of an imminent return to the Land of Israel.

In quiet moods, Mother sometimes also sang us *her* mother's song about a flower that had lain neglected on the road for *two thousand years*—the phrase that had come to figure in the Jewish national awakening as a marker of the end of dispersion and beginning of ingathering. Both she and her mother, Fradl, knew it had been composed by Eliakum Zunzer, who was actually present at Fradl's first wedding; but they sang it as a folk song, part of the repertoire of reaching for Zion that stretches back to Psalms 126 ("When the Lord restores the fortunes of Zion—we see it in a dream—our mouths shall be filled with laughter, our tongues with songs of joy ... ") and 137 ("If I forget you, O Jerusalem, let my right hand wither; let my tongue stick to my palate ... if I place not Jerusalem above my chiefest joy").

On my frequent flights to Israel, particularly when I was traveling alone to a conference or meetings, I would think of our plane as that lovely bird flying home after a visit to Bialik's window. Hard as it may be to romanticize an actual El Al flight, what with teenagers nervously excited about their upcoming gap year or Birthright trip and bearded men summoning one's seatmates for a prayer minyan, and though I no longer kiss the ground as I did on my first arrival—since we are ushered right into the terminal and no longer get to step on the tarmac—the miracle of the recovered Jewish homeland is never lost on me. It ranks among the human wonders of the world.

I don't know anyone more independent than I have felt myself to be for most of my life, yet I happily experience that freedom as a rooted freedom—rooted, first and foremost, in my being a fortunate Jew and a fortunate citizen of Canada and the United States. Nor is that the sum of my good fortune: I had the good fortune to marry a fine man who would father and help me raise children who are better than their parents and see them in their turn raise grandchildren perhaps better still. Part of *their* joy in life and contribution to society will depend similarly on the gratitude they feel and express for the good fortune of their birth. So many others would like to have what has come down to us, and what is ours only to appreciate, and to work to deserve.

GRATITUDE

$\mathcal{C}$ustomary acknowledgments will not suffice for this memoir, which is itself largely an expression of thanks for the good fortune that no amount of good works can requite. Philosophically and psychologically, I believe in the value of gratitude, but above and beyond the moral and practical benefits it bestows, my life has taken the form of an unpayable debt. To record it is not yet to settle what I owe.

This is no false humility on my part. I have chronicled some of what I've accomplished, trying not to embellish or play it down, but readers will have seen that lucky circumstance frequently afforded me the means and opportunity to do what I did. My parents gave me life and then saved it. My older brother absorbed the anxiety I did not understand enough to feel. A great country that denied so many others extended refuge to our family. All of this was unearned bounty in a time of slaughter.

That last point, about our place of refuge and citizenship, was actually a rare point of contention with my father, who welcomed all other opinions or arguments but asked me never to criticize Canada. Once, having come across the record of its cruel immigration policy in wartime, I reproached my father with the evidence of how very few Jews our country had admitted when it mattered most. My father said, "Yes, but we were four of them." He honored our personal debt over the larger question of right and wrong. I did not bow to his judgment then, but just as he had grown to see his own father's greater wisdom, so, too, I learned from him to elevate gratitude over grievance, and to understand that democracies, though they sometimes act badly, are no less precious and no less in need of our protection.

Through this personal account, I convey my hope that my fellow citizens and people everywhere share my appreciation for the traditions of freedom that some of us inherit and others acquire. With the decline of formal expressions of gratitude like daily prayer and the Pledge of Allegiance, the obligations attending them are likewise in danger of disappearing to the point where people born into this gift no longer realize that it must be reinforced and defended.

THIS BOOK ALSO THANKS THE many individuals who have shown me kindness in word and deed. That not all of them figure by name in the narrative reflects only my unsystematic choice of some episodes over others in the process of writing and revising. I hope that what I have written about my association with the Avi Chai Foundation conveys my continuing indebtedness to its founder, Zalman Bernstein, to its succeeding chairmen, Arthur Fried and Mem Bernstein, to members of the board and the staff.

As concerns the memoir directly, it is pure pleasure to thank Roger Hertog, founder, and Eric Cohen, executive director of the Tikvah Fund for their support of this project and of the work I have been doing since my retirement from Harvard in 2014. I have felt part of a community of independent thinkers who inspire one another to keep learning and teaching as they learn. "Tikvah" is hope, and the hope that is Tikvah has certainly inspired hope in me.

Neal Kozodoy published serial chapters of the work in progress in Tikvah's online magazine *Mosaic*, giving me the benefit of his wisdom and elegant editorial oversight. He inspired whatever is best in this book. When Adam Bellow undertook to publish the whole under his new imprint, he wisely encouraged me to shore up the social and cultural background and make the memoir more of a witness to its times. I also thank Sue Kahn who read an early draft of the sections on my Harvard years, and the readers of *Mosaic* who offered me invariably helpful comments on the chapters as they appeared.

When it comes to family, I run into a problem. As I have written elsewhere, the "*phoo, phoo, phoo*" approach to the praise of family (spit three times to ward off evil spirits), inherited from my mother and who knows how many generations before her, does not permit the counting of Jews and certainly not of one's children or grandchildren, and generally discourages the kind of pridefulness that some people believe is incumbent upon us. I will risk saying that my greatest good fortune rests in my husband, Len; in our children, Billy, Jacob, and Abby, and their basherte; in our loving in-laws and the grandchildren we share who are as varied and radiant as stars in the firmament. Their presence brightens my life and the world.

I do not say enough in this book about my siblings, David Roskies and Eva Raby, or their spouses and marvelous children. Our family extends to admirable cousins in Australia, South Africa, and of course Israel; we sometimes meet and connect across continents. The Jewish family has always been the foundation of the Jewish people and may ours continue to grow and flourish.

When I realized that this memoir would be more valuable as cultural testimony than personal disclosure, I eliminated a chapter devoted to women friends, some now deceased and others, may they enjoy long years, who continue to sustain me. Like dear Ann Charney and Gita Rotenberg who already figures in the book, they tend to be tough-minded (like my mother). Although I never belonged to a group like the one enjoyed for a time by the estimable Cynthia Ozick, Johanna Kaplan, and Norma Rosen, I did find a warm literary friend in Janis Bellow, and I may one day take up that part of the story.

The working title of this book when I began it was *To the Graduating Class*. My elementary school principal Shloime Wiseman often said, "More than the calf wishes to suck, the cow wants to suckle." Never having studied Talmud, I did not realize that these words were spoken by the great Rabbi Akiva when he was imprisoned by the Romans and was weighing the dangers involved in imparting Jewish texts to his students—dangers to them both. The World War II writings with which I was familiar showed that the same fraught conditions still prevailed nineteen centuries later, when Mira Bernstein in the Vilna Ghetto continued teaching her class of one hundred and thirty as its numbers dropped to seven; she died with the last. Teaching Jewish texts was a privilege never to be taken for granted.

Every precious new class is a chance to share my appreciation for important literary works. If I sometimes teach as if my life depended on it, that is how it feels to me. The conditions in which I taught were, for the most part, at the farthest remove from those terrible times, but today's students inherit a much less robust academy than the one I entered. Quite reasonably, many of the most independent-minded among them have ceased even to consider an academic career, while those already in the field feel under increasing threat.

It was unimaginable to me that informers could emerge from among my colleagues, and yet, as the changing climate on campus began to require the suppression of "incorrect" views, the first denunciation came, along with outright attempts to silence me and others.

The decline in American civic culture that I record in the last part of this book was by no means inevitable and, I would like to think, is still not irreversible. I dedicate this book to my students—and theirs—in the hope that they will retrieve and revive the precious freedoms that are being lost. I wish them strength.